NO!

AGAINST ADULT SUPREMACY

ANTHOLOGY

STINNΞY DISTRO

First published online by Stinney Distro, 2016.
First published in London, 2017 by Dog Section Press and Active Distribution
Printed by Što Citaš, Zagreb, Croatia

ISBN 9780993543531

Anthology design by Matt Bonner revoltdesign.org
Dog Section Press logo by Marco Bevilacqua

CONTENTS

PREFACE

Intellectual property is a legally fabricated monopoly, confining culture and science, and violently depriving the poorest and most marginalised from access to critical resources. The fictions of copyright and patent are despotic attempts to monopolise the mind; outrageous constraints on intelligence and creativity; and a destructive protectionist scheme for the profit of power.

Stinney Distro

These zines were originally published online free of charge and copyright. We've put them in print so that they might reach a different audience, because we believe print has a different impact to electronic editions. To do so, we've had to put a small cover charge on this anthology; however, the reader should rest assured that the charge is simply to cover the costs associated with printing. All of the publishers involved in producing this edition operate on a strictly not-for-profit basis, and this print edition stays true to the spirit of the original project.

We encourage the reader to pass this book on to a friend once they've finished with it.

INTRODUCTION

Every hierarchy, every abuse, every act of domination that seeks to justify or excuse itself appeals through analogy to the rule of adults over children. We are all indoctrinated from birth in ways of "because I said so." The flags of supposed experience, benevolence, and familial obligation are the first of many paraded through our lives to celebrate the suppression of our agency, the dismissal of our desires, the reduction of our personhood. Our whole world is caught in a cycle of abuse, largely unexamined and unnamed. And at its root lies our dehumanisation of children.

NO!

AGAINST ADULT SUPREMACY

Issue 1

Children's Oppression, Rights, and Liberation

Samantha Godwin

Excerpt: academia.edu/2046034/Childrens_Oppression_Rights_and_Liberation (Citations Omitted)

The legal, political, scientific and media discourse prevalent in previous generations promoted the idea that race and gender are biologically determinate categories with biologically determined attributes, characteristics, and social roles. Historically, many anthropologists and psychologists believed they had found physical evidence that non-white people had an inferior capacity for reason and rationality. These supposed differences fit into an imperialist ideology of a 'white man's burden' that justified the systematic oppression of indigenous peoples through-out the world. Black people were said to be intellectually and morally inferior to white people and as a result, unable to take care of themselves without the supervision of their white slave owners. The myth of a biological basis for male domination over women has persisted for even longer. Both those who defended the historical relegation of women to second class citizen status under the law and the contemporary anti-feminist backlash have relied on a belief (often backed by superficially scientific-looking evidence of the inferior female mental capacities) that men are more capable, at least on average, of fulfilling a variety of important social rules than are women. Anti-Suffragette propaganda held that women's minds were not suitable for politics or public life. These supposed mental differences were said to causally explain why women were excluded from politics. This reasoning was also used to normatively justify female exclusion from politics as a necessary consequence of having to protect women in general and from the burdens of public responsibility in particular.

In addition to the paternalistic justifications for white dominance over black people and male dominance over women - arguments that fit the pattern of "group A must have legal power over group B for the best interests and protection of group B" - the white chauvinist and male chauvinist ideologies also employed a somewhat different normative justification: an appeal to the good of society, where the subordination of black people and women was said to be necessary for society to function. Defenders of slavery for instance claimed that the institution of slavery was necessary for a functioning society and economy. Similarly, the subordination of women to their husbands was widely held to be necessary for the stability and wellbeing of the family, and hence, society at large. In both instances, the biological differences between subordinate and dominant demographic groups was said to both causally explain the social relations of domination and subordination, while also providing a normative justification for why those social relations were good, natural, and desirable.

Today, the subordination of children to adults in general and their parents in particular is similarly seen as being both caused and justified by children's inferior mental faculties. Both the paternalism argument (children must be subordinate for their own good) and the social necessity argument (children must be subordinate for the good of society) are advanced to support the legal disabilities of children. The parallels with "scientific racism" and sexist neurological theories should be obvious: we are frequently told that children and adolescents are mentally inferior due to their underdeveloped brains, and this inferiority renders them incapable of behaving rationally or responsibly; in the past, precisely the same claims were advanced against women and black people.

Many people will instinctively reply that the racists and male chauvinists of nineteenth century were wrong about black people and women, whereas our scientifically superior contemporary society is right about children and adolescents. There are good reasons however not to leap to this conclusion.

A chief way the black civil rights movement and women's rights movement responded to racist and sexist stereotypes was not to deny that there are discernable differences between races and genders that might (mistakenly) be called upon to justify social hierarchies, but that social hierarchies themselves produced these differences. In The Mismeasure of Man, Stephen J. Gould argues that measurable "intelligence" does not casually explain the inferior social status of racial minority groups, rather the inferior social status of racial minority groups contributes to their relatively worse average performance on "intelligence" tests: the characteristics that racists appealed to in order to causally explain the conditions of white dominance could themselves be causally explained by the fact of living under white dominance. In Guns, Germs, and Steel: The Fates of Human Societies, Jared Diamond argued that Eurasians have been politically dominant over the rest of the world's population not because of some biological, cultural, intellectual or moral superiority, but because of their geographic advantages; resources like horses, metals, and sufficiently large populations to develop disease resistance structurally advantaged them against populations who lacked those resources.

Similar explanations have also been advanced for gender differences and hierarchies. The cultural materialist anthropologist Marvin Harris argued that patriarchal, male dominant family arrangements arose when agricultural societies developed livestock driven iron plows: men were better equipped for this type of more efficient farming that became economically dominant, and so their social dominance followed from their control of the most efficient means of production. In The Dialectic of Sex (1970), Shulamith Firestone offers a different explanation where she argues that while the physical differences between male and female roles in reproduction explain how male dominance developed, the feminine character traits cited as reasons why male dominance should persist are themselves products of female oppression.

The purpose of these arguments is not to show that it is impossible to explain the status of subordinated demographic groups in reference to their biological differences. Rather, it is to demonstrate that there are social structural or material explanations that can also account for the social hierarchy and the perceived differences between demographic groups. Given two possible explanations – one sociological, the other biological (where the variables are impossible to control; we cannot take a child and put him or her in some other experimental social arrangement, nor can we put an adult in a social position identical to a child in our society) – there is no way for us to determine how much of children's childishness is the result of their innate attributes and how much is the result of their social position.

What does it really mean when we say that a child's brain is "still developing"? This is often construed to suggest that the changes that go on in a child's brain over time are teleological in nature – they begin at a low level of development and lead to the end point of a superior adult level of development, so we only give people adult rights and responsibilities once they have fully reached that superior level. This narrative, however, has minimal scientific support. The reality is that there is no fixed adult level of brain development where brains plateau – rather, brains continue to change over the course of someone's lifetime. Myelin levels in the brain, often cited as 'proof' that the teenage brain is still developing, not only continue to increase through teenage years, but well into middle age, at which point they decline.

Psychologist Robert Epstein surveyed the literature on adolescent neurology studies and concluded that they were misrepresented in the popular press in several ways: the changes observed continue to take place through our lives, and research has thus far only shown correlations between behavior and neurology, but has not demonstrated causality, and it is well known that experience can alter brain anatomy, and studies are often simply misrepresented and overstated. Epstein notes that while all of our behavior, thoughts and feelings are in some way reflected physically in our brains, it does not follow that something particular about our brains is the cause of those actions or emotional states. According to Epstein, environments, studying, diet, exercise, stress, and many other activities alter the brain – so if adolescents have problems, pointing to brain differences does not show that their brains caused the problems, as the problems could cause the brain differences. There are also numerous differences between child and adult mental capacities where children actually have superior mental abilities. Visual acuity peaks at the onset of puberty, and incidental memory abilities peak near twelve years old before declining, so young people actually have an organic advantage in learning new things. Intelligence researchers J.C. Raven and David Wechsler using different intelligence tests found that "raw intelligence" scores peak between age thirteen and fifteen and decline through life. Needless to say these differences between child and adult mental capacities have not been prominent in political and media discourse about children's capacities and rights.

The focus on the difference between adults and children ignores what is at stake from a social justice perspective in according children equal rights. Even to the extent that there are significant natural differences in capacity between most adults and most children, these differences do not necessarily justify all or most of the social structures that privilege adults against children. Just as biological differences between men and women do not determine the specific socio-economic (and, historically, legal) advantages of men over women (such as coverture), the biological differences between adults and children do not determine the form that children's legal status takes with regard to adults. Even if we were to grant for the sake of argument that, implausibly, all people under the age of eighteen have inferior mental capabilities to all those over eighteen, this is hardly an argument for assigning civil rights only to those with superior mental capabilities over eighteen. Reasonable people rightly recognise that those allegedly (or even demonstrably) more rational and intelligent should not enjoy greater rights than those with lesser capacities for rationality and intelligence – we do not see legal caste hierarchies arranged by IQ points or brain size as legitimate or just ways of organising a society.

Despite the considerable variability in the roles children have occupied in society, people continue the mistake of thinking children's status is something inherent to children, rather than a condition imposed on them by the state and society. For instance, in Schall v. Martin, the Supreme Court permitted pretrial detention of children for longer periods than permitted for adults, under the theory that such detention was not punitive, but merely regulatory, in part because children have fewer liberty interests than adults – they are always in some sort of custody. Do children really have fewer liberty interests as an inherent result of their childhood, or has the state already deprived them of their liberty under its 'regulations'? It would seem that the Schall Court did not find any pre-trial punishment of children because children are generally treated in a way that would be recognised as punitive if applied to an adult. In this case, the status of a child's liberty is the result of a child's legal status, not a child's biology.

It is dangerous from the viewpoint of someone concerned with wrongly depriving others of liberty to assume that children's apparent capacities necessarily exclude them from possessing rights, when their effective capabilities are constrained by the way they are treated in society. If a child were capable of exercising equal rights competently, how would we be able to recognise it in a society that deprives them of any opportunity to do so? If we cannot tell whether or not children are capable of exercising rights in a society that enables them to do so, because we are only familiar with children in the context of a society that prevents them from exercising equal rights, then the assumption that children are naturally incapable of having rights is unjustified.

Prevailing Attitudes Towards Children

There are additional reasons to be suspicious of the common impulse to accept research that seems to confirm adult assumptions about children. Dismissing out of hand the possibility that children could exercise greater control over their lives is attractive, easy, and convenient. It is convenient because it is easier for adults to deal with children if children have few state-enforceable rights that can be mobilized against adults when adults attempt to control their lives against their wishes. Many adults also tend to just really like the idea that children are child-like and profoundly unadult-like: that they are cute, innocent, irresponsible, and dependent without the possibility of autonomy. Educator and child rights' advocate John Holt writes:

> When one person sees and deals with another not as a unique person but as an example of a type, whether Celebrity, Black, Sex Symbol, Great Genius, Artist, Saint, or whatever, he diminishes that person and makes it hard for any natural relationship to grow between them. This is what we do to children when we see them as Cute, Adorable, Innocent. For the real child before us we substitute some idea of Childhood that we have in our minds and deal with that. Often, when we label someone in this way, we invest him with magical properties, sometimes bad, sometimes good. Men often do this to women they consider beautiful. Having turned the child into an ideal abstraction, many parents and teachers tend to look at him much as Rocket Control in Houston looks at a moon shot. They have a trajectory (life) all mapped out for this child, and they are constantly monitoring him to see whether he is on the path or whether he needs a little boost from this rocket (psychologist) here or a sideways push from that rocket (learning specialist) there. They have their own precise notions of what a child should be. They tend to slip very easily into condescending sentimentality as I have described.

Holt's observation reveals what we in some ways already know, that adults judge children according to what plans and expectations the powerful adults in their lives – their parents and teachers – have for them. If children are not under parental control – following a parent-defined path rather than their own desires – adults judge them to be out of control. If it is often thought that if children are left to their own devices they will make a mess of their lives, this is in part because parents, teachers and other adults presume to define what is valuable in their children's lives and what would constitute making a mess of them. The widespread liberal belief that the state should remain neutral between differing conceptions of the good is inconsistently dropped when it comes to dealings with children – most adults imagine instead that there is either an objectively appropriate way for children to behave, learn, and grow up, or that each parent's subjective and arbitrary preferences for their children's conduct should be given force despite also thinking that even a democratically elected state should not impose its beliefs of how to live one's life on its citizenry.

When children deviate from adult expectations, from the idealised abstracted version of what a child is, it can cause cognitive dissonance: the problem is felt to be with the child and not with the idea of what a child should be and how children should act. To find an example of this we need look no further than the way adults react with horror to children's use of foul language when the same language used by an adult would leave them unfazed. Just as children's apparent capabilities and behaviors are limited by societal constraints, societal views of children and the impressions they make on adults are similarly informed by the social conventions that affect how adults think about children. This is all the more reason to be skeptical of our own intuitions about what children are capable of. Recent research strongly suggests that older adults actually prefer reading articles that seem to confirm inferior traits in young people. One way this could be explained is that people in a position of privilege find it affirming and convenient when they receive information that seems to confirm that their privilege is natural and not arbitrary.

Parenting is a Conflict of Interest

Kathleen Nicole O'Neal

Since becoming involved with youth liberation, I have encountered an attitude from a number of parents that has consistently left me baffled. They have expressed this attitude in a variety of ways that probably sounded like fine rhetoric to the person making the statements but which has consistently struck me as either disingenuous or betraying a deep lack of understanding of what youth liberation is really about.

Here is a sampling of the sort of statements to which I refer: "As a parent, I am on the frontlines of advocating for children while you are dealing with theory." (This might be less disingenuous coming from someone that attempts to put some sort of youth autonomy-centered philosophy at the core of their parenting, but alas this person was not such a parent.) "As a parent, I can speak to my child's need for boundaries and discipline." "You'll feel differently when you are a parent." These statements are not only a prime example of the authoritarian impulses of the people making them, they are also patently absurd upon reflection. This is because parenting is not a qualification for discussing the rights of youth, it is a conflict of interest.

One is often seen as bolstering his case when he takes a stand despite having interests to the contrary. This is why the millionaire that supports higher income tax rates, the poor person that doesn't believe in government assistance for people like himself, the white person speaking out in favor of affirmative action programs for racial minorities, and the person of color who opposes affirmative action programs tend to be seen as either a.) lacking a true appreciation of their own self-interests or b.) acting from a higher and more noble set of values than immediate self-interest but never as c.) deeply corrupted by their own interests.

There are also individuals who come to make a judgment about a situation as a more or less neutral party with nothing that she personally stands to gain or lose depending on the outcome of the situation. We think of the ideal judge and jury in a court case as having interests of this type. Their very neutrality can bolster their claims about a situation.

Parents advocating for their "right" to arbitrarily punish their children and control their lives are not taking either type of stand. They are not taking a stand that goes against their self-interest and they are not coming to a decision about their values from a place of neutrality. Guardianship and minority give parents power at the expense of their children. There is therefore nothing especially noble or wise about parents arguing for the maintenance of these institutions in their current form – it is simply one example among many of powerful people attempting to protect their interests at the expense of those they have power over. Saying "As a parent I know what is best for my child" is no more noble than saying "As a slave owner I know that emancipation doesn't suit the Negro" or "As a logging executive I know that we don't need environmental regulation." Even if the statements were valid, we would be right to be highly suspect about the motives of the person making the claim.

When we hear someone speaking of his or her role as a parent as a justification for beliefs about youth that many youth themselves would likely find oppressive or even abusive we should never accept that as good enough and we should never defer to their judgment on those grounds alone. If anything, that person's status as a parent should make us more suspect about his or her motives for supporting youth oppression. When discussing youth liberation, parenting is not a qualification. It is a conflict of interest. It is important that no one ever trick us into thinking of the position of a parent as necessarily pro-youth or even neutral. We cannot be bullied into silence by those whose class position vis a vis youth betrays their true motives for advocating for their continued oppression.

Cheating is a Moral Imperative

Cevin Soling

You have been kidnapped and dragged off to a remote location where your abductors have tied you to a chair. One of your captors is seated in front of you. He holds up ten flash cards and informs you that he is going to ask you a series of questions and the answers are printed on the backs of the cards. He assures you that once he has finished asking these questions, you will be released. There is a catch, though. For every question you get wrong, he will signal his accomplice to cut off one of your fingers. As he begins to read the first question, you notice there is a mirror on the opposite wall where you can see the reflection of the text on the card. Because you have been taught that cheating is dishonest, you interrupt your kidnapper and let him know that you are able to read the card and that he must conceal them better so that you cannot inadvertently cheat. He adjusts himself accordingly and proceeds to ask you a series of dry and uninspired questions on topics that hold no interest for you, while his accomplice menacingly holds out a set of cutting pliers.

While cheating is technically wrong, everyone should cringe at this conception of morality because it fails to account for context. In this example, cheating is not only justified, it is necessary because it aids a helpless victim who has been involuntarily subjected to unreasonable conditions. Unfortunately, this kind of clarity is absent when it comes to compulsory education.

One of the most salient features of all public schools is the importance of grades. Because grades are the currency and sole commodity of schools, they are used both to motivate and punish. They are a major component of a student's portfolio and have the potential to impact their future. Educators might try to stress the value of "learning" over grades, but that is a complete farce. When learning is not commensurately represented by grades, students rightly feel cheated by the system and become apathetic. To insist on valuing learning over grades is offensively disingenuous and hypocritical. It is akin to telling workers at McDonald's that they should care more about doing their job than their salary.

Students have no input regarding how or what they learn, and they are alienated from the work they do at school. Except for a few rare assignments, students are not inspired by their work, and any personal attachment they could have is undermined by the fact that they must compromise their efforts to meet the demands and expectations of the person who grades their work.

It's important to bear in mind that students prepare for tests with the intention that they will retain the material just long enough to take the test and then forget most of what they learned soon afterwards. This completely undermines the purpose and value of testing. Advocates of testing who denigrate cheating conveniently fail to acknowledge this. Testing demands that students view knowledge as a disposable commodity that is only relevant when it is tested. This contributes to the process of devaluing education.

The benefits of cheating are obvious – improved grades in an environment where failure is not an opportunity for learning, but rather a badge of shame. When students do poorly on a test, there is no reason for students to review their responses because they will likely never be tested on the same thing ever again. The test itself is largely arbitrary and often not meaningful. Organisations such as FairTest are devoted to sharing research that exposes the problems of bad testing practices.

The main arguments against cheating in school are that it is unethical, promotes bad habits, and impacts self-esteem through the attainment of an unearned reward. None of these concerns are even remotely valid because none consider the environment. Children are routinely rounded up and forcibly placed in an institution where they are subjected to a hierarchy that places them at the bottom. Like the hostage, they are held captive even if they are not physically bound. They are deprived of any power over their own lives, including the ability to pursue their interests, and are subjected to a barrage of tests that have consequences for each wrong answer.

Maintaining ethics is part of an unwritten contract of being a willing participant in a community. Students placed in school against their will and routinely disrespected have no obligation to adhere to the ethical codes of their oppressors. Cheating is an act of resistance, and resistance against oppressive powers should be encouraged and celebrated, rather than deemed a "bad habit" or an unethical act. The concern regarding self-esteem that is highlighted by The Child Study Center as promoting the "worst damage," lacks any scientific support whatsoever.

If students feel bad for cheating, it is because the environment has created a set of conditions where cheating is necessary and justifiable. For this same reason, many students are proud that they cheat. Cheating often requires creativity in terms of execution as well as ingenuity to avoid being caught. It also serves as a statement of disdain against an arbitrary and repressive institution. For these reasons, cheating can be a source for pride that boosts self-esteem. Given this construct, cheating is not simply something many students do: it is something all students in compulsory schools should do. Cheating is a moral imperative.

Punishing students for cheating is completely misguided. People should be most concerned about the student who does not cheat. They are the ones who appear to have internalised their oppression and might lack the necessary skills to rally and lobby against abuses of power that are perpetrated by governing bodies. Cheating should be recognised as the necessary and logical outcome of an arbitrary and oppressive institution. Punishing students who cheat is yet another abuse of autocratic power. In a healthy society, people ridicule and shame those who force children to endure the kind of environment that demands they must cheat.

Excerpt from
Undoing the School-to-Prison Pipeline
Damien Sojoyner

The analytical construction of the STPP provides an easy and accessible narrative pertaining to prisons and public education. In general, the STPP argument states that schools unfairly discipline non-white youth, particularly Black youth, when compared to students of other races. Studies demonstrate that Black students have higher rates of suspensions, detentions, and expulsions than their peers (Wald & Losen, 2003). Further, there is increasing evidence that Black students within the same schools are disproportionately given more severe forms of discipline than their white peers for the exact same offenses (Jackson, 2012). The results of these forms of punishment often lead to Black students either being pushed out of school or arrested on campus. Hence, school discipline policies and legal constructs serve to funnel Black youth through the STPP.

The history of STPP research and its associated campaign is complicated by its development in the midst of anti-prison movements across the United States. While decades-long organising efforts by the likes of Critical Resistance, A New Way of Life, and the Southern California Library have explicit ties to historic, economic, political, and social projects that aim to radically alter society through the abolishment of prisons, the STPP discourse is not invested in the same goal. Further, the STPP is framed ahistorically, often missing critical racial, class, gendered, and sexed analyses that are needed to understand the root causes, including the development of education malaise and subsequent expansion of prisons within the United States. In this manner, the STPP discourse cannot begin to address a central theme and line of inquiry posed by Ruth Wilson Gilmore (2007) that is key to any analysis of prisons:

> This book is about the phenomenal growth of California's state prison since 1982, it asks how, why, where, and to what effect one of the planet's richest and most diverse political economies has organised and executed a prison-building and filling plan that government analysts have called 'the biggest… in the history of the world.' (p. 5)

While community organisations across the country have been fighting to identify and eradicate the multilayered connections between the nation's schools and prisons, this has not been the articulated aims of the STPP discourse. For example, the central document that laid the groundwork for the discursive framing of the STPP, Deconstructing the School-to-Prison Pipeline (Wald & Losen, 2003), details a funneling mechanism that transfers minoritised youth from schools to prisons but neglects to interrogate the coalescence of schools and prisons including the political, economic, racial, gendered, and sexed complexities that undergird both of their foundations. This narrow understanding of the relationship between schools and prisons has become increasingly popularized within the past decade. Philanthropic organisations and national and state government offices have highlighted the pipeline as a reformist attempt to assuage the demands of community and neighborhood organising. The STPP discourse has not only been used by government officials to describe the relationship between schools and prisons, it has also been repackaged as a non-threatening, ubiquitous, rhetorical device for community organisers.

This disturbing trend follows in an eerily similar path as the development of the "Schools not Jails" campaign during the late 1990s. As argued by Camille Acey (2000), the Schools not Jails movement undercut the radical and valid critique that students and community members had regarding the function of school in the United States. According to Acey (2000):

> The slogan "education not incarceration" grew out of the link between university student anti-Proposition 209 activism and grass-roots high school student activism. In the mid- to late 1990s, a number of student walkouts and protests were led throughout the state of California. The main emphasis of university students was on increasing access to the university for poor, working-class communities of color and promoting more relevant curricula. High school students from those communities voiced concerns over insufficient educational resources, declining economic opportunity, and the growing criminalisation of their generation. Often, many of the organisations came together to develop more comprehensive, radical critiques of these issues and strategies for political education. Though it is often believed that SNJ [Schools not Jails] is a variation on "education not incarceration," I would argue that that it is a corruption.

In recent years, the co-optation of the STPP discourse has shifted the conversation away from key historical issues that constituted the generative core of radical community organising. Over the past ten years, conferences and workshops have convened non- profit organisations, academic scholars, philanthropic foundations, and legislative bodies to analyze causes and solutions to the STPP. To date, the primary answer to the STPP has been to focus on student behavior and policy transformation; that is, the response has been to focus on the way that discipline policies are levied out based upon racialised conceptualisations of student behaviour (Kim, Losen, & Hewitt, 2010). An underlying logic of these solutions is that by altering behaviors and certain policies, students will no longer be pushed out or arrested. Subsequently, these strategies would help to greatly reduce students' chances of being sent to prison.

While there is general agreement that Black students are unfairly disciplined within the realm of public education and that predominately Black schools are mired in a labyrinth of policing procedures, I argue that the STPP framework provides an overdetermined, analytic model and an undertheorised solution set to address issues that are both historical in nature and extremely complex. Specifically, the STPP is a concept that is predicated upon an analysis of power that follows an arc whereby the supposed beholders of power have complete control of the "other" - Black youth. Similar to Cedric Robinson's (2007) critique of Foucault's analysis of power, the same argument can be made with respect to the STPP. Specifically, Robinson (2007) states:

> It is as if systems of power never encounter the stranger, or that strangers can be seamlessly abducted into a system of oppression. In our own interrogations this amounts to the presumption that the exposing of the invention of race subjects is a sufficient method for recognising and explaining difference. (p. xii)

The glaring problem with the STPP's framework is that it never accounts for the possibility that the structure of public education is responding to the actions taken by Black students that are perceived to threaten the status quo. In this regard, the criminalisation of Black youth is not only intentional, but it is in response to direct agitation on the part of Black people. Thus, strategies to address the STPP that focus on shifting behaviors serve to legitimate the idea that disciplining student behavior is necessary, as long as the mechanisms do not push students out of school or entail arrests.

While the STPP framework may challenge the basic tenant that the meting out of discipline is disproportional, it fails to challenge the ethos of anti-Blackness as foundational to the formation and enactment of school discipline. Through a brief cull of the annals of contemporary history, which the STPP framework completely disregards, I will demonstrate that the modes of current school discipline (e.g., policing and expulsions) have developed in an attempt to suppress assertions of Black culture, Black autonomy, and Black liberation movements within schools. Very simply, the attention to reforming student behaviour belies the complicity of state officials, private capital, and philanthropic organisations to undermine efforts by Black communities to dictate the parameters of Black education.

Recognising that historical processes stretching back over two centuries account for the education of Black people in the United States, the basis of support for my argumentation rests on evidence amassed between the 1940s and 1970s in Southern California. This time period was of great significance as it marked a mass influx of Black migrants from the U.S. South to California.

Moreover, Los Angeles is important during this moment as the site where intense violence was enacted upon Black communal organisations that advocated for social change (Widener, 2010). It was also during this time period in Los Angeles that education was a hotly contested area in terms of the terrain of ideological governance. That is, while Black communities in Los Angeles conceptualised and used public education as a space to develop alternative models of cultural expression and organising, city officials, planners, and private capital lobbied for and responded with brute force and policy tactics to undermine liberation movements of Black Angelinos. Looking through two important documents – the Welfare Planning Council's report on "Youth Problems and Needs in the South Central Area" (WPC, 1961) and the "Police in Government" course manual taught by officers within the Los Angeles Police Department (LAPD) (Los Angeles Police Department, 1974) in predominately Black high schools – we achieve a nuanced understanding of the complex relationship among Black communities, city leaders, and public education.

In addition to the influx of Black migrants and the level of violence enacted upon Black communal organisations in Los Angeles during this time period, Southern California (and Los Angeles in particular) is a critical site to examine because over the last 50 years, it has become the region of choice in regards to the testing and development of models that foster enclosure linkages between education and prisons. Ranging from the highly marketed anti-drug "D.A.R.E" program to truancy tickets that mandate arrests and carry exorbitant fines, policy makers in Southern California have been at the cutting edge of creating policy and perfecting extralegal measures to ensure the subjugation of Black education. While these programs have been exported nationwide and lauded as models of public safety and/or crime prevention, it is necessary to understand the social and political context from which they developed. It is only then that we can refine our analysis beyond seductive, rhetorical devices and empty reformist concessions such as the STPP. Moreover, understanding the social and political context enables us to begin the "heavy lifting" of developing concrete strategies that explore the multifaceted nature of education and re-root movements for social change back to Black communities.

Anarchism and Youth Liberation

Marc Silverstein

Children in today's society are uniquely oppressed, but for the most part their oppression goes unnoticed even by people who consider themselves progressives or radicals. The fact that the relations between children and adults are based on inequality and compulsion is considered a separate issue from oppressions based on race, gender or sexual orientation, because it is considered somehow natural. Children are seen as incapable of making decisions for themselves and running their own affairs, due to their supposed lack of experience and immaturity, and therefore it is considered legitimate for adults to exercise some kind of authority over them. Anarchism, which is based on the principles of individual sovereignty, non-coercion, free association and mutual aid, can play an important role in helping to formulate an anti-authoritarian theory of parenting, education and child-rearing, and to begin the process of liberating children from an oppressive society.

The first kind of authority that children face while growing up is that of their parents. Parents have legal guardianship over their children from the moment they are born until they turn 18. Most parents hold an authoritarian and hierarchical view of their relation to their children. They see their kids as their property, who are to be nurtured, protected, kept in line, restrained, disciplined, rewarded or punished as the parents see fit. Anarchists would oppose this conception of the child, since children are not seen as autonomous individuals in their own right, but mere appendages of their parents. Mikhail Bakunin, the Russian anarchist, put it succinctly: "Children do not constitute anyone's property: they are neither the property of the parents nor even of society. They belong only to their own future freedom."

Some parents use the justification that they are "over-protective" or they "care about their children too much" to excuse the stifling atmosphere of the nuclear family. It is with the nuclear family that gender roles are created and re-inforced, and where authoritarian ideologies are passed down to the next generation. Neurotic and anti-social personality traits are also produced in children as a consequence of the nuclear family's puritanical suppression of sexuality. Oftentimes, parents will force their children to follow their particular religion, i.e. Judaism, Christianity, etc. or political affiliation, i.e. Republican, Democrat, etc. In the Jewish religion, boys at 13 are usually pressured or outright coerced into having Bar Mitzvahs, which is the sign of "becoming a man". Hanukkah and Christmas are religious celebrations which children are forced to partake in, and they are not given any opportunity to make up their own mind about their religious or political beliefs.

Around the age of 5, children are shipped off to schools, or "youth concentration camps" as anarchist writer Bob Black accurately called them. In these institutions children are monitored closely by their teachers, who make sure to report any kind of "suspicious" behavior. The purpose of school is to thwart any signs of free-thought or individuality, by forms of subtle or not-so-subtle coercion. If children "misbehave", they are punished by being sent to the office, detention, suspension, expulsion, or bad grades. In most private middle and high schools, and in a growing number of public schools, there is a dress code that children have to follow. Sometimes they are even forced to tuck in their shirts or wear a belt. Tattoos, dyed hair, piercings and other attempts to create an individual identity are often met with the fierce hostility of principals and administrators.

The relation of the administration to the students is almost exactly like that of a boss to his workers. He owns the institution, he sets the "standards of conduct", and tries to create a "productive work environment". It is not considered a good idea to question those in authority, and the anger of the students are channeled into acceptable forms such as student government or the official student union, which are similar to modern AFL-CIO unions in the workplace. Student government may call for minor reforms, but in no way calls into question the very existence of schools, or the possibility of abolishing coercion altogether, which the anarchist critique calls for.

It is also quite interesting how much schools and prisons have in common with each other. In both prisons and schools, the following criteria apply: an authoritarian structure, dress code, pass needed for going from one part of the facility to another, emphasis on silence and order, negative reinforcement, emphasis on behaviour, extrinsic reward system, loss of individual autonomy, abdridged freedoms, and little participation in decision making.

This begs the question: what can children do to fight back against the particular forms of oppression they face in their daily lives? The most important thing is to create a subversive atmosphere in the home, school, and workplace (high-school students are often forced to work in shitty, low-paying jobs like McDonalds). Let other young people know how you feel about parental coercion or about how you are treated by adults. Class consciousness is essential. Children need to recognise that they are a uniquely oppressed class vis a vis the oppressing class which dictates the conditions of their existence. To paraphrase the Preamble to the IWW Constitution, the oppressed class and the oppressing class have nothing in common.

Disobedience can be expressed in small ways (kind of like sabotage in the workplace) by refusing to pledge allegiance, to participate in prayer (in religious schools), or by choosing to write school essays on, for example, Youth Revolt Throughout History,

Emma Goldman, or the case of Katie Sierra (a 15-year old anarchist suspended from school for wearing homemade anti-war shirts and for trying to start up an anarchist club) and delivering them in front of class. Educate yourself outside of school by talking with others, reading, and sharing your ideas and experiences. You can make flyers and distribute them or paste them up around the school. You can start up a zine by yourself or with others, and distribute it at school. High-school general strikes or Reclaim the Streets can also be planned; even if they are over seemingly reformist issues (curfew, uniforms, etc.), they have the possibility of radicalising more and more students.

There are many creative possibilities: for instance, a group of anarchists close to where I live took a sign from a kennel that said "Obedience Training" and unfurled it over a local high school. To the extent that such things are successful, parents and administrators must feel like they can not get away with stuff that they could get away with before, that they are being closely watched and monitored by the children they formerly oppressed, that they are slowly losing their grip of power and authority over youth, and that youth are no longer an amorphous mass of docile sheep, but class conscious, intelligent, committed, and organised, and are prepared to take their lives into their own hands and to abolish all masters once and for all.

Anarchism has a lot to offer youth liberation. Its basic principles of anti-authoritarianism and non-coercion are powerful weapons in the arsenal to free children from their state of slavery and bondage. Anarchism also offers youth liberation the insight that it cannot be content with just abolishing parental coercion, it must also create liberatory alternatives. This is an example of the revolutionary dual power strategy, where the new society is created out of the shell of the old. Contrary to the official view, education does not equal schooling, and kids can create a whole self-organised infrastructure of counter-institutions for learning, growing, and developing themselves – on a basis of full equality and freedom. Genuinely "free skools" can be created, where classes are strictly voluntary, and children can choose to study a particular subject with others, children or adults, who happen to be an authority on the topic. As Colin Ward put it in his book Anarchy in Action, they will be "schools no longer" but popular laboratories of liberation.

NO!

AGAINST ADULT SUPREMACY
Issue 2

Youth Liberation and Deschooling
An Interview with Carla Bergman

Carla Bergman is a community artist, curator and writer who mucks around with her partner and two unschooling kids in East Vancouver, unceded Coast Salish Territories. Currently, she is the director of the Purple Thistle Centre and has worked with youth creating projects, mentoring, facilitating workshops and making a variety of publications for the past fifteen years. She is on the Board of the Institute for Anarchist Studies. Carla co-founded the art and activist publication RAIN, worked with car free day Vancouver as a core organiser and co-founded the Thistle Institute, an alternative to university, in 2011. She is currently working on a film about the Thistle and Youth Liberation, to be completed late 2014. She was one of the editors of the AK Press book: Stay Solid: A Radical Handbook For Youth.

You really center trust when you talk about youth liberation and oppression – why?

C: John Holt has a great quote about this: "Trust children. Nothing could be more simple - or more difficult. Difficult, because to trust children we must trust ourselves - and most of us were taught as children that we could not be trusted."

I think that kids start off their lives trusting everyone around them; it's how they learn from others and how they receive love. And then, over time it often gets eroded… I don't think it's because they learn to distrust, indeed that does happen, but I think it begins with not being trusted. It's obvious that a largely accepted notion in society is that kids are not to be trusted. I think this is one of the most damaging and brutal forms of discrimination against kids and youth.

I think trust happens in all kinds of subtle ways, and it's relational. I can use the Thistle as an example of how it might look in the most obvious, concrete way. One thing that separates the Thistle from many other youth projects is that the youth on the collective each have keys to the space and are free to use them anytime. The youth don't have to go through some big formal interview process, or sign over their life; we just ask that if they are new to the space to hang out a bit and get to know us first, and sometimes, you get the keys on your first night there. This contributes to a wonderful environment of shared trust and kindness – a space filled with friendship.

Trust is one of the most important foundations for all relationships and communities, and if we are not trusting our kids, the most vulnerable folks in our communities, then we are setting up to fail as radical inclusive humans.

You've talked about how power relations between kids and adults can't just be flattened out or eliminated – can you say more about that?

C: I always say, and it's deeply sincere, that it has been through the act of parenting that I have been truly radicalised. As anti-authoritarians we have to ask ourselves: how do kids fit into our praxis? I am put to test every single day to not oppress my kids. As one of the adults in my house I hold almost all the power and it's good, fucking hard work figuring out how to be solid, how to be a mentor, and how to have a thriving life as well. For me this isn't about just being permissive and nice, because as parents we can do all kinds of fucked up manipulation and oppression with a gentle sweet smile on our faces.

So, we always say that we strive to be a relationship/family centered home. I see that as an alternative to centering kids, which I think can lead adults into the fantasy that we've checked our power at the door, and that it's all good. It's not that easy. I come to every single day with my kids with years of socialisation and fuckedupness. It's deeply embedded and nuanced, and it takes care and dedication to unlearn and to do well. Mistakes happen, a lot. But those are OK too, because we show our kids that we're not some god(dess) on a pedestal really early on and more than that, we show them that humans make mistakes, and in fact it's how we learn. I think of my relationships with my kids (and all the young folks in our lives) as relationships that matter and that means I don't take it for granted that we're friends just because I say so. I have to work at it, as I would with any good pal. I think solidarity begins at home – we need to be solid, kind, and caring there if we're going to try to extend those values to the broader world.

You have a militant stand against schools and schooling, and people assume this means you won't work with anyone involved in the school system, but your stance is a lot more nuanced. Can you explain how you think about this?

C: My stance is that I am a strong supporter of folks who are school resisters, because folks who resist compulsory schooling (and all its problems) have in almost every case centered kids as a group that deserve liberation. I can really get behind that and I'm passionate about it.

I think it's also important to emphasize that youth and compulsory schooling are not isolated from the rest of society, so I think it's imperative to look at the entire system and how school and youth oppression fits into the entire dominant culture pie and how it intersects into all forms of oppression. For example, when you add capitalism, work, class, race, patriarchy, colonialism and all the rest into the mix, it's really clear that the situation is complex and there isn't room for simple black-and-white judgments. The bottom line is that most parents/caregivers have to work and so kids need some care, some place to be. In many places around the world it is illegal to homeschool/unschool and it's a criminal act to leave your kids at home alone in many places. Just a few weeks ago in the US, a single mom was put in jail because her 9 year old was at the park alone. With all this in mind, I support all movements and struggles of resistance and reform when it comes to creating better conditions for kids and that includes movements to make schools less fucked up places. Most schools are places that warehouse kids and oppress them in terrible ways. At the same time, I have nothing but mad respect for those folks who tirelessly and passionately show up to these institutions daily to support kids and to try and make it better for them.

Ultimately, my personal work and activism is about creating alternatives to school, so I am less interested in the binary between school or no school and more interested in rethinking entirely how we can create free, accessible spaces and projects for and by youth. I want to challenge the conditions that underscore youth oppression by having our communities sincerely engage kids into the architecture of all areas of society, and that's going to mean directly challenging ageism against children and youth. It's worth emphasising that most folks don't even include youth oppression (childism) on their list of oppressions. We have lots of work to do, and it's going to have to be together and it's going to have to be lead by youth.

Where do you think radical pedagogy and critiques of education go wrong?

C: In lots of cases, critiques or new models of education or of pedagogies can replicate the same kind of ageism and hatred of kids that happens in conventional institutions. If we don't begin from a sincere place of believing that kids deserve the same respect and treatment we'd give any other adult then we are doomed to repeat shitty forms of aggression and oppression.

The equation of learning to education is the crux of the problem; I like to center the idea that kids are learning all the time, and that we can all learn by doing. This isn't a new idea; Tolstoy wrote about it during the rise of modern schooling over 150 years ago. I started using the #checkyourpedagogy hashtag on twitter because I have noticed that a lot of radicals are still thinking about kids as empty vessels that need to be taught everything. The problem I see a lot is that critical and radical pedagogy methods don't really get to the heart of the problem (childism) and so the practice is often condescending and comes from a place that assumes youth need to be radicalised, or educated about social justice.

I think really sharing power and being sincere about youth liberation means never being attached to an outcome, and most pedagogies are all about an outcome that connects back to the teacher's plans. This is where deschooling can come in. To me deschooling just means having horizontal and friendly relationships between learner and mentor – centering relationships. When it's going well, learning and sharing knowledge moves in all directions, sideways, up and down. It's organic, relationship-based, fluid and deeply nuanced. This may seem super obvious, but the reality is that our entire education system is based on the opposite of that, it's basically just one direction: going down – expert to beginner.

The Thistle project (all the classes, workshops, the buying of supplies, etc) is run by a crew of youth, yet somehow the youth at the Thistle are not seen as folks who can teach anything about organising, or share the skills that they mentor at the centre. I can't tell you how many times I hear from well-meaning adults wanting to teach the Thistle youth this and that about organising. In contrast, other than silkscreening, we rarely receive an email asking the youth to come share their knowledge on running a dynamic and vibrant project. That sucks, right?

It really points to how undervalued their work and knowledge is. I think it's probably a (shitty) normal response because it's coming from an internal ageist place of "isn't that sweet, the kids practicing organising!" I often have to point to all the failed adult-run projects around town just to show that it's ageist to think the youth at the Thistle aren't fucking kicking some serious ass at organising! I think there are clear parallels with the ways other oppressions play out, like the ways that women's work and knowledge gets systematically marginalised and discounted.

How can folks learn more about deschooling and youth liberation?

C: I say just get busy doing it, get out there and engage with kids, learn together, make shit and have fun! And don't worry too much if you don't know what to do, or how to do it well – just be a good person, follow their curiosity, be open and listen lots! I am constantly learning how to do this work. I fuck up more than I care to admit and I am always learning and sometimes that happens from witnessing other adults do it well, but mostly that learning comes from the kindness of younger folks meeting me where I am at and letting me stumble and learn from experiencing alongside them.

I like to turn to folks like Tolstoy or Emma Goldman – both were staunch critics of compulsory schooling – to emphasise the point that people have been resisting, criticising, and creating alterna¬tives to modern factory schooling since its inception. I think that's important to realise and to remember. Resisting schooling/schools, or trying to rethink how we can live better with the youngest folks in our lives is not a privileged act: it's a sincere attempt to understand fully what school is about, who it is benefiting and more than that, who it is hurting. Modern schooling is steeped in colonial and capitalist logic and deeply oppressive to children, and there's a long history and vibrant legacy of resistance to the dominant models of education.

If it is something you're interested in researching there are lots of books written about school resistance and the problems with compulsory schooling. There are also tons of resources on how to create the alternatives. The core folks I turn to are Ivan Illich (critic of institutions, including schooling), John Holt (founder of the term unschooling and creator of alternatives to school), and a super popular book, primarily for youth, is by Grace Llewellyn called: The Teenage Liberation Handbook: How to Quit School and Get a Real Life and Education. A terrific go-to reader edited by Matt Hern, Everywhere All the Time, is definitely worth a read and includes a lot of youth voices. There are also tons of free resources online, and so many brilliant projects all over the world. I'd suggest doing a quick online search with keywords like: deschooling, school resistance, youth liberation, free schools and unschooling and you'll find great stuff.

You Did Not Turn Out Fine

James C. Talbot

In public forums on the internet, we can certainly have lively debates over whether Hitler was a hero, or whether or not the holocaust ever occurred. Oh, yes, we could find a debate over whether slavery ever existed in the U.S.. We might even get an argument that the Earth is flat and always has been. And, given what has also yet to become common knowledge, we can still find arguments in favor of hitting young children as a form of punishment.

For example, those who developed through their formative years having adopted as a part of their belief system that adults hit children as an acceptable practice will take on this treatment of children as a belief not dissimilar to the religious beliefs they've adopted during this same stage of development. And these are beliefs that tend to become deeply ingrained.

Those who happen to overcome and evolve beyond such irrational belief systems seem to be the exception to the rule. Sadly, it would seem that few children are able to avoid early childhood brainwashing to a particular religion or orientation. Typically, our little ones will buy into what we feed them lock, stock and barrel.

Herein lies the problem of change in the face of overwhelming evidence. Let's liken this change to telling a grown man that his name is actually Archibald instead of Joe. Lot's of luck. It's going to take awhile, no doubt and repeated efforts are in order. So, once again, let's try driving home the facts that carry with them the hope of breaking through just a few more of those bigoted obstacles still standing in the way of social progress.

To begin with, I feel it's most important to make it very clearly known to any and all concerned, that the debate on spanking within the scientific and academic communities is dead, and has been for a number of years now. The most substantial indicator of this development is evidenced by the fact that virtually every professional organisation in the U.S. and Canada concerned with the care and treatment of children has taken a public stance against the practice of spanking.

Based on the overwhelming accumulation of research conducted over the past 50+ years linking spanking to a number of risk factors, the professional consensus against this practice has grown to world-wide proportions. Even to the extent that Sweden, Finland, Austria, Norway, Croatia, Denmark, Hungary, Israel, Cyprus, Netherlands, Bulgaria, Germany, Latvia, Iceland, Romania, Greece, New Zealand, Venezuela, Spain, Portugal, Chile, Uruguay, and Ukraine have legislated total bans on spanking, with Italy, South Africa, Scotland, Canada, and Ireland apparently in the process of following suit. It should also be noted that every industrialised country in the world has banned spanking in schools. The evidence is in, and the evidence has found against the practice of spanking in a compellingly conclusive manner.

Just as one might find supportive views toward spanking being promoted (typically) on web sites sponsored by fundamentalist Christian sects, so can one find supportive views promoting Homophobia, Racism, Misogyny, and other 'hate group' propaganda. Because of the fact that the actual agendas of these sites are often deceptively disguised by organisational titles such as, 'Family Council', 'People's Choice', 'Rights and Freedoms', etc., people are forced to exercise a highly judicious discernment of the information being made available on the Internet. Some web surfers have had to learn the hard way that the Internet abounds with persuasive presentations of 'facts and figures' that can prove to represent nothing more than religious, political, or philosophical attempts to spread self-serving misinformation.

Having spent 30+ years examining/evaluating the research on this issue of spanking children, I am able to state with a high degree of confidence that there has never been a peer-reviewed study that has been able to establish the efficacy of spanking as a means of long-term behavior modification; as an effective teaching modality; as an effective punishment; or as a means of instilling self-discipline. Nor have there been published research findings in peer-reviewed professional journals that served to refute previous research. This previous research found spanking to be associated with a risk for undesirable emotional consequences; a risk for physical injury; a risk of counter-productive behavioural outcomes; a risk for the onset of dependence on external controls; and a proclivity toward authority-directed behaviour. Moreover, there has never been research data produced finding that spanking carries no risk to the quality of the parent-child relationship (and I should add that conservative editorial reviews of previous research findings do not constitute actual research, as is sometimes claimed to be the case).

Nevertheless, there are some spankers who will find reasons to dismiss, ignore, or discount the research findings of field conducted experimental studies related to the Social Sciences. Well, it's especially these folks that I'd like to address concerning alarming new research findings, which represent the most severe consequences of physical punishment yet discovered – while doing so in the form of documented scientific proof.

These revelations have come through studies in brain research having provided CAT SCAN pictures showing an abnormal lack of brain development (within the portion of the brain responsible for emotional functioning) in children who had been subject to spankings as a punitive measure. For the sake of sample homogeneity, the researchers chose subjects for their study that had been categorised as 'abused' children. Common sense tells us that this does not eliminate the possibility of a lesser degree of brain damage occurring to spanked children who are subjected to a lesser degree of non-injurious violence. In other words, it would be ludicrous to assume that a child must first suffer bruises, cuts, or welts (or other injuries), before brain damage can take place as a result of the physical punishments. Rather, it is much more logical to deduce that acts of physical aggression toward young children can disrupt, or prevent, the optimal conditions necessary to facilitate a normal process of healthy brain development.

As far as I'm concerned, this new area of research (apparently not yet freely available on the Internet) represents the most compelling, undeniable reason that's yet been discovered to persuade parents to stop (or never start) striking their children as a punitive measure. And I hope any pro-spankers reading this feel the same way. It's difficult to imagine any parent who would be willing to treat their child in a way that might carry even a remote risk of causing a measure of brain damage to their child.

But, in spite of having said all of that, we actually shouldn't need research to end the practice of striking children any more than we needed research to end the practice of striking wives. As a society, there was no need for research findings to convince us of the harmful effects associated with the practice of wives being physically punished.

Instead, when society reached the point of being no longer willing to grant social tolerance to the tradition of husbands physically disciplining their wives, our decision to do so was based on our having progressed socially into the higher morality of a greater humanity. Perhaps our next step ahead in forward progress should come by way of reaching a decision to begin recognising children as also being deserving of those same protections against being struck.

No longer do we see any adult members of our society remaining outside the jurisdiction of the protective laws once enjoyed by only the more privileged and 'deserving' (namely white males who made the laws), regardless of race, gender, religion, ethnic group, or sexual orientation. None of our adult citizens remain legally unprotected from being violated through harassment, threats, defamation, discrimination, or being victimized by violence to any degree or form. So, given our heritage of bestowing a greater humanity upon those of a lower social status by welcoming them as our equals in the eyes of the law (in terms of violent treatment), would it be so out of character for us to also shelter the younger, weaker members of our society by allowing them to join those of us already sharing in the security and comfort of safety that's provided under the umbrella of legal protections from violence?

Bringing our little ones into the fold really doesn't seem all that magnanimous if we keep in mind that we've already been willing to share the shelter of our umbrella of assault laws with even the most vicious of hardened adult criminals. After all, children are the very last segment of our shared human collective who still remain as fair game for being subjected to acts of physical aggression. We display a strange sense of priorities when we don't allow the prison guard to break-out a paddle and start whacking away on the disobedient buttocks of a sociopathic death-row inmate who kills for the rush it gives him, yet we find helpless, defenceless young children as deserving of such treatment.

Fact is, we define corporal punishments of prison inmates as 'cruel and unusual punishment', 'guard brutality', or 'aggravated assault'. And, should the physical punishments be repeated as a routine punitive measure, such a treatment of prisoners would fall under the definition of 'torture'. Why would a murderous inmate be less subject to physical discipline than a helpless 3-year-old child? Logically, morally, humanely, and scientifically, the debate on spanking is dead... save for those who would object to further social progress.

As we evolve as a society, we have to keep in mind that historically there was a time when it was acceptable to legally own other people; a time when the mentally ill were generally considered to be possessed by evil spirits; a time when men legally shot each other in officiated duels; a time when public hangings were attended as a family outing complete with picnic basket; a time when public floggings were considered acceptable punishment; a time when it was a gentleman's agreement that husbands should not beat their wives with a switch that was 'bigger-round than your thumb' (which later became known as 'the rule of thumb'); and there was a time when there were no laws against parents severely beating their children (killing children was unacceptable, of course, but an occasional accidental maiming as a result of disciplinary measures was tolerated).

Obviously, we no longer permit these punishments. The time has come for us to yet further our level of social sophistication by coming to a general agreement that any degree of physical punishment used against children is as socially unacceptable and repugnant as those past violent behaviors we have chosen to put behind us.

Stop Caging Kids
Nathan Goodman

This week marks the 2014 National Week of Action Against Incarcerating Youth. Across the country, actions will be held to protest everything from the criminalisation of queer and disabled youth to the isolation of youth in solitary confinement. Ultimately, what activists are protesting is systematic child abuse by the state.

Kids are being locked in cages by the government all across the country. The consequences are devastating. According to a report from the Justice Policy Institute:

A recent literature review of youth corrections shows that detention has a profoundly negative impact on young people's mental and physical well-being, their education, and their employment. One psychologist found that for one-third of incarcerated youth diagnosed with depression, the onset of the depression occurred after they began their incarceration, and another suggests that poor mental health, and the conditions of confinement together conspire to make it more likely that incarcerated teens will engage in suicide and self-harm. Economists have shown that the process of incarcerating youth will reduce their future earnings and their ability to remain in the workforce, and could change formerly detained youth into less stable employees. Educational researchers have found that upwards of 40 percent of incarcerated youth have a learning disability, and they will face significant challenges returning to school after they leave detention. Most importantly, for a variety of reasons to be explored, there is credible and significant research that suggests that the experience of detention may make it more likely that youth will continue to engage in delinquent behavior, and that the detention experience may increase the odds that youth will recidivate, further compromising public safety.

So the state is engaging in violence that scars young people physically and mentally, and hurts their economic prospects; and this practice may even increase rather than decrease the chance of future crime. Moreover, according to the same report, most of these youth are not even a threat to others, as "about 70 percent are detained for nonviolent offenses."

Once incarcerated, youth are subjected to severe abuses. For example, many youth are isolated in solitary confinement, which is widely recognised as a form of psychological torture. According to the American Civil Liberties Union:

Solitary confinement can cause extreme psychological, physical, and developmental harm. For children, who are still developing and more vulnerable to irreparable harm, the risks are magnified – particularly for kids with disabilities or histories of trauma and abuse. While confined, children are regularly deprived of the services, programming, and other tools that they need for healthy growth, education, and development.

The impacts of solitary on adults are harmful enough. "It's an awful thing, solitary," wrote John McCain, "It crushes your spirit and weakens your resistance more effectively than any other form of mistreatment." Subjecting youth to this kind of torture is monstrous.

Incarcerated youth are also all too often raped and sexually assaulted by guards. According to David Kaiser and Lovisa Stannow, "4.5 percent of juveniles in prison and 4.7 percent of those in jail reported such [sexual] victimisation – rates that ought to be considered disastrously high." Their risk was higher in youth detention centers, "minors held in juvenile detention suffered sexual abuse at twice the rate of their peers in adult facilities." Most of this abuse is committed by guards employed and paid with tax dollars:

Some 2.5 percent of all boys and girls in juvenile detention reported having been the victims of inmate-on-inmate abuse. This is not dramatically higher than the corresponding combined male and female rates reported by adults or juveniles in either prison or jail. The reason why the overall rate of sexual abuse (9.5 percent) was so much higher in juvenile detention than in other facilities is the frequency of sexual misconduct by staff. About 7.7 percent of those in juvenile detention reported sexual contact with staff during the preceding year. Over 90 percent of these cases involved female staff and teenage boys in custody.

Government employees are committing child sexual abuse against caged victims. These guards are often repeat offenders. "In juvenile facilities, victims of sexual misconduct by staff members were more likely to report eleven or more instances of abuse than a single, isolated occurrence." All of this data comes from research conducted by the government's own Bureau of Justice Statistics.

The impacts of the state's systematic caging and abuse of children are not equally distributed across the population. The Center for Children's Law and Policy documents many studies showing the racially disparate impacts of youth incarceration and juvenile justice policies. LGBTQ youth also face disproportionate impacts from the juvenile justice system. According to an article in The Nation:

The road to incarceration begins in pretrial detention, before the youth even meets a judge. Laws and professional standards state that it's appropriate to detain a child before trial only if she might run away or harm someone. Yet for queer youth, these standards are frequently ignored. According to UC Santa Cruz researcher Dr. Angela Irvine, LGBT youth are two times more likely than straight youth to land in a prison cell before adjudication for nonviolent offenses like truancy, running away and prostitution. According to Ilona Picou, executive director of Juvenile Regional Services, Inc., in Louisiana, 50 percent of the gay youth picked up for nonviolent offenses in Louisiana in 2009 were sent to jail to await trial, while less than 10 percent of straight kids were. "Once a child is detained, the judge assumes there's a reason you can't go home," says Dr. Marty Beyer, a juvenile justice specialist. "A kid coming into court wearing handcuffs and shackles versus a kid coming in with his parents – it makes a very different impression."

Queer and transgender youth are treated differently by the justice system before they are even tried and convicted. Once incarcerated, they face brutal violence. From beatings to victim blaming to bigoted slurs from guards, queer and transgender youth are regularly abused in juvenile corrections facilities.

Some of America's youth incarceration problem begins in the schools. "Zero-tolerance" policies in public schools criminalise violating school rules, producing what is often called the school to prison pipeline. The racially disparate impacts of this school to prison pipeline are well documented, and they often criminalise minor infractions.

Outside of school, youth are often directly targeted by police thanks to ageist laws like curfews. Laws often restrict freedom of movement and bodily autonomy for youth, and justify this coercion through condescending and paternalistic platitudes. In a particularly appalling recent case of paternalism sending youth to prison, a transgender girl was sent to an adult prison without charges or trial, because the state had power over her as her "guardian." The desire to protect youth provides ideological cover for the state to treat them even more abusively than it treats adults.

The American state is uniquely punitive in some respects. According to Amnesty International, "The United States is believed to stand alone in sentencing children to life without parole." Amnesty identifies "at least 2,500 people in the US serving life imprisonment without the possibility of parole for crimes committed when they were under 18 years old." Before turning 18, these youth were permanently separated from society, permanently sent to violent hellholes.

The essence of imprisonment as we know it is throwing away a human being, treating them as disposable. Prisoners are subjected to violence, abuse, and torture. They are held in austere and inhumane conditions. And they are kept out of the general public's sight. They are punished rather than being made to make amends or provide restitution to victims. It's bad enough to treat any human being this way. To treat children this way is unconscionable.

Stop caging kids.

NO!

AGAINST ADULT SUPREMACY

Issue 3

Young and Oppressed

Brian Dominick and Sara Zia Ebrahimi

While most common oppressions, such as sexism, racism, classism, heterosexism, even speciesism, have been identified, widely acknowledged, thoroughly discussed and deeply analysed, one oppression remains largely untouched. This fact is astonishing given that the group oppressed by this ignored injustice is one to which every adult human has once belonged. It is the one oppression with which all humans can identify, having suffered from it directly. It is not an oppression of a tiny minority to which few will ever belong. It is not the oppression of people who can be blamed themselves - by any stretch of the imagination - for being among the oppressed.

The oppressed group is that of young people - *all* young people.

As we will further demonstrate, adults and adult institutions in our society regularly commit acts of abuse, coercion, deprivation, indoctrination and invalidation against young people. From the moment of conception, young people are oppressed by their elders, entirely based on the difference in age, via a process known as "ageism."

As an oppression in need of acknowledgment and understanding, ageism is vital to oppression theory. Yet its overall framework has long been ignored. Sure, many an author has attempted to discuss the relationship between parent and child, teacher and pupil, detention centre officer and detainee, etc. But when has it been stated that adult society, as an institution, oppresses the young regularly, consistently, and without exception? And when has it been stated further, in any detail, that this oppression is vital to, and largely born of, society's need for maintenance at such absurd, atrocious levels?

Let's face it: when adults look at oppression theory, they do so from a "grown up" perspective - one which sees right over the heads of even their own children. While the Left takes great pride in its defence of women, the impoverished, racial and religious minorities, etc., it fails to realise that among the most thoroughly and widely oppressed are society's young. In our struggle for true liberation, we can leave no one behind - especially not those to whom the torch of revolution shall be passed. That is why ageism needs to be recognised.

Which brings us to why ageism is unique among oppressions: we are all directly its victims. It is not at all presumptuous to claim that the one oppressive dynamic of which we have all been on the receiving end is that of ageism. Indeed, we are all victims of every oppression acted out in our society. But none other than ageism claims each of us like a man carves a notch on his headboard, like a bombardier a stencil on his airplane, a capitalist a dollar in his bank account.

That is significant. When we step back and observe the social engineering performed by society's institutions upon its members, oppressions are plainly spotted in the tool chest of the dominant. Among those oppressions which help maintain the power positions of the wealthy white Christian heterosexual male elitist adult, ageism is universal. It is also, unlike the others which are interchangeable, completely indispensable to society's maintenance of individual apathy.

In order to be a permanent victim of an unjust society's power structure - that is, accepting and not resisting one's own victimisation - one must be engineered as a child to remain docile in the face of oppression. Certainly young people who are impoverished, female, African American, gay or otherwise in position to be oppressed, are conditioned for disempowerment. But what about white male children of upper class parents? Why do they show the same signs of submission and apathy when confronted by oppressors? Why do they, by and large, fail to expose and resist injustices, both in concept and in everyday encounters? Could it be because, as children, they undergo a rigorous process of indoctrination, both formal and informal, in schools, on television, at church, in the home? Could it be because they have been abused and coerced by legal systems, parents, teachers, police? Because they have been invalidated by overpowering institutions and individuals whose purpose it has been to teach them of their "incompetence," their "worthlessness"? Could they be so as a result of having been deprived of their right to self management, of simple needs, indeed of love and understanding and support? Could it be, at last, because throughout childhood and adolescence they have been treated as adult society has seen fit for its young - ignored, conditioned, neglected, brutalised, violated and compelled?

Then, as adults, they reproduce their own suffering, this time inflicting it upon those the society of which they are now full members has traditionally oppressed. As adults, they are offered power over - if no one else - the people on whose behalf few stand: their children, their younger neighbours, their adolescent customers, their voiceless constituents.

It is clear that ageism is not just another oppression. In some cases (few would disagree) age difference, aside from being the basis for oppression, is a justification for special treatment. Surely children require guidance as they learn for themselves about social realities. In many cases, clear bounds need setting by adults, for the child's safety and indeed for her or his benefit. But how much more often than not does the relationship between adult and young person - between adult institution and the young population - become counterproductive, destructive, outright violent? Why are these inequities not exposed, denounced and struggled against by those of us who regularly fight other oppressions?

These issues, equal in importance to the full examination of ageism itself, are in dire need of discourse. With that in mind, we hope to present, from our own biased perspective as young people, what we see as the issue: What is ageism? How does it manifest itself in practice? What are its results?

Political Ageism

Few oppressions are more obvious than those perpetrated by governments. From laws to bureaucracies, the manipulation factor in state systems is staggering. The most blatant mechanism employed by government towards the oppression of its subjects is certainly the legal system. Consistently, it is laws made specifically against young people which most flagrantly display the state's contempt for their youthful attitudes; mindsets which by their nature contradict prevailing social values and norms. After all, young people are one of the only oppressed groups which the US government not only discriminates against in an official capacity, but towards whom it does so unabashedly and without apology. The list of things the state will not allow people to do based on their age is seemingly endless. At the same time, the rights and "equality" of most other oppressed groups are lauded and, at least to some extent, protected by government agencies.

There is little validity to the argument that young people, due to their inexperience, need to be protected from themselves by agents of the state. It is the government's own interests which require defence from young people's natural lack of subordination and submission. Hence, authoritarian structures are forced to protect themselves by containing the expression of free thought and activity by children and adolescents. As a sort of insurance policy, the government stunts self-confidence, individuality and creativity at the earliest age possible, knowing full well that its resurgence in adult life will then be unlikely. People must be trained for submission when they are most vulnerable to impression, which happens to be when they are young.

The government displays its contempt for young people's ability to determine the courses of their own lives by trying to restrict their access to everything from R-rated movies and ear piercing to alcohol and tobacco. Conflicting with the concurrent pressures introduced by the market economy - which encourage participation in "risqué" entertainment, exotic fashion and drug usage - the imposition of such limitations is counterproductive at best, probably even devastating. The mixed messages conveyed by the two wings of the establishment that possess the farthest-reaching influence pit (commercially manufactured) impulse against (state-imposed) inhibitions, and the confused results are ruinous.

Another outstanding and pressingly current example of legal ageism is the rash of curfew laws which is presently sweeping the nation. While crime rates hover at mid-

1970s levels, violent incidences have become increasingly concentrated among the young community, particularly in urban areas. Rather than take an approach which could be labeled even slightly rational, many local governments have decided to pass new laws and further restrict the rights of young people. Though laws will never keep young people indoors, they will surely keep them out of places where they can safely meet and recreate. Meanwhile, the boredom, frustration and despair felt by many young people is only fuelled and aggravated. This is a clear example of coercive power used to deprive young people of the freedom to act as they choose, regardless of whether harm would be done to themselves or someone else (the usual accepted criteria for determining legislation).

As few clear-minded folks would dispute, modern states have managed with alarming success to master the art of indoctrination. Without using severe and boisterous methods of brainwashing, the government has achieved the relatively efficient production of numbed minds, conditioned for obedience, servitude and, in turn, the perpetuation and magnification of state power. Not only does the state define the curricula which will be imposed upon any student whose parents cannot afford private school (and upon many whose can), but it forces them to attend classes in Eurocentric barbarism, as dictated by powerful adults who define education standards. Those mental factories which the government does not control it at least regulates.

In the classroom, the student learns, above all else, that learning is boring, degrading and difficult. Based on quantitative systems of instruction, even the most progressive mainstream schools educate young people of little else than submission, assimilation and conformity. It's not what you learn that counts, it's how much you can prove you know. More still, as education standards and expectations regress, the rule is who knows more, not if anyone knows anything of relevance.

The enforced process of hand-raising, through which the student demonstrates her or his subservience to the teacher, is a classic display of the demeaning relationship promoted by formal scholastic activity. The teacher, at the same time, is an adult who is chosen unpluralistically and given ultimate authority - not only in the sense of "expertise" but also of "power." That is, the class is being run by someone who is vastly different in age from the students, and was chosen not because of leadership competence but knowledge alone; charisma, compatibility and attitude being irrelevant.

While the teacher is dictating many rules and little important knowledge, the students are being stratified and segregated. Young people begin the process of discrimination by gender, class, race, etc., which reflects the attitudes of parents and teachers, before they are in grade school. "Boys are good at math and science, girls needn't so much as try their best." "Black students do not possess the capacity to learn as well as whites, so we might as well spend less energy trying to teach them." The pattern is irrational, but it has been consistent and unwavering for centuries.

Although experimentation with a progressive concept known as "inclusive education" is now being undertaken around the country, the separation of students according to their perceived ability to learn is still dominant throughout most US schools. Elites are formed of "gifted" students who display a propensity to learn at a faster pace, while "normal" students are herded into overcrowded classrooms across the way from those tagged "disabled." Do these distinctions haunt the adult lives of students grouped as such because they were originally accurate or because they became self-fulfilled prophecies during childhood and adolescence? Furthermore, in case the labelling system does not sufficiently stabilise a young person's self-image, requiring that his or her class ranking be included on every high school transcript does the trick.

Formal education, whether it be collegiate or secondary, is wonderful practice for one experience which can be looked forward to by prospective adults: routinisation. School teaches people to fall into line, obey rules and, most of all, to qualify. Whether one learns anything or not, one had better pass the final; whether one works a fulfilling job as an adult, one had better bring home a paycheck.

Other government institutions practice ageism as well. There is little argument on the Left that the US military - any military, for that matter - uses severe forms of indoctrination, coercion and invalidation, whose effects overshadow even those of the most thorough scholastic "education." The recruitment practices of the armed forces are diabolical in their use of propaganda and outright lies, as well as their focus on young people, not so much for the acquisition of strong, young bodies as impressionable minds. Save for professional criminality, the military is often seen by America's poor to be the only way out of poverty, a fact illustrated by disproportionate numbers of Latino, Afro-American and working class recruits. And again, the military complex instills the same biases and psychological effects as the education system, only with much greater severity. The broad effects of military service on the individual young person, not to mention whoever s/he is manipulated or forced or bribed into killing, are clear and disastrous.

As our world becomes more and more technologically advanced, it has become increasingly difficult for individuals to maintain any sense of individuality. As humanity is herded and oppressed as a whole, it is the young who receive the most trampling. As if the isolation felt by adults is not enough, their needs are often fulfilled by the state (over which adults at least have some power) far prior to the needs of their children. We live in a system where even those adults whose voices are allowed hearing receive very little from the power structure which holds them down. So how can we (especially those of us on the Left) have gone so long without recognising that young people, whose voices are seldom heard if ever, are even more severely oppressed by that same, inherently violent system of authority and subordination?

Economic Ageism

Anytime an economic apparatus exists which is not specifically designed for equity it will oppress certain groups in society. Throughout the world one of the groups most heavily oppressed by nearly all economic systems is that of young people. In relation to the work force, young people are violated in several ways. At times they are excluded from the workplace; at other times they are forced against their will to become a part of it. Moreover, at the other end of the assembly line, primarily in the market system, capital* exploits the paradoxical combination of young people's youthful open-mindedness and their desire to assimilate.

In a system of centralised capital, whereby wealth and power are manipulated by interests other than those of society as a whole, the individual's needs are automatically excluded from the concern of those coordinating the flow of capital. Whether an economy is public but coordinatorist or "free" but private, young people constitute the last group to have a say in the management process (again regardless of how little voice most adults may have). Therefore, as they are ignored by the rule makers, the economic activity of young people is drastically restricted, perhaps more so than any other oppressed group.

Where politics collide with economics, the state has substantial influence over the economic freedom of young people. The system of compulsory education, whereby young people are forced to work without pay, is similar to slavery, the product being the student her or his self. Prior to the age of 16, people are neither allowed to work at a regular job nor to leave school. Even after 16 adolescents are offered a limited spectrum of opportunities in the workplace, almost never including work which could possibly be considered empowering.

Although child labor laws were originally created to protect young people from exploitation by business and parents, and they undoubtedly serve that purpose today, in many cases they also prevent adolescents from obtaining money legally and without soliciting parents. And while family incomes vary, they are hardly indicative of the amount of money children will be allowed. Still, when children below age 16 are permitted to work, most commonly in the family business or farm, their labour is heavily exploited by parents who treat them as capital. This demonstrates the importance of a substantially deep look at economic institutions as a whole in their relationship to young people. Any time the capitalist system can exploit, it will, and those with no recourse are by definition most vulnerable.

Of course, there is a fundamental difference between young people and adults where this matter is concerned. Namely, young people are still socialising (or being socialised) at a rapid pace, and thus schooling is of greater importance than the production, through labor, of other goods. However, the fact remains that the education apparatus is an industry, and the chief labourers - not teachers or administrators but the students themselves - are not rewarded for their labour in the same way workers in other industries are. In this case, the students are not necessarily alienated from the fruits of their labour (i.e., themselves), but are alienated from the process by which production takes place.

While young people in the US are kept from earning money, they are simultaneously bombarded by specifically-geared commercialism and its introduction of "wants." Of course, many young people see their wants fulfilled by parents who are willing to appease the desires of large corporations as well as those perceived interests newly instilled in their child (which isn't to say that such children are not oppressed by capital simply because they can satisfy their material desires). However, this process forms a significant group of young people in whom wants are being commercially conjured but who themselves cannot allocate the material manifestations of those desires - that is, they simply can't afford all the things they're told they desire.

Such is not meant to imply that society should pity those young people who cannot afford the latest fashions and the action figure or video game of the month, so long as they have sufficient clothing and entertainment. Rather, we should recognise that it is a primary purpose of private capitalist institutions to take advantage of young people's culturally reinforced need to conform and their search for identity, as well as their relatively free minds whose desires and initiatives are malleable.

One of the market's most manipulative and socially-destructive weapons is its elimination, via the "entertainment industry," of the community and family relations which previously raised children without heavy commercial interference. We have seen the substitution of seemingly realistic film and television for actual experience.

More subtly, the commercial aspects of the modern market serve to manipulate or even eliminate the community and family relation as well. A 30-second douche advertisement on TV, in which an imaginary daughter confronts her make-believe mother with simulated feminine problems (e.g., the "not-so-fresh feeling"), actually replaces an entire conversation between real-life mother and daughter. Not only does the adolescent woman, as viewer, no longer think she needs to discuss certain personal things with her mother, but now she even knows the name of the product she is supposed to use.

The contradiction of want creation and accompanying restrictions from the ability to satisfy those wants places young people in a position which is even more blatantly discriminatory than capital's obvious abuse of women and minority races. Yet, while the Left adamantly supports the rights of those oppressed groups to have access to satisfactory amounts of wealth and privilege, young people's right to economic independence is almost nowhere advocated.

As young people are forced into dependence on parents and (often) the paternal state, their own potential is neglected and invalidated. Meanwhile, the state system forces them into a subjective conditioning process while young people are economically manipulated to, in all their social activity, serve the interests of capitalists.

In an alternative economy, the production of labourers could easily be taken into account as such, and the producers rewarded for their efforts. Such an economy could separate young people's consumption rights from those of their parents, thus circumventing the problem of misappropriation of excessive or inadequate amounts of goods to those young people. Furthermore, by eradicating markets and capital, we could eliminate misguiding commercial pressures and the inheritance of intemperate or deficient wealth.

Cultural Ageism

Taking a look at communities in our society, generally identified by race, ethnicity, heritage or religion, it is plain that the institutions within these communities oppress young people regularly. Particularly by respecting coercive and invalidating traditions, whereby young people are treated as less than whole, groups identified as communities intimidate and violate their younger members.

Simply speaking, the very fact that young people are so often born into communities which are identified as somehow separate from others is oppressive. The idea that differences in race, for example, are even acknowledged at all is oppressive, as it creates an immediate identity crisis experienced early on in a child's social development. That a child's skin pigmentation differs from another's is one thing; that such characteristics are of importance in life is another matter altogether, undoubtedly initiating a pattern of heavy distress. Soon, as the child grows, the race factor becomes accepted, and all the social strife it causes seems natural. But it remains unnatural, a truth even radical theorists are still having trouble understanding. We teach young people of colour to take pride in their race, which may well serve to "empower" them as individuals; but doing so also perpetuates the myth that race is a rational concept in and of itself. Children do not understand the idea of race until they are taught it's perceived importance by adult society, a kind of informal indoctrination.

Then, of course, there is formal indoctrination. Judaism and Christianity both contain official structures by which young people are trained to accept dogmatic "truths" which have relevance to them not because the concepts are rational per se, but because they are hereditary. So we have a situation where young people, once again, are born into oppressive systems, inheriting them from parents who promote their relevance only because those parents themselves were born into them.

As children are taught one religion (the religion), they learn that they must live in accordance with the dictates of that religion - the only acceptable manner. To do otherwise would yield Hell or worse. Such manipulative power is highly coercive, and it sees that choice is removed from the individual student, a quite invalidating condition.

Moreover, many religions have formal "rites of passage" by which young members are graduated into "adulthood". This systematically segregates children from adults in an official capacity, denying the younger indoctrinees the validity of full-fledged membership in the culture, and forcing upon the adolescents the responsibilities of religious maturity.

Community identification is also the basis by which parents usually decide to perform circumcision on male children. Circumcision is among the most painful acts any human will likely experience, and the psychological trauma, not to mention physical mutilation, has deep-rooted effects both psychologically and socially. Indeed, those circumcised will later be offered positions as oppressors when they might chastise a fellow young male's uncircumcised penis in a high school locker room. Circumcision performed for social reasons is a form of child abuse, based on cultural standards.

Many community-based programs, in which young people's participation is often encouraged if not enforced by parents and other adult community members, have oppressive aspects. Organisations like the Boy Scouts and Girl Scouts, despite facilitating some positive learning experiences, encouraging social activity and introducing young people to diverse cultures, are noted for their narrow conceptions of community and family, as well as their strict foundation in Judeo-Christian doctrine. By forcing young members to wear uniforms, salute the American flag and pray to the other god, these groups forego their progressive potential to enter the business of mind-molding.

Formal scholastic sports, again despite their positive potential, also serve to oppress many young people. By restricting access to participation based on athletic ability, they invalidate any young person who cannot "make the team." Further, among those who are not excluded, a competitive mindset is encouraged. Winning is rewarded while losing or even tying is punished, externally by adult coaches and internally between team members. Instead of encouraging teamwork and communitarian ethics, school athletic programs teach young people to look out for themselves, regardless of who else might be hurt.

Many leftists tout the merits of community identification, which no doubt exist. But the idea that individuals should inherit such identifications rather than acquire them by personal choice as they grow is absurd; that skin colour or place of birth or bloodline are determining factors of community identification is a ridiculous and damaging injustice which must be further addressed.

Interpersonal Ageism

It is in the kinship sphere of social activity that interpersonal relations are formed. This sphere also houses the most direct oppressions of young people, and it is where internalised oppression among and between young people primarily takes place. Inside personal relationships, the young person contends not only with oppressions from adult family members and friends but also siblings and peers.

The most obvious forms of ageism are perhaps those perpetrated by parents and legal guardians. Not unlike a corporation or bureaucracy, the family unit is a top-down hierarchical institution. Parents play the roles of absolute managers in a cell where level of authority is determined by seniority.

Before we investigate the relationship between parent and child, let us expose a few notions which set the stage for active oppressions but are rarely identified as oppressions themselves.

First, we must take into account the reasons for which parents typically have children. While the reasons themselves do not necessarily ensure oppression during the actual life of a young person, they potentially promote oppressive attitudes and behaviour towards children by their parents. In this age, parents seldom produce children for economic reasons (though this is not unheard of), but child-bearing is nonetheless often carried out largely for the selfish benefit of the parents themselves.

All too commonly, children are a source of entertainment, toys with which "mature" adults can play and still be respected by their peers. Children are also used by parents as cohesion between themselves while their own partnership is else wise failing. Parents also intend to live vicariously through their children, having their offspring achieve things they never could. And at risk of defying politically correct normalcy, it is our assertion that single parents or lesbian/gay couples often conceive or adopt children in order to make social statements. That isn't to imply that such people are incapable of being suitable parents, but rather that human life should not be produced for use as political or social protest signs.

Of course, oppression is not predetermined in all cases, and the reasons for which children are born are not all for the advantage of the parent at the expense of the child. But there is a significant relationship between parents' intentions, which are often just to appease cultural expectations of adulthood, and the methods by which families socialise their offspring.

Another component of parenthood which is taken for granted but as such is no less oppressive is the notion that children are wards of parents or guardians. "Ownership" of children is determined simply by their physical origin or by legal documentation which grants control to otherwise unrelated adults. Certainly children need protection, and to some extent guidance, but that this should be dictated by one or two or even three individuals is preposterous. Pluralism is so often lacking in familial relationships, but this is rarely connected to the narrow social and personal characteristics of those raised in such an unpluralistic manner. Again, we clearly see tradition conflicting with the actual needs of young people, depriving them of diversity for the sake of parental self-satisfaction via the idea that children exist as personal property.

In the debate over "family values," where is the voice of children, the very people most affected?

It is in the context of family that gender and other roles are first accumulated. Children acquire their sense of self in large part by mimicking the actions of their parents, the rationalisation coming much later in life. Hence, when parents exhibit roles of dominance and submission based on sex, their children will adopt similar roles as they grow socially. For instance, a young female who repeatedly observes her mother depending on her father financially, emotionally, etc., is likely to become dependent on males herself, abandoning any potential for independence. Similarly, a male who constantly witnesses his father's dominance, coercion and abuse of his mother will probably espouse an over-powerful role in future relationships with women. Role imposition is a type of informal indoctrination.

While the gender roles delegated to young people have been exposed and explored by feminists quite sufficiently, it must be noted that gender assimilation is a process controlled by parents and other adults, thus making them ageist as well as sexist. Unlike adult women who fall pray to sexism, the sex roles of girls are directly dictated by adults, those who society acknowledges universally as having legitimate authority over young people.

Young people also experience ageism when parents and other adults inflict feelings of guilt, shame and worthlessness, causing psychological dysfunction, an indisputable example of invalidation. Using guilt and manipulation as tools, parents coerce young people into performing tasks which they themselves lack the desire to carry out. When children are not acting on the dictates of their parents, they are often called "unhelpful" or "no good," regardless of the fact that they are seldom offered or even shown the benefits of equitable participation in the function of family.

Parents are hardly seen as friends by their children, but rather as figures of authority. This is a loss for both child and parent, depriving them of a potentially wonderful and equally rewarding relationship based on trust, openness and companionship. Instead of this ideal, mistrust of adults is learned as a defence mechanism (often a necessary one). Coupled with the "generation gap" (which is not at all inherent to familial relationships, but is unique to those in which parents deny their children respect, camaraderie and understanding), the actual basis of parent-child relationship activity is oppression-ridden.

Sexual abuse between adults and children, during which the elder takes advantage of the young person's impressionability and lack of understanding, as well as physical size, are acknowledged as widespread. But it must be stated that this is an oppression founded strictly on age differences. By understanding paedophilia, we can begin to recognise the extent to which adult dominance over the young actually reaches. More importantly, knowing how common such abuse actually is, we can realise how common and widespread less extreme and less apparent abuses must be.

All forms of child abuse must be recognised as something aside from ordinary violence. Besides being the victim's first introduction to cruelty, abuse causes children to inherit a pattern of violence, prompting them to act similarly towards their peers and, in adulthood, towards their own children. Even more directly than most oppressive activities, child abuse has been clinically proven to be self-perpetuating.

Anyone who believes parents and guardians possess legitimate authority over "their" children must either overlook the severity and frequency of these violations or deem them acceptable. The only remedy for this dynamic, which has likely existed throughout human history, is the elimination of parental authority. The role of parent as dictator must be replaced by nurturer. With humans, nurturing consists mainly of oversight, with guidance and control limited to a minimum.

All known social oppressions can be shown to possess a phenomenal characteristic known as "internalised oppression" whereby members of the oppressed group actually oppress each other in unwitting service to their interested oppressors. The internal self-destructive activities of the black community are among the most obvious examples of this. Also, the self-perpetuation of dependent and submissive activity among women, through defining each other by their relationships to men, is yet another example of internalised oppression.

Among young people, there are several such examples. Segregated almost entirely from valuable interaction with adults, much socialisation takes place strictly between and among groups of children - yet they mirror relationships indicative of adult society. Young people consistently form cliques at school, practicing exclusion and limiting their own exposure to variety. They invalidate and even abuse each other verbally, physically and sexually based on racist, classist and sexist assumptions. Of late, it has also been noted that the most recent generation of young people insists on invalidating achievers in the classroom. Low scholastic achievement is often rewarded with acceptance while high achievement is penalised by exclusion. All these activities and many more are carried out solely based on association by age.

Now That We Know...

This indictment of adult society, the first part to a manifesto of sorts, is by no means complete. Many volumes could (and hopefully will) be written on these matters. There is much more to discuss and investigate regarding ageism in theory and practice. For now, identifying the most glaring applications and most basic theories will have to suffice.

Of course, this essay wouldn't have been written had its authors not honestly believed there was hope for change and progress. If we can agree to acknowledge the existence of ageism as a far-reaching, powerful and thus significant oppression, we can perhaps initiate discourse on the liberation of young people, an act equal in importance to the liberation of all other oppressed groups.

Let's face it: young people are the future; they always have been. It is the values and perceptions instilled in young people which will carry over into adult life and dominate social activity therein.

One idea is that adults should instil as few values and perspectives as possible, thus freeing the "nature of youth" to develop on its own in a free manner of socialisation, in the absence of indoctrination and social engineering. Already the topic of discussion and debate in certain, limited forums, this idea has become known as "youthism," whereby the free-spirits, open minds, curiosities and reasoning capacities, along with the desire for freedom, so often found in our young before they are extensively engineered by the dominant forces of society, can be nurtured not by dictators or even leaders but by free association. Indeed, we are all born anarchists, defiant to irrational oppressions, but are then moulded by social forces largely beyond our control.

What would happen if these dominant forces never were allowed to dig their claws into the minds and hearts of our young? Would children reach the conclusions that classism, sexism, authoritarianism, racism, etc. are rational and just on their own accord? Is it possible that they might never recognise that power should be inequitably distributed among individuals and groups?

Might we find that the corruption of adults begins with the corruption of children, a reciprocal and indeed cyclical process? And might we see that the nurturing process, delicate yet vital, is in dire need of revolution?

Youth Rights 101
Kathleen Nicole O'Neal

Why Youth?

Some people may wonder why I focus so disproportionately on youth issues. After all, young people are not the only people oppressed, either collectively or individually, in our society. Structural forces and individual prejudices often conspire to keep women and people of colour from being as successful as many white males. Heterosexism is still inscribed into our nation's law codes and animates the belief systems of many people. The situation of disabled and elderly Americans bears many similarities to that of youth (albeit with some key differences). People of size are increasingly scapegoated under the guise of a "war on obesity" that conveniently doubles as a war on them. Rural people are oppressed both by the condescending attitudes of non-rural people and the very geographic realities of rurality. The poor economy is an increasingly oppressive force in the lives of more and more Americans, including those who would have once been known as middle class or even wealthy. And individuals of all demographic groups are oppressed by the military, medical, and prison industrial complexes as well as social mores which prize conformity over critical thinking and individuality. So why focus on youth?

I focus on youth because minors are the only group of individuals in our society that almost everyone – left or right, religious or secular, educated or ignorant, authoritarian or libertarian – is openly comfortable treating as a subject class. Youth are the only group of people in the United States for whom there is widespread consensus that segregating them from the rest of society, denying them legal rights, keeping them economically dependent, and turning arbitrary authority for them over to other people is not a necessary evil but the best possible way we individually and collectively can hope to relate to them. I focus on youth because the ills of sexism, racism, heterosexism, ableism, classism, sizeism, rural oppression, poverty, and the military, medical, and prison industrial complexes are complicated and exacerbated by the status of minority. I focus on youth oppression because it is taken for granted and therefore invisible despite its ubiquity.

I focus on youth because the critical theoretical eye that has problematised the idea of biologically essentialist gender roles and racial identities has not problematised much of the ageist pseudoscience surrounding discourses about child development. I focus on youth because those who decry the warehousing of our elders and people with disabilities in nursing homes and assisted living facilities do not draw parallels with the warehousing of our youth in schools and other institutions. I focus on youth because most libertarians see no contradiction in talking about arbitrary and oppressive state power on the one hand and using the phrase "parents' rights" on the other. I talk about youth because a commitment to human liberty and social justice demands youth liberation and those who claim to support human liberty and social justice rarely acknowledge this. I focus on youth because there is a more organised effort in our society to extend liberty and dignity to animals than to human children. I focus on youth because ageism is one of the greatest unexamined black marks on American society in the early twenty-first century. I focus on youth because if I don't few people will. And as long as all of these things are true I am a radical youth liberation supporter first, last, and always.

Youth Rights vs Child Protection

"Youth rights" can be difficult to pin down. The term itself is vague (although no vaguer than most terms used to describe more established social movements and philosophies). Youth rights is difficult to pin down primarily because there are a number of philosophies similar in some respects to youth rights that ultimately differ in critical enough ways to distinguish themselves from youth rights. There is also a great deal of ideological diversity within the youth rights movement itself. Those differences may be highlighted in more depth elsewhere on [The Youth Rights Blog], but this post is intended to focus on the commonalities that make us youth rights supporters as opposed to something else. Youth rights is, like feminism, first and foremost a frame for viewing issues (in this case issues affecting young people). It emphasises the prevalence of ageism as a key prejudice affecting the lives of young people. It problematises institutions like the family and compulsory education which are central in the lives of youth. It calls into question assumptions that most thinkers about childhood, education, and the family take for granted about children's capacities. Most critically, youth rights thinkers tend to regard child abuse and child protectionism as two sides of the same coin.

In the words of philosopher Howard Cohen, "Child protection has been concerned with the quality of care of the child, and therefore with the fitness of the caretaker. It has not been concerned with fundamental questions about the nature and limits of adult authority over children. It is the sense that the ways in which adults control children and make decisions for them are themselves a part of the mistreatment and oppression of children which is absent from the ideology, and is ignored by the government when it becomes involved." To paraphrase psychologist Richard Farson, we believe that we best protect youth by protecting their rights. That which undermines the right of young people to autonomy and self-determination (even under the misguided assumption that it is for their own welfare) demeans, oppresses, and endangers them. Child abuse and child protectionism are two sides of the same coin.

Youth rights supporters believe that youth don't usually need protection from themselves – they need protection from the social, political, legal, economic, and cultural forces that make them a subject class. We recognise that, as has been the case with people with disabilities, when youth need protection it is usually from the institutions such as schools, the family, and social services agencies that were ironically enough set up for the purpose of protecting them. This is because it is impossible to truly protect someone within a framework that denies them liberty, autonomy, and self-determination and thereby deprives them of the ability to meet their own needs and desires and to protect themselves.

NO!

AGAINST ADULT SUPREMACY
Issue 4

Why We Can't Wait

Adam Fletcher

"Freedom is never voluntarily given by the oppressor;
it must be demanded by the oppressed."
I look at the people around me
and see the prisons and traps
we are all stuck.
From an early age we are taught and trained:
sit still, hold on, walk (don't run),
and be quiet.
Whatever you do, be quiet.

So we do. We go to polite schools or content jobs.
We type and read and feel nice.
Our hair is nice and our hearts are nice.
We live nice lives.

But what if…
what if we were shown the whole picture
from the first day?
What if they said
"Hey, when you're poor, you're screwed.
If you're black, you're facing an uphill road.
If you're female, you're up a creek.
Oh, yeah, and you'll be young too!
Let's not even go there!"

What if we could awaken all people to the chains that tie them down?
What if everyone saw that
we are responsible for holding ourselves down?
What if the message of systematic and deliberate oppression
was exposed and the entire society
– everyone everywhere-
saw that young people are
looked down upon,
frowned upon,
sat upon
and shat upon?

Then they become adults.
The world turns.
They start pooping on youth...
and the cycle continues.

We've gotta speak up, act up, and quit
putting up, giving up and settling down.

We cannot wait any longer.

Its time to get up, stand up, scream out loud and dream out loud.
We've gotta break outta the chains that hold us down.
We've gotta stand up for what is ours:
Freedom.
To earn, to learn, to speak, to serve.

We've gotta tie people together
instead of tearing them apart.
We're taught that we're not the same because we are
young and old
black and white
educated and ignorant
rich and poor.

But we're the same.
And that's why young people have got to be free.

No one is free until everyone is free.
Free Youth Now.

On Play and Development

Benjamin Fife

In 1978 a collection of writings by the Russian psychologist L.S. Vygotsky was published in English for the first time. Among these writings was a new translation of an important article he wrote on play and its relationship to development. The 1978 publication offered American psychologists and educators new ways of thinking about child development.

Partly due to the cold war, access to Vygotsky's ideas had been very limited in the United States. Only one important article of his had been published in English up to that point, and that was in 1962, twenty eight years after his death. In the seventies, Alexander Luria, an influential neuropsychologist and a student of Vygotsky's convinced a group of American academics to publish a collection of Vygotsky's essays called Mind In Society: The Development of Higher Psychological Processes.

It is remarkable reading his essays now to think about how well they have held up over time (They were written in the late 1920s and early 1930s). I find chapter 7 of his book, The role of play in development, very useful for thinking about how play relates to cognitive and socio-emotional development.

If there is something in my summary of Vygotsky's work that you find useful or interesting, consider checking out his wonderful book.

Understanding play helps to understand children's changing relationships to their own needs.

Vygotsky begins his chapter The Role of Play in Development reminding readers that if we see play only as something children are doing for enjoyment, then we miss an important aspect of play – its relationship to development. At the same time we should keep in mind the parts of play that are about children's needs and motivations – including the need for pleasure and fun. Vygotsky's goal is to form a complete picture of play, what play makes possible, and what play allows to happen later in life.

Vygotsky wants to make sure that children's motivations are fully considered when thinking about play and development. He highlights a constant relationship between need, motivation and development in play. Specific needs that children are motivated to satisfy through play change as a child grows.

Play and Development: Developing the capacity to wait.

Part of what changes in children as they grow older is how long they can wait before a need is satisfied. Vygotsky writes "No one has met a child under three who wants to do something a few days in the future."(p. 93)

When a very young child can't have something she wants or can't do something she wants to do she gets upset immediately. Maybe she even tantrums. She might be able to be distracted by a skilled and lucky caregiver, but that is not the same as being able to wait.

As a child gets older she starts to recognise that there are some needs that can't be satisfied right away. Vygotsky sees play as the first activity that allows a child to hold off on having a need satisfied. For Vygotsky, play is the activity in young children that in older children and adults becomes the experience of having an imagination. To Vygotsky imagination as experienced by older children, adolescents and adults is "play without action."(p. 93)

What is play made of?

Vygotsky argues that two things – imagination and rules – are necessary components to play. Even play that seems to have no rules and seems very connected to reality, has both imagination and rules if you know where to look.

Take for example a pair of siblings playing a game they call "being siblings". They hold hands, talk the same, dress the same, maybe the older one talks in authoritative ways to the younger one about things that belong to them, and things that belong to other people. It might not seem at first that there are a lot of rules or much imagination – but Vygotsky sees it differently. In this kind of play, the children are distilling rules about what it means to be siblings – they are taking the things that people don't notice in day to day life, and making them the rules of play. They are also imagining what is different to adults and to others about the relationships siblings have with each other from the relationships they have with the rest of the world. The game allows them to figure out, through the use of imagination, the meaning of being sisters instead of just living the day to day experience of being sisters.

Any play with imagination has rules. Playing house involves rules of how members of the family behave. Whatever the imaginary game, be it cops and robbers, or space explorers or mom and baby, or monsters attacking the town, rules are there. Often these are not rules that the child comes up with ahead of time but rather rules that emerge from the imaginary situation the child presents – rules about who wins and how, rules of how monsters, babies, mommies, and townspeople act.

For Vygotsky games are activities where rules and imagination are always present and where each helps to make the other. Even later games that seem to be all rules and no imagination – games like chess – actually contain both. Accepting the rules of the game, "here we are in a scenario where knights move like this and bishops move like this and the game ends when one of us captures the other's king," means entering into a shared imaginary situation.

For Vygotsky what defines something as an imaginary situation is the fact that a person accepts some rules and the rules limit the possibilities for action.

According to this theory developmental progress in play goes from a child having games that look mostly like imaginary situations but have hidden rules to having games with clear rules and a less obvious imaginary situation.

When does play in an imaginary situation start?

Play in an imaginary situation usually starts around 3 years old. This is about the time when a child goes from reacting mostly to the environment to being motivated by cognitive factors as well. Of course there is variation in the ages when children start to play – but a huge amount of brain development happens between 2 and 3 that allows for new kinds of thinking to emerge at about 3 years old.

A three year old can plan in a way that a 2 year old simply cannot yet. Vygotsky gives the example of a 2 year old who is facing at a stone. An adult asks him to sit on the stone and he has a very hard time following the directions. The task is difficult because planning the actions required to turn around first and then sit down is cognitively too complex. The stone is right there in front of him and he's committed to doing something with it. If he turns around he won't be able to see it anymore and figuring out the interaction with the stone will be incredibly difficult. Where two year olds are generally motivated by what they see in front of them, three year olds can often begin to hold a plan in mind and figure out the steps needed to make that plan happen.

Objects and Motivation

For most children under about three years old objects in the environment contain their own inherent motivation. For an infant, everything is to be explored with every sense. For the toddler, objects in the environment are recognised and are associated with a concrete use. Doors are for opening, stairs are for climbing, bells are for ringing. Everything that the under three year old child perceives in her environment is in itself a motivation to do something; to approach or to avoid – to interact with in a concrete way.

It is usually only at about age three when something a child perceives can start to be used in an imaginary scenario – for example a stick can be ridden as if it were a pony. What is happening when a child starts to play this way is a giant cognitive step from early childhood. Unlike before, a child at play can now see an object in her environment and act based on what she is thinking about rather than based on what she is seeing. This allows children to start taking actions based on meaning rather than perception.

What is happening in preschool aged play?

Vygotsky sees something special happening at preschool age – specifically thought and objects become separate allowing children's actions to begin to come from their ideas instead of their reactions to things.

Little by little objects in the world that have some similarities to things a child is thinking about can be used in play as if they were the things the child is thinking about. So a stick, because a child can swing a leg over it and pretend to ride it, can become a play horse, and a piece of wood, because it is about the right size and shape, can become a baby doll.

This is a transitional stage – and it is important to remember that what the child is doing here is at times for the child hard work. It is also important to remember that the object the child picks to stand for the thing she is thinking about has to have some of the same properties as that thing and it has to be able to be used as if it were the thing, not just any object in the environment will do.

The Object to Meaning Ratio

Vygotsky has a math-like formula for understanding what is happening here. One of the things that is special about being human, he says, is that we can make meaning out of objects. We can look at a clock and where an animal might see a round thingy with two straight thingies in it, we can distinguish a clock, and know what the parts of it are and its specific uses. He proposes that for people there is an object to meaning ratio. Early in life, when we are infants and toddlers the object value in the ratio is higher and the meaning value is lower. Later in life the meaning value can be higher and the object value is lower. Play is the activity in development that allows for that change to start to happen. Meaning enters into how a child understands her environment when the child starts to use objects as if they were something else – when the stick, because of how it is used starts to mean "horse."

The Limits of Play

Where an adult can take a match and put it on a table next to a postcard and say to another adult "OK, so imagine the horse is here and the barn is here" and be understood, that kind of symbolic communication isn't available to a preschool child. The stick isn't a sign for horse the way the adult uses the match as a sign for horse. The stick's meaning comes from the fact that it can be used as if it were a horse. This difference for Vygotsky highlights how play is a transitional activity between the way very young children experience the world in terms of the situations they are in, and the way adults can have abstract thoughts that don't have anything to do with real-life situations.

Play and Later Development

Play also paves the way for later, more complex, relationships children will have to meaning through activities like writing. In play a child makes a thing stand for something else without knowing that is what she is doing. Later activities like reading and writing will be based on doing that same thing with awareness; making one thing (for example the word "tree" written in pencil) call up an idea about another thing (the tree outside my window) with the full knowledge that is what you are doing.

Play allows creative things to happen. It gives young children their first opportunity to take the meaning of something they know about from one environment and put it in a new reality. For example it allows a child to ride her pony in her classroom, even if the pony is a stick, or to be a nurse in her bedroom taking her teddy-bear's temperature with a crayon. Play also allows a child to both have pleasurable experiences and to delay pleasurable experiences at the same time.

Take for example the child who really wants a pony but can't have one for the usual reasons of space, money, and everything else that stops us from buying every child a pony. Imaginary play allows her to have the experiences she imagines having if she did have a pony, and to tolerate the fact that she has to operate within a certain set of external rules that doesn't allow her to have a real pony. She also gets to come up with the rules of play herself that are involved in the experience of having a pony. Where in a lot of childhood experiences following a rule feels like giving up on pleasure, in play coming up with the rules of play and then following them becomes the source of pleasure in itself. Vygotsky sees here the seeds of both self restraint and self determination.

What Changes in Play Look Like

A preschool child's relationship to her own actions changes through play. In the play of a young preschool age child all of the actions the child takes will more or less mirror the activities she is imagining. When she is pretending to eat toy food from toy plates she will usually do all of the things that she would do when eating from real food from real plates. As play progresses, her actions will take on more diversity and things she with her body will start to stand for actions instead of just mimicking them.

Let's return to the example of the older preschool child playing at riding a pony using a stick. Maybe stomping her feet quickly while standing in place becomes the way she rides the pony very very fast. She isn't imitating the action here so much as doing something that has elements of how she thinks about "riding a pony" (the loudness of the stomping, the speed of moving her feet). Action in play also has a ratio type relationship to meaning. For the younger child action determined meaning, for the older child meanings were assigned to actions.

Play as a Preview

Vygotsky sees play as a place where children can experiment with what comes next developmentally. For him play represents a "zone of proximal development," a time when a child can experience being developmentally older than she is in other parts of her life. In that way play is probably the single most important activity that prepares children for future developmental progress. Actions children take in the imaginative realms of play give them opportunities to set goals, develop plans, and see activities through. Outside of play a child might not be ready to do some of the things she can do inside of play, but once she does them in play she is well on the road to doing them in other areas of her life.

For example, a child with anxiety about sleeping in her own bed may be able to participate in a game where a caregiver plays at putting her to sleep in her own bed and she plays at falling asleep. While intending this as a game, the child may really be able to fall asleep. In such a game she might be able to have her first sense of being able to do something she could not do before. Over time this play skill could transition into becoming a day to day skill she can use.

In another instance a child who cannot yet read may play at reading a book to a friend or stuffed animal. The play may include explaining the pictures, turning pages, checking to make sure the stuffed animal or friend is paying attention, and telling a story in a way that links specific moments with specific feelings. Each of these may be things that the child cannot yet do outside of the play scenario. Play, by the way it provides an imaginary scenario in which a child performs real actions frees a child from some of the constraints of everyday life and allows her to do things she can't do elsewhere.

Ultimately Vygotsky sees two very important developmental skills emerging from play:

abstract thought – which he sees as developing from play in imaginary situations;

and the ability to differentiate work from play and to work creatively within sets of rules – which he sees coming from the development of rules and experimentation with relationships to rules within imaginary scenarios.

In this way it is play that for preschool age children sets the fundamental groundwork for later complex thought and motivated action.

Against School

John Taylor Gatto

I taught for thirty years in some of the worst schools in Manhattan, and in some of the best, and during that time I became an expert in boredom. Boredom was everywhere in my world, and if you asked the kids, as I often did, why they felt so bored, they always gave the same answers: They said the work was stupid, that it made no sense, that they already knew it. They said they wanted to be doing something real, not just sitting around. They said teachers didn't seem to know much about their subjects and clearly weren't interested in learning more. And the kids were right: their teachers were every bit as bored as they were.

Boredom is the common condition of schoolteachers, and anyone who has spent time in a teachers' lounge can vouch for the low energy, the whining, the dispirited attitudes, to be found there. When asked why they feel bored, the teachers tend to blame the kids, as you might expect. Who wouldn't get bored teaching students who are rude and interested only in grades? If even that. Of course, teachers are themselves products of the same twelve-year compulsory school programs that so thoroughly bore their students, and as school personnel they are trapped inside structures even more rigid than those imposed upon the children. Who, then, is to blame?

We all are. My grandfather taught me that. One afternoon when I was seven I complained to him of boredom, and he batted me hard on the head. He told me that I was never to use that term in his presence again, that if I was bored it was my fault and no one else's. The obligation to amuse and instruct myself was entirely my own, and people who didn't know that were childish people, to be avoided if possible. Certainly not to be trusted. That episode cured me of boredom forever, and here and there over the years I was able to pass on the lesson to some remarkable student. For the most part, however, I found it futile to challenge the official notion that boredom and childishness were the natural state of affairs in the classroom. Often I had to defy custom, and even bend the law, to help kids break out of this trap.

The empire struck back, of course: childish adults regularly conflate opposition with disloyalty. I once returned from a medical leave to discover that all evidence of my having been granted the leave had been purposely destroyed, that my job had been terminated, and that I no longer possessed even a teaching license. After nine months of tormented effort I was able to retrieve the license when a school secretary testified to witnessing the plot unfold. In the meantime my family suffered more than I care to remember. By the time I finally retired in 1991, I had more than enough reason to think of our schools – with their long-term, cell-block-style, forced confinement of both students and teachers – as virtual factories of childishness. Yet I honestly could not see why they had to be that way. My own experience had revealed to me what many other teachers must learn along the way, too, yet keep to themselves for fear of reprisal: if we wanted to we could easily and inexpensively jettison the old, stupid structures and help kids take an education rather than merely receive a schooling. We could encourage the best qualities of youthfulness – curiosity, adventure, resilience, the capacity for surprising insight – simply by being more flexible about time, texts, and tests, by introducing kids to truly competent adults, and by giving each student what autonomy he or she needs in order to take a risk every now and then.

But we don't do that. And the more I asked why not, and persisted in thinking about the "problem" of schooling as an engineer might, the more I missed the point: What if there is no "problem" with our schools? What if they are the way they are, so expensively flying in the face of common sense and long experience in how children learn things, not because they are doing something wrong but because they are doing something right? Is it possible that George W. Bush accidentally spoke the truth when he said we would "leave no child behind"? Could it be that our schools are designed to make sure not one of them ever really grows up?

Do we really need school? I don't mean education, just forced schooling: six classes a day, five days a week, nine months a year, for twelve years. Is this deadly routine really necessary? And if so, for what? Don't hide behind reading, writing, and arithmetic as a rationale, because 2 million happy homeschoolers have surely put that banal justification to rest. Even if they hadn't, a considerable number of well-known Americans never went through the twelve-year wringer our kids currently go through, and they turned out all right. George Washington, Benjamin Franklin, Thomas Jefferson, Abraham Lincoln? Someone taught them, to be sure, but they were not products of a school system, and not one of them was ever "graduated" from a secondary school. Throughout most of American history, kids generally didn't go to high school, yet the unschooled rose to be admirals, like Farragut; inventors, like Edison; captains of industry, like Carnegie and Rockefeller; writers, like Melville and Twain and Conrad; and even scholars, like Margaret Mead. In fact, until pretty recently people who reached the age of thirteen weren't looked upon as children at all. Ariel Durant, who co-wrote an enormous, and very good, multivolume history of the world with her husband, Will, was happily married at fifteen, and who could reasonably claim that Ariel Durant was an uneducated person? Unschooled, perhaps, but not uneducated.

We have been taught (that is, schooled) in this country to think of "success" as synonymous with, or at least dependent upon, "schooling," but historically that isn't true in either an intellectual or a financial sense. And plenty of people throughout the world today find a way to educate themselves without resorting to a system of compulsory secondary schools that all too often resemble prisons. Why, then, do

Americans confuse education with just such a system? What exactly is the purpose of our public schools?

Mass schooling of a compulsory nature really got its teeth into the United States between 1905 and 1915, though it was conceived of much earlier and pushed for throughout most of the nineteenth century. The reason given for this enormous upheaval of family life and cultural traditions was, roughly speaking, threefold:

1 – To make good people.
2 – To make good citizens.
3 – To make each person his or her personal best.

These goals are still trotted out today on a regular basis, and most of us accept them in one form or another as a decent definition of public education's mission, however short schools actually fall in achieving them. But we are dead wrong. Compounding our error is the fact that the national literature holds numerous and surprisingly consistent statements of compulsory schooling's true purpose. We have, for example, the great H. L. Mencken, who wrote in The American Mercury for April 1924 that the aim of public education is not

"to fill the young of the species with knowledge and awaken their intelligence... Nothing could be further from the truth. The aim... is simply to reduce as many individuals as possible to the same safe level, to breed and train a standardised citizenry, to put down dissent and originality. That is its aim in the United States... and that is its aim everywhere else."

Because of Mencken's reputation as a satirist, we might be tempted to dismiss this passage as a bit of hyperbolic sarcasm. His article, however, goes on to trace the template for our own educational system back to the now vanished, though never to be forgotten, military state of Prussia. And although he was certainly aware of the irony that we had recently been at war with Germany, the heir to Prussian thought and culture, Mencken was being perfectly serious here. Our educational system really is Prussian in origin, and that really is cause for concern.

The odd fact of a Prussian provenance for our schools pops up again and again once you know to look for it. William James alluded to it many times at the turn of the century. Orestes Brownson, the hero of Christopher Lasch's 1991 book, The True and Only Heaven, was publicly denouncing the Prussianisation of American schools back in the 1840s. Horace Mann's "Seventh Annual Report" to the Massachusetts State Board of Education in 1843 is essentially a paean to the land of Frederick the Great and a call for its schooling to be brought here. That Prussian culture loomed large in America is hardly surprising, given our early association with that utopian state. A Prussian served as Washington's aide during the

Revolutionary War, and so many German- speaking people had settled here by 1795 that Congress considered publishing a German-language edition of the federal laws. But what shocks is that we should so eagerly have adopted one of the very worst aspects of Prussian culture: an educational system deliberately designed to produce mediocre intellects, to hamstring the inner life, to deny students appreciable leadership skills, and to ensure docile and incomplete citizens – all in order to render the populace "manageable."

It was from James Bryant Conant - president of Harvard for twenty years, WWI poison-gas specialist, WWII executive on the atomic-bomb project, high commissioner of the American zone in Germany after WWII, and truly one of the most influential figures of the twentieth century – that I first got wind of the real purposes of American schooling. Without Conant, we would probably not have the same style and degree of standardised testing that we enjoy today, nor would we be blessed with gargantuan high schools that warehouse 2,000 to 4,000 students at a time, like the famous Columbine High in Littleton, Colorado. Shortly after I retired from teaching I picked up Conant's 1959 book-length essay, The Child the Parent and the State, and was more than a little intrigued to see him mention in passing that the modern schools we attend were the result of a "revolution" engineered between 1905 and 1930. A revolution? He declines to elaborate, but he does direct the curious and the uninformed to Alexander Inglis's 1918 book, Principles of Secondary Education, in which "one saw this revolution through the eyes of a revolutionary."

Inglis, for whom a lecture in education at Harvard is named, makes it perfectly clear that compulsory schooling on this continent was intended to be just what it had been for Prussia in the 1820s: a fifth column into the burgeoning democratic movement that threatened to give the peasants and the proletarians a voice at the bargaining table. Modern, industrialised, compulsory schooling was to make a sort of surgical incision into the prospective unity of these underclasses. Divide children by subject, by age-grading, by constant rankings on tests, and by many other more subtle means, and it was unlikely that the ignorant mass of mankind, separated in childhood, would ever reintegrate into a dangerous whole.

Inglis breaks down the purpose – the actual purpose – of modem schooling into six basic functions, any one of which is enough to curl the hair of those innocent enough to believe the three traditional goals listed earlier:

1) The adjustive or adaptive function. Schools are to establish fixed habits of reaction to authority. This, of course, precludes critical judgment completely. It also pretty much destroys the idea that useful or interesting material should be taught, because you can't test for reflexive obedience until you know whether you can make kids learn, and do, foolish and boring things.

2) The integrating function. This might well be called "the conformity function," because its intention is to make children as alike as possible. People who conform are predictable, and this is of great use to those who wish to harness and manipulate a large labour force.

3) The diagnostic and directive function. School is meant to determine each student's proper social role. This is done by logging evidence mathematically and anecdotally on cumulative records. As in "your permanent record." Yes, you do have one.

4) The differentiating function. Once their social role has been "diagnosed," children are to be sorted by role and trained only so far as their destination in the social machine merits – and not one step further. So much for making kids their personal best.

5) The selective function. This refers not to human choice at all but to Darwin's theory of natural selection as applied to what he called "the favoured races." In short, the idea is to help things along by consciously attempting to improve the breeding stock. Schools are meant to tag the unfit – with poor grades, remedial placement, and other punishments – clearly enough that their peers will accept them as inferior and effectively bar them from the reproductive sweepstakes. That's what all those little humiliations from first grade onward were intended to do: wash the dirt down the drain.

6) The propaedeutic function. The societal system implied by these rules will require an elite group of caretakers. To that end, a small fraction of the kids will quietly be taught how to manage this continuing project, how to watch over and control a population deliberately dumbed down and declawed in order that government might proceed unchallenged and corporations might never want for obedient labour.

That, unfortunately, is the purpose of mandatory public education in this country. And lest you take Inglis for an isolated crank with a rather too cynical take on the educational enterprise, you should know that he was hardly alone in championing these ideas. Conant himself, building on the ideas of Horace Mann and others, campaigned tirelessly for an American school system designed along the same lines. Men like George Peabody, who funded the cause of mandatory schooling throughout the South, surely understood that the Prussian system was useful in creating not only a harmless electorate and a servile labour force but also a virtual herd of mindless consumers. In time a great number of industrial titans came to recognise the enormous profits to be had by cultivating and tending just such a herd via public education, among them Andrew Carnegie and John D. Rockefeller.

There you have it. Now you know. We don't need Karl Marx's conception of a grand warfare between the classes to see that it is in the interest of complex management, economic or political, to dumb people down, to demoralise them, to divide them from one another, and to discard them if they don't conform. Class may frame the proposition, as when Woodrow Wilson, then president of Princeton University, said the following to the New York City School Teachers Association in 1909: "We want one class of persons to have a liberal education, and we want another class of persons, a very much larger class, of necessity, in every society, to forgo the privileges of a liberal education and fit themselves to perform specific difficult manual tasks." But the motives behind the disgusting decisions that bring about these ends need not be class-based at all. They can stem purely from fear, or from the by now familiar belief that "efficiency" is the paramount virtue, rather than love, liberty, laughter, or hope. Above all, they can stem from simple greed.

There were vast fortunes to be made, after all, in an economy based on mass production and organised to favour the large corporation rather than the small business or the family farm. But mass production required mass consumption, and at the turn of the twentieth century most Americans considered it both unnatural and unwise to buy things they didn't actually need. Mandatory schooling was a godsend on that count. School didn't have to train kids in any direct sense to think they should consume nonstop, because it did something even better: it encouraged them not to think at all. And that left them sitting ducks for another great invention of the modem era: marketing.

Now, you needn't have studied marketing to know that there are two groups of people who can always be convinced to consume more than they need to: addicts and children. School has done a pretty good job of turning our children into addicts, but it has done a spectacular job of turning our children into children. Again, this is no accident. Theorists from Plato to Rousseau to our own Dr. Inglis knew that if children could be cloistered with other children, stripped of responsibility and independence, encouraged to develop only the trivialising emotions of greed, envy, jealousy, and fear, they would grow older but never truly grow up. In the 1934 edition of his once well-known book Public Education in the United States, Ellwood P. Cubberley detailed and praised the way the strategy of successive school enlargements had extended childhood by two to six years, and forced schooling was at that point still quite new. This same Cubberley – who was dean of Stanford's School of Education, a textbook editor at Houghton Mifflin, and Conant's friend and correspondent at Harvard – had written the following in the 1922 edition of his book Public School Administration: "Our schools are... factories in which the raw products (children) are to be shaped and fashioned... And it is the business of the school to build its pupils according to the specifications laid down."

It's perfectly obvious from our society today what those specifications were. Maturity has by now been banished from nearly every aspect of our lives. Easy divorce laws have removed the need to work at relationships; easy credit has removed the need for fiscal self-control; easy entertainment has removed the need to learn to entertain oneself; easy answers have removed the need to ask questions. We have become a nation of children, happy to surrender our judgments and our wills to political exhortations and commercial blandishments that would insult actual adults. We buy televisions, and then we buy the things we see on the television. We buy computers, and then we buy the things we see on the computer. We buy $150 sneakers whether we need them or not, and when they fall apart too soon we buy another pair. We drive SUVs and believe the lie that they constitute a kind of life insurance, even when we're upside-down in them. And, worst of all, we don't bat an eye when Ari Fleischer tells us to "be careful what you say," even if we remember having been told somewhere back in school that America is the land of the free. We simply buy that one too. Our schooling, as intended, has seen to it.

Now for the good news. Once you understand the logic behind modern schooling, its tricks and traps are fairly easy to avoid. School trains children to be employees and consumers; teach your own to be leaders and adventurers. School trains children to obey reflexively; teach your own to think critically and independently. Well-schooled kids have a low threshold for boredom; help your own to develop an inner life so that they'll never be bored. Urge them to take on the serious material, the grown-up material, in history, literature, philosophy, music, art, economics, theology – all the stuff school teachers know well enough to avoid. Challenge your kids with plenty of solitude so that they can learn to enjoy their own company, to conduct inner dialogues. Well-schooled people are conditioned to dread being alone, and they seek constant companionship through the TV, the computer, the cell phone, and through shallow friendships quickly acquired and quickly abandoned. Your children should have a more meaningful life, and they can.

First, though, we must wake up to what our schools really are: laboratories of experimentation on young minds, drill centres for the habits and attitudes that corporate society demands. Mandatory education serves children only incidentally; its real purpose is to turn them into servants. Don't let your own have their childhoods extended, not even for a day. If David Farragut could take command of a captured British warship as a preteen, if Thomas Edison could publish a broadsheet at the age of twelve, if Ben Franklin could apprentice himself to a printer at the same age (then put himself through a course of study that would choke a Yale senior today), there's no telling what your own kids could do. After a long life, and thirty years in the public school trenches, I've concluded that genius is as common as dirt. We suppress our genius only because we haven't yet figured out how to manage a population of educated men and women. The solution, I think, is simple and glorious. Let them manage themselves.

NO!

AGAINST ADULT SUPREMACY
Issue 5

America and the Beating of a Black Child

Stacey Patton

It's not surprising that a black mother in Baltimore who chased down, cursed and beat her 16-year-old son in the middle of a riot has been called a hero. In this country, when black mothers fulfil stereotypes of mammies, angry and thwarting resistance to a system designed to kill their children, they get praised.

"He gave me eye contact," Toya Graham told CBS News. "And at that point, you know, not even thinking about cameras or anything like that - that's my only son and at the end of the day, I don't want him to be a Freddie Gray. Is he the perfect boy? No he's not, but he's mine."

In other words, Graham's message to America is: I will teach my black son not to resist white supremacy so he can live.

The kind of violent discipline Graham unleashed on her son did not originate with her, or with my adoptive mother who publicly beat me when I was a child, or with the legions of black parents who equate pain with protection and love. The beatings originated with white supremacy, a history of cultural and physical violence that devalues black life at every turn. From slavery through Jim Crow, from the school-to-prison pipeline, the innocence and protection of black children has always been a dream deferred.

The problem is that Graham's actions do not assure that her son, and legions like him, will survive childhood. Recall the uncle who in 2011 posted a video recording of himself beating his teenage nephew for posting gang messages on Facebook. Acting out of love and fear for his life, he whipped the teen, but months later he was found dead anyway.

Praising Graham distracts from a hard truth: It doesn't matter how black children behave – whether they throw rocks at the police, burn a CVS, join gangs, walk home from the store with candy in their pocket, listen to rap music in a car with friends, play with a toy gun in a park, or simply make eye contact with a police officer – they risk being killed and blamed for their own deaths because black youths are rarely viewed as innocent or worthy of protection.

If there were an easy way to keep black children safe from police, out of prisons, morgues and graves, we would not have spent the past three years in an almost endless cycle of grieving the loss of young black people: Trayvon Martin, Renisha McBride, Rekia Boyd, Jordan Davis, Michael Brown, Tamir Rice, Freddie Gray and, and, and... the list is too long to fit into my word count.

This celebration of Graham reflects a belief that black youths are inherently problematic, criminal and out of control. The video also supports the idea that black fathers are absent, suggesting that all we need is an angry black mom to beat the "thug" out of an angry young man – and everything will be fine.

What is so disturbing is that white supremacy is let off the hook. A militarised and racist police force is not the problem. Systemic racism - from the War on Drugs to racial profiling, from hyper segregation to community divestment - is not the issue. The message becomes: Black children's behaviour is the true enemy of peace.

This distracting conversation turns the spotlight back to black youth. If only Freddie hadn't run; if only his parents had beaten him; if only he was perfect, maybe he would still be with us. And the praise of Graham reflects a belief shared across race lines that beating black children is the only way to keep them safe from the dangers of a racist society, or from stepping out of line. Rather than embracing her son Michael, rather than hearing and seeing his pain and assuring him that she's got his back, Graham beat and shamed him in front of the world.

The public shaming and devaluing of black children has a long heritage. On Nov. 8, 1893, the Anderson Intelligencer, a South Carolina newspaper, reported that a black boy was caught stealing a lunch that had been left inside of a horse buggy. The locals tied the boy up in a stall and called his mother. Upon her arrival, the 200-pound mom was told of the trouble her son made. She then exclaimed, "Dar now, told you so, tank de good Lord I dun got you dis time. I bin trying to git hold of you for six munts and you git away from me ebery time. Bit I got you now, tank de Lord."

The mother asked for a whip or cowhide, but was given a buggy trace. She stripped her son's pants, bent him over a cross bar and beat him. The reporter noted, "Those licks and those yells were awful to hear and awfuller to behold." And then the mother "lynched him while other humane gentlemen looked on and approved. That darkey will never steal another lunch from that stable nor any other stable."

While Graham did not literally lynch her son Michael, she metaphorically strung him up for the world to see - in hopes of keeping him alive. We can all appreciate the pain and fear in her cry that "I don't want my son to be a Freddie Gray." This is every black mother's cry heard over hundreds of years in America. From the plantation moms who whipped their kids so white masters and overseers wouldn't more harshly do the same, to the parents during Jim Crow who beat their children to keep them safe from the Klan and lynch mobs, these beatings are the acts of a people so desperate and helpless, so terrorised and enraged, that heaping pain upon their children actually seems like a sane and viable act of parental protection.

The intensity of this fear is integral to the history of black Americans. Just as black parents have "the talk" with their children, listing survival tips for when they are confronted by white authority, black corporal punishment has been encouraged as the only way to make black children acceptable to society.

The recent killings of unarmed black people, including children, has elevated black parents' fears and questions about how to protect their kids, and intensified debates over corporal punishment. All of this happens against the backdrop of American hypocrisy: a culture that routinely cites Martin Luther King Jr.'s embrace of nonviolence yet celebrates militarised police, corporal punishment, and the daily violence directed at black children; a culture that disempowers black parents, that criminalises them, and blames them for everything from low graduation rates to poverty. Only hip-hop is a bigger problem if you believe people like CNN's Don Lemon.

At the same time, American society has empowered principals who suspend and use corporal punishment, and police who wield their batons and guns to control black children.

Beatings are not transformative. They don't empower. They simply punish the victims and accelerate the trauma, bringing the pain from the streets into the home. This form of "discipline" makes children only more vulnerable to violent behaviour, and increases the risk of the very behaviours that will get them in trouble at school and in the streets - the behaviours that parents think beatings will prevent.

Where is celebration of moms whose children have been at the forefront of peaceful protests? Where is the celebration of black mothers and fathers who have been organising against police violence, against food injustice, and against the violence and looting in Baltimore and beyond? The history of the civil rights movement is one of parents and children joining together on the front lines of the struggle for justice, not one of black parents beating their children. Yet this is the image captivating the nation.

What's most tragic is that Graham said that she unleashed on her son after making eye contact with him on the street. Tragically, Freddie Gray's offence that led to his killing was that he made eye contact with police. A look from and the mere presence of black bodies leads to violence and death, and that is the real crime, which no amount of shaming or corporal punishment will fix.

Youth Against Liberation: An Exploration

Sven Bonnichsen

Not all youth support Youth Liberation. In fact, a large percentage would be against Youth Liberation - even after being introduced to its ideas. See, granted many youth simply haven't encountered the ideas of Youth Liberation, and so they just go along with the flow. But resistance to YL, by youth, runs deeper than that. My thinking here is highly influenced by the book "Right-Wing Women" by Andrea Dworkin. It's 1971, the second wave of feminism is cresting, and the slogan "Sisterhood is Powerful" is hitting the streets. There's this feeling among radicals that with 51% of the population, women are going to be an unstoppable force. All we need to do is raise women's consciousness, and they'll surely be on board with the cause.

But, it comes as a slap in the face to discover that not all women are on board with feminism. There are people like Phyllis Schlafly (in particular) who defend the notion of wives being subordinated to their husbands. Why is this? The Marxist Feminists fall back on the concept of "false consciousness" - which to my mind is rather patronising, and un-disprovable. Once you basically say that a person is wrong because they're deluded, there's no further room for argument.

Dworkin argued that Right-Wing Women are basically offered a better deal. It's the sexual revolution, and one segment of the feminist movement is feeling disillusioned, getting the sense that they're just getting exploited and used by "free love" men. So the choice looks like this: be the property of just one man, who has some obligations to care for you - or be the property of all men, none of whom owe you squat. From that perspective, it makes a lot of sense to me why a lot of women would want to stick with the "traditional" patriarchal arrangement.

Back to youth. You're 16, legal adulthood is just two years away. You can either make a fuss and fight for your rights - taking lots of flack from parents, teachers, and society in general along the way - or you can simply wait out your time, ageing out of minority. It's the path of least resistance. And all the privileges of adulthood are just waiting, shining in front of you; the fee-for-entry seems to be putting up with the 18-year hazing of childhood just a little longer.

Furthermore, youth are well-practiced at taking the point of view of adults. It's the dynamic of dissociation. The five year old protests, "I'm not a baby!" The eleventh-graders avoid hanging out with the tenth-graders, to avoid the stigma of being associated with one's inferiors. Most people spend the first 18 years of their lives not thinking of themselves as minors at all - but rather, practicing thinking like adults.

I've listened to youth condemn Youth Liberation, talking about how children aren't competent to vote. Or about how they support the curfew, because youth are bound to get in trouble. It's rather amazing: the speaker never seems to doubt their own intelligence and good nature - but their opinion of their peers is abysmal. I can't help but wonder: what portion of this is actually based on observation - and what portion is based on the powerful image of youth-as-inferior propagated by adult society?

In terms of talking about the "deal" that society presents youth (be a rebel and suffer, or be patient and get enormous privilege), I'd be remiss if I didn't mention the deal offered to religious youth. Secular society offers up legal status for putting up with minority. Religious communities (many of them) offer up heaven. "Honour your father and mother…" (which means "obey", I believe), is the fifth of the Ten Commandments. If you believe in the bible, then YL is seemingly a rebellion against God.

Religion offers a complete world-view that can be very difficult to argue with. The worldview offered by most YL thinkers, by contrast is very limited. Our area of focus tends to be limited just to a few legal rights, and a period of one's life that may only be 2-4 years long. I think our ranks remain thin partly due to this. Notice that the YL movement is being far outpaced by the Christian Youth movement. Ironically, some of these youth groups are also dubbed "Youth Liberation"!

It need not be so, however. YL has the potential to offer up a very expansive world-view: one that is not merely about a few years of one's life, but rather encompasses what it means to be an adult, how to do well at having a family of one's own, a vision of justice and fairness that takes it's strength from the principle that no person is property (and we must continue working to wipe out the vestiges of people-as-property), a world-view whose truth is firmly rooted in verifiable historical events.

A world-view is a powerful thing. Feminism, Marxism, Freudianism, Re-evaluation Counselling, and other such philosophies are compelling largely because they give you a lens - through which it becomes possible to interpret the world around you. The sense of control provided by being able to make sense of the world is intense.

The Student Left: A History

Tom Watts

The history of the oppression of youth goes back to the origins of society, the imposition of the Patriarchy, and the division of society into classes (freeman and slave). But at every stage in the development of class society, youth have, in rebelling against their specific oppression as youth, played a role in the overall class struggle and helped to advance the struggle of humanity to liberate itself from all oppression.

History advances in waves and several revolutionary waves have swept across America, each gaining in depth and force. And in each, youth have been the most active element and have increasingly come to the fore as youth in their own cause and under their own organisation. Between the high tides there have been periods of retrogression but each new wave builds upon the last: Each revolutionary generation stands upon the shoulders of the preceding generation and takes the struggle higher.

From the early days of European colonisation of America, Native American youth played the most active role in resisting the colonisers. It has become a Hollywood cliche for the Old Chief to say that he cannot control the "young bucks." In reality, many young braves did rise rapidly to become leaders of rebellions and whole Indian armies, such as Teedyuscung of the Lenape, Oceola of the Seminole, and Blue Jacket and Tecumseh of the Shawnee. [Actually Blue Jacket was originally a white youth adopted into the Shawnee nation after being taken captive.]

Masses of white youth came to America as indentured servants, many of them to die under the harsh conditions of servitude, and many of them ran off to join the Indian nations as did many black slave youth. Most of the slaves that were kidnapped and brought on the "middle passage" from Africa were youth, or children, and many of them died along the way, or shortly after arrival in the new land. Conditions of living for slave children were deplorable. They were denied any type of family life, and usually their parents were worked for very long hours, and they had little time or energy left to rear their children, who were often raised under the care of older children or women too old for the masters to exploit another way. When they got sick they often died.

Both white indentured servants and Black slaves played an active role in Bacon's Rebellion of 1676, which was a foretaste of the War of Independence a century later. Youth organised as the "Mohawks" played an important role in the popular movement led by the "Sons of Liberty", as did student leaders like Aaron Burr and Alexander Hamilton. Tom Paine was a young English radical who came to America and became the Revolution's most noted propagandist along with young Thomas Jefferson who drafted the Declaration of Independence.

But the Revolution was dominated by and served the interests of the rising middle class and land owners, and youth, women, indians, and slaves, as well as those without property, were counted out from the liberty that was won. To the new dominant classes of capitalists and landlords, freedom meant freedom to trade and develop the productive forces in ways that would maximise their profits. This meant exploiting the unpaid labour of youth under slavery or on the family farm and exploiting the barely-paid labour of youth as workers in mines and mills.

The Abolitionist Movement gave rise to the first leader of a radical student movement in the U.S., Theodore Welt, of the Lane Theological Seminary in Cincinnati, Ohio. In 1833-34, he organised the sons of slave holders to publicly speak out against the institution of slavery at meetings of students. Eventually, he and his core group were expelled, and they transferred to Oberlin College, were they continued their abolitionist activities and helped to organise the "Underground Railroad." They also campaigned for the right of free speech on campuses. Abolitionist youth fought in Kansas and were with John Brown in the raid on the arsenal at Harper's Ferry, when he attempted to initiate guerrilla warfare to overthrow slavery in the South. During the Civil War, millions of youth (black, white and indian) answered the call to take up arms against slavery. But the Civil War, which was a continuation of the American Revolution, did not address the issues of youth liberation, women's liberation or even racism, class oppression and exploitation, or genocide against the Native Americans. The oppression and exploitation of youth intensified after the war as many tens of thousands were forced into taking jobs in factories where they worked twelve and thirteen hour days for half pay. In the South, former slave plantations were turned into semi-feudal manors were poor whites and blacks worked the land as sharecroppers, including the unpaid hands of children and youth. In the North, factory owners like Simon Slater competed to see who could exploit children the most, even recruiting orphans as young as seven or eight years old to work in their "sweat shops." In Rhode Island, where Slater had his mills, the census in 1875 listed 1,258 factory workers under twelve years old. The Industrial Workers of the World (IWW), organised in 1905, took on the issue of child labor, and on August 3, 1913, Mother Jones of the IWW led a march of factory children from New York City to Washington, D.C. to protest child labor and demand free public education. The Socialist Party had been founded in 1901 by Victor Berger, Eugene Debs and Morris Hillquit. In 1905, Jack London, Upton Sinclair and other students founded the Intercollegiate Socialist Society (ISS). Sinclair wrote that, "only a few institutions would let us in under our own evil name, and we had to disguise ourselves as open forums and social science clubs" [Prospect for Youth, p. 143]. After the First World War, the ISS was reorganised as the Student League for Industrial Democracy (SLID). In a pamphlet titled the Revolt of Youth published in 1923, Dr. John Holmes wrote:

Our young people have come to the time when they propose to be free from the domination of their elders – free to follow their own courses and seek their own goals... to my way of thinking, this declaration of independence is as glorious as all previous declarations of the same kind; and the youth movement, which embodies it, not a terror, but a great hope to humanity" [Ibid, p. 144].

Early in 1933, a split in the SLID led by the Young Communist League (YCL) led to the formation of the National Student League (NSL). The first action of the NSL was a student expedition to Harlan County, Kentucky, where miners were engaged in a tough armed struggle with company goons known as the Harlan County War. This was followed by an NSL-led student strike at Columbia University over the expulsion of the editor of the Columbia Spectator. In October of 1934, The YCL led several successful student strikes and demonstrations in the Chicago high schools protesting racial discrimination. And in general the YCL was active on many fronts of the rising workers' movement during the depression, particularly in building the unemployed councils and in celebrating events such as International Worker's Day (May 1st), International Women's Day (March 8th), and International Youth Day (August 31st). SLID continued under socialist leadership, but it continued to work with the communist-led NSL on issues such as combating racism and kicking Reserve Officer Training Corps (ROTC) off campus. Eventually SLID and NSL re-merged to form the American Student Union (ASU). Throughout the 1930's mass student protests against war and fascism rocked American campuses. During the April 12,1935 student strike, 10,000 students rallied in New York City against war and fascism. In November, 20,000 rallied on the different campuses in the city. Together with other progressive student and youth groups, the ASU organised the walkout of a million collage students in protest of the war in Europe in April of 1937.

In 1934, the American Youth Congress (AYC) was formed under the slogan "Peace. Freedom and Progress," and it adopted "The Declaration of the Rights of American Youth" at its second congress on July 4th, 1935. Together with ASU, AYC succeeded in getting the American Youth Bill before the 74th Congress and organised a demonstration of more than 1,000 youth in front of the capitol to demand passage of the bill. It was not passed. Both ASU and AYC participated in the American League Against War and Fascism (ALAWF), which had been established in 1933. By 1939, ASU had a membership of some 12,000 students, 400 of whom volunteered to go to Spain to fight fascism with the Abraham Lincoln Brigade.

In 1959, SLID changed its name to Students for a Democratic Society (SDS). In June of 1962, SDS leader Tom Hayden presented a sixty-one page document to the SDS convention at the AFL-CIO camp at Port Huron, Michigan. It became known as the Port Huron Statement, and some 100,000 copies were eventually distributed by SDS. In April of 1965, SDS drew 20,000 students to Washington. D.C. in what was up until then the largest anti-war demonstration in the capital's history. For many students, the revolution had begun in 1964, during the "Freedom Summer" in Mississippi, organised by the Student Non-violent Coordinating Committee (SNCC). More than 2,000 Mississippi black youth were organised into forty-two two-month "Freedom Schools" that stayed open despite KKK terror, while other students organised voter registration. SNCC leaders Stokeley Carmichael and H. Rap Brown would sum up that the SNCC civil rights approach was wrong and mired in middle-class liberalism and subtle white racism, and they launched the Black Liberation Movement taking their cue from Malcolm X, who was assassinated in 1965. Also inspired by Brother Malcolm were the Black Panther Party (BPP), born in Oakland, California when Bobby Seale hooked up with Huey P. Newton at the local junior college in 1966. The Panthers added a new dynamic into the American left by popularising the Little Red Book (quotations From Chairman Mao), and openly advocating and practicing armed self-defence. Parallel to the Black Panthers, and allied with them, were other ethnic based revolution organisations centred among oppressed youth, such as the Young Lords Party (YLP), later the Puerto Rican Revolutionary Workers' Organisation (PRWO), The Young Patriot Party (YPP), composed of hillbilly white youth, La Raza Unida Party (Chicanos), l Wor Kun (Chinese), and others including the American Indian Movement (AIM). Dennis Banks and George Mitchel founded AIM in 1968, consciously patterning it after the Black Panthers. The Panthers, by their example and through the liaison work of Bob Avakain, had a profound influence on the SDS, just as SDS was having a profound influence on the growing anti- Vietnam War movement. Picking up the chant first raised by SNCC outside the U.S. Army induction centre in Atlanta, SDS rocked the ivory towers of academia with "HELL NO WE WON'T GO!" and "HO – HO – HO CHI MINH, THE NLF IS GOING TO WIN!" Student takeovers of buildings at Columbia and Harvard in the spring of 1968, led by SDS and the Black Student Union (BSU), the student wing of the Black Panthers, led to the rapid growth of both organisations and severely hurt government attempts to sell the war as "winding-down." Coupled with the Tet Offensive by the National Liberation Front (NFL) in Vietnam, it marked the turning point in the war. That spring marked the high tide of revolution internationally and the 1968 Democratic National Convention in Chicago was a showdown between youth and the Cold War Liberal Establishment. Contrary to the popular impression, the young demonstrators in Chicago were not, for the most part, the hard core of the American left. The Black Panthers and most militants had heeded SDS's call to stay away. The overwhelming majority of demonstrators were unaffiliated with the revolutionary left. Many were supporters of anti-war candidate, Eugene McCarthy, or had come for the Yippie!

Festival of Life. According to the official Walker Report, of the 668 persons arrested, 75.8% were twenty-five years old or younger (64% were under 18) and roughly half were from Chicago or its immediate suburbs. Forty-three percent were workers and less than a third were students. Only 39 out of the 668 had been previously arrested for political activity.

Following its convention after Chicago, SDS split apart into numerous factions, one of which, led by the political line of Bob Avakain, regrouped in the 1970's as first the Attica Brigade and later as the Revolutionary Student Brigade. Following the formation of the Revolutionary Communist Party in 1975, it became the Revolutionary Communist Youth Brigade. Other factions tended to form other Marxist-Leninist parties such as the Communist Workers' Party, Communist Party (ML), etc. – joining the alphabet soup of the fractionalised American Left. Most of these formations have since passed out of existence.

In response to the revolutionary upsurge of the 1960's and early 1970's, certain concessions were made to youth, such as lowering the voting age to eighteen and discontinuing the draft, in practice (though it can be reinstituted at any time). Most importantly, there has been an acknowledgement that youth are a social, and potentially political, power which must be considered.

The issue of Youth Liberation was raised in this upsurge and the results can be seen in changes in the custody laws and the U.N. Convention on the Rights of the Child, but it has yet to win decisive victories, and only another and more powerful wave can accomplish this. The student left is at present quite weak, as is the left generally in the U.S. The Youth Liberation Movement will have the task of rejuvenating it, which will ground it more firmly in youth issues and a youth perspective, but it is important not to narrow or negate the revolutionary scope of the student left in doing this. Youth should discuss and deepen their understanding of this heritage and prepare to enrich it as they move forward to prepare a tidal wave of youth liberation in the 21st century.

Unschooling and Anarchism

Idzie Desmarais

I don't really separate the different aspects of my life: every belief, opinion, and interaction is intertwined with all other parts of who I am and how I live. So although I might not talk about it specifically all that often in my writings, my anarchist views – my belief that humans have the innate ability to control their own lives and as such do not need to be, and are happier without being, ruled – infuse everything that I write and think, including what I write and think about unschooling.

I find it interesting that my becoming anarchist went hand-in-hand with my embracing of unschooling. Coming out of a not-so-great time in my early to mid teenage years, a time characterised by feelings of depression, of feeling like an outcast, and of not knowing who I was as a person or what I should be doing, I started reading extensively about both unschooling and anarchism. And, not long after I decided, with both relief and a new found conviction, that unschooling really had been the right thing for me, and really was an amazing way of looking at and living education, I finally found a political view that truly spoke to me, that felt right in the most fundamental way.

For me, the questioning of the education system – something so close to the hearts of so many people, something almost universally heralded as an amazing achievement for a democratic country, and the best way to Get An Education – and the realisation that it was not only not the best option, but something truly horrible to inflict on the vast majority of youth, really startled me, and led me to start questioning all the other rarely examined or thought about aspects of society. That questioning, starting with unschooling, was a process that led me very organically to rethinking almost every aspect of life and how we live in this world. It was pretty mind-blowing. So as you can see, for me unschooling and anarchy have always been tied especially closely together.

Radical unschooling is a philosophy that recognises that children are people, too, and as such have a right to control their own thoughts and activities, and by extension their own education and learning. Parents thus abdicate their role of authoritarian presence, dictator and teacher, in favour of becoming their children's partner, supporter, helper, and guide. It removes hierarchy from the family unit, and replaces it with mutual co-operation.

Anarchism is the belief that individuals are fully capable of being self-governing, so do not need to be ruled, controlled, or governed. Taken from An Anarchist FAQ: "anarchism is a political theory which aims to create a society within which individuals freely co-operate together as equals. As such anarchism opposes all forms of hierarchical control as harmful to the individual and their individuality as well as unnecessary."

So to me, unschooling is basically putting anarchy into practice in daily life. It's going past the philosophy and the can-it-really-work and proving that people, even children, are far more capable of controlling their own lives than anyone gives them (us) credit for.

Yes, I most definitely realise that unschoolers are not all anarchists. Most aren't (though there are definitely more anarchists in your average group of unschoolers than you'd find in your average group of random people). I just find that, from my point of view, the two philosophies are extremely complementary. Both emphasise living in co-operation, living in freedom. Both involve a lack of dependence on the State or other higher authorities.

At their core, what both unschooling and anarchy mean to me is living in (when possible), and striving for (when necessary), true freedom. If anarchy is getting rid of all forms of domination and oppression, hierarchy and authority, then unschooling, the freeing of children from school and the empowering of children and teens by giving them back their own lives, is an important part in moving toward an anarchist, co-operative society.

NO!

AGAINST ADULT SUPREMACY
Issue 6

Confession and Execution

Corey Hutchins

A few miles off I-95, past acres of brown-and-white fields where blackbirds circle overhead, this small town in the heart of Deep South cotton country isn't known for much. It has a post office and a few churches, some abandoned houses and some nicer ones, ramshackle trailers and cotton fields. After church on a recent Sunday there, George Frierson was scuffing a shiny black dress shoe across some gravel at a railroad crossing. Back when he was a kid the rail line split this tiny, rural town along racial lines. But for blacks like him growing up in Alcolu, the train tracks signified something even more sinister than segregation.

Frierson is a local historian and community activist who works at the nearby Oak Grove Missionary Baptist Church and serves on the county school board. The general area he was marking with his shoe was the scene of a double murder in 1944. Two young white girls out picking flowers had their skulls bashed in and were found in a nearby water-filled ditch. Police said their killer used a railroad spike, and for the culprit they fingered a 14-year-old black boy named George Stinney Jr., whom a witness said had been seen talking to the girls earlier that day. The sheriff's deputies who snatched Stinney up said he confessed to the crime when they took him in for questioning. The boy's parents, who lived in a company house, were run out of town the day he was arrested and didn't see their son until his trial. An all-white jury sentenced the teenager to death after 10 minutes of deliberation. The trial lasted two and a half hours in the Clarendon County courthouse where a local tax commissioner preparing for a State House run in an election year was appointed to represent him. No witnesses spoke in his defence. That summer, fewer than 90 days after the girls were killed, the State of South Carolina shocked George Stinney Jr. to death in an electric chair that could barely fit his small frame. He was the youngest person executed in 20th century America.

About four years ago, a white local attorney named Steve McKenzie read a newspaper account about the execution. No written record of a confession has even been produced, according to McKenzie and others who have researched the case, and nearly all the transcripts, files and records related to the prosecution have vanished except for some handwritten notes. Part of the new petition to re-open the case also hinges on that alleged confession between a black teenager, alone in a room with multiple white sheriff's deputies in the Deep South, pre-Miranda rights era of 1944.

"The only thing that we are aware of is an oral confession," McKenzie says. "To me, any time you put a 14-year-old in that situation and you put it in that era, then the chances of this confession either being coerced or the person being manipulated by the people who were actually doing the interrogation would be very, very high. You're talking about white men in the Jim Crow South with a 14-year-old boy. It wasn't even close to being an even playing field."

Obviously no can say for sure what happened in the room where the deputies questioned George Stinney Jr. 70 years ago. The officers are dead, and Stinney is dead. But one thing can be said about the circumstances in which the teenager's alleged confession was used in the swift trial that led to his execution. In 1944, there was no body of scientific evidence, research or psychology to suggest that people would ever confess to a crime they didn't commit. Now, there's plenty.

These days, no murder trial in the United States could ever take just two and a half hours, as Stinney's trial did in 1944. And when it comes to the confession part of it, modern defence attorneys have a bench of experts at their disposal, some of whom have devoted their life's work researching it. One of those is Kassin. In 1985, he wrote a landmark article that laid out three categories of false confessions and why someone would ever admit to a crime they didn't commit. One category is a voluntary confession, typically given by someone looking for attention. Another is an internalised confession, when interrogation tactics lead someone to believe they might have actually committed an act they haven't.

The third is called a coerced compliant false confession. "These are cases where innocent people who know they're innocent are in a situation of interrogation that is so stressful, they've been there so long and they're sleep deprived and they're so tired and they are being yelled at and being called a liar and there may have been threats or promises that have been made or implied, and basically, in a nutshell, the situation has become so bad that they use confession as the only way to get out."

Oftentimes, Kassin says, a part of it is something known as myopic decision making: when someone is under duress, he or she will do what's expedient to get out of a bad situation with little or no regard for future consequences. "Innocent people trust that their innocence will ultimately work them out," he says, adding that someone who knows they've done nothing wrong can sometimes believe that once the interrogation is over, the crime is fully examined and investigated, the police will see the evidence clearly points in another direction, and everything will be OK once they get a lawyer."

That, and myopic decision making, is much worse with young people than adults, Kassin says. They'll ask if they can call their mom and are told they can when the interrogation is over. Getting out becomes the urgent problem they need to solve and so they say whatever it might take to get them out of the situation. It certainly isn't beyond the realm of possibilities that Stinney was up against the same or similar circumstances and psychology in 1944. "Research couldn't be clearer: kids are much more shortsighted in their decision making than they are focused on longterm consequences," Kassin says. "A 14-year-old fits perfectly into that model."

Just as no one can know how Stinney's alleged 1944 confession to the sheriff's deputies came about, or if it even did, the same could be said for what the jurors in the case were thinking when they reached their verdict, sentencing a black teenager to death for the killing of two white girls in a segregated Deep South town that wanted revenge. Steve McKenzie, the lead lawyer working to have the Stinney case re-heard, in order to right what he sees as a moral wrong, had a rather shocking confession himself when asked about that specific aspect of the trial. "If I would have been sitting on that jury I probably would have convicted him too," he told me. "I'll tell you why: It's simply because the white community was expecting justice and they had what they thought was a confession. So why doubt what the police officers were saying? You had two sheriff's deputies that said he confessed. For the white community, as far as they were concerned it was done, the girls were dead and let's execute the murderer and move on. And that's what they did."

"I was born in Alcolu, and all young black males knew about this story from our youth," Frierson said outside the church as he looked out over a cotton field across the highway. "I wasn't born at the time of this incident, I'm not that old. But I'm considered a historian, so I started out on this juncture to see the facts of this case, not as an advocacy or activism point of view. And then it evolved into the activism. When I started out I just wanted to be sure that the facts that I heard all my life are correct." It turned out that facts were funny things. People believed the ones they wanted to believe. "I won't say that the white community doesn't know, but they won't admit to what they do know."

He doesn't think Stinney killed anybody. At around 95 pounds, there was just no way the skinny 14-year-old could have beaten those girls to death, he believes, and then hauled them several hundred feet from the murder site and dumped them in a ditch. "There has never been any statements about any blood attributed to Mr. Stinney in this case," Frierson says. "It never, ever was alleged that there was any bloody clothes, blood on him or whatever." But Frierson is also keeping his own secrets about the case. "There are some things that are not reported anywhere that I know to be facts that I am not at liberty to speak of, like who the real perpetrator was," he said at one point. "I think they call that defamation of character or slander."

Criminalising Gender Nonconforming Youth

Jerome Hunt and Aisha C. Moodie-Mills

Gay, transgender, and gender nonconforming youth are significantly over-represented in the juvenile justice system – approximately 300,000 gay and transgender youth are arrested and/or detained each year, of which more than 60 percent are black or Latino. Though gay and transgender youth represent just 5 percent to 7 percent of the nation's overall youth population, they compose 13 percent to 15 percent of those currently in the juvenile justice system.

These high rates of involvement in the juvenile justice system are a result of gay and transgender youth abandonment by their families and communities, and victimisation in their schools – sad realities that place this group of young people at a heightened risk of entering the school-to-prison pipeline. Despite the disproportionately high rates of gay and transgender youth entering the juvenile justice system, our nation's schools, law enforcement officers, district attorneys, judges, and juvenile defenders are not equipped to manage the unique experiences and challenges that these young people face. As a consequence, the system often does more harm by unfairly criminalising these youth – imposing harsh school sanctions, labelling them as sex offenders, or detaining them for minor offences – in addition to subjecting them to discriminatory and harmful treatment that deprives them of their basic civil rights.

Angela Irvine of the National Council on Crime and Delinquency in conjunction with the Equity Project, which works to ensure gay and transgender youth in the juvenile justice system are treated with fairness and respect, have both generated groundbreaking research on the experiences of these youth in the system over the past few years. This issue brief offers a high-level summary of some of their findings, as well as others, to explain the disproportionate pipelining of gay and transgender youth into the juvenile justice system, the bias and discrimination they face once within the system, and the steps that the federal government and state and local juvenile courts can take to ensure that gay and transgender youth are treated with dignity and respect.

Family rejection, homelessness, and failed safety nets

Research shows that gay and transgender youth entering into the juvenile justice system are twice as likely to have experienced family conflict, child abuse, and homelessness as other youth. This trend is partly due to the fact that youth today "come out" at younger ages, often to families that may not accept gay and transgender people. Since these youth still depend on their families to meet their material needs, family rejection can leave them emotionally and physically vulnerable, particularly if they find themselves cast onto the streets with nowhere to turn for support.

Many gay and transgender youth leave their homes of their own accord to escape the conflict and emotional or physical abuse that can ensue – 26 percent report leaving their homes at some point – but more often, they are pushed out and into the juvenile justice system by their own families. Interfamily conflicts stemming from parents' refusal to accept a child's sexual orientation or gender identity often result in the first contact these young people have with the justice system. According to the Equity Project, prosecutors frequently file charges against these youth for being "incorrigible" or beyond the control of their parents or guardians, based largely on the parent's objections to their sexual orientation. This practice unfairly criminalises gay and transgender youth because of their identity rather than because of their behaviour.

Further, family discord that casts these youth from their homes can send them cascading through social safety nets not adequately equipped to support them. Programs designed to keep children and youth off the streets, such as foster care, health centres, and other youth-serving institutions, are often ill-prepared or unsafe for gay and transgender youth due to institutional prejudice, lack of provider and foster-parent training, and discrimination against gay and transgender youth by adults and peers. As a result, many youth run away from these placements, actions that could also land them in the custody of the juvenile justice system.

Gay and transgender youth who flee hostility and abuse at home and in temporary placements are most likely to end up homeless, which is the greatest predictor of involvement with the juvenile justice system. Gay and transgender youth represent up to 40 percent of the homeless youth population even though they only compose 5 percent to 7 percent of the youth population overall, and 39 percent of homeless gay and transgender youth report being involved in the juvenile justice system at some level.

Out of despair and a need for survival, homeless gay and transgender youth are more likely to resort to criminal behaviours, such as drug sales, theft, or "survival sex," which put them at risk of arrest and detainment. These youth are also at an increased risk of detainment for committing crimes related to homelessness, such as violating youth curfew laws and sleeping in public spaces. Family rejection, which sets off a tragic chain of events for many gay and transgender youth, is at the core of these issues. Caitlin Ryan of the Family Acceptance Project at San Francisco State University, whose research has brought to light the negative impacts that family rejection can have on gay and transgender youth, emphasises the need to provide opportunities to help support and strengthen families in order to promote nurturing environments for gay and transgender children. Early intervention can help families and caregivers reduce the risk of these youth entering the juvenile justice system. It is important that law enforcement officials, district attorneys, judges, and juvenile defenders seek ways to keep gay and transgender youth and their families together, rather than pushing for incarceration.

Biased school discipline policies

Unfortunately, schools do not always provide a reprieve for youth experiencing family rejection. According to the Gay Lesbian and Straight Education Network's School Climate Survey, 84 percent of gay and transgender students report being verbally harassed, 40 percent physically harassed, and 19 percent physically assaulted.

What's more, gay and transgender students report astonishingly low levels of confidence in their school administrators and often do not report incidents because they expect the situation will not improve or fear it might even become worse. This is not surprising considering that one-third of bullied gay and transgender students who reported bullying to school officials said the administrators did nothing to address the issue. In fact, school officials in many ways exacerbate these problems and place further stress and burden on gay and transgender youth by disproportionately doling out harsh school sanctions against them for minor disciplinary infractions. The school and juvenile justice systems have become inextricably linked in recent years with schools relying heavily on law enforcement to manage what in the past were school discipline issues. The consequence of this conflated discipline system is that it unduly criminalises youth of colour and gay and transgender youth.

School discipline policies across the United States are under heightened scrutiny because of the disparate impact they have on youth of colour, particularly black boys. Data released this spring from the U.S. Department of Education's Office of Civil Rights show that harsh school sanctions – such as zero-tolerance policies, which lead to suspensions and expulsions of students for even the most minor offences – perpetuate a school-to-prison pipeline that disproportionately criminalises youth of colour.

Hidden among these school discipline data are thousands of gay and transgender youth who bear a double burden of disparate impact. A groundbreaking study published in 2010 in the medical journal Paediatrics revealed that gay and transgender youth, particularly gender nonconforming girls, are up to three times more likely to experience harsh disciplinary treatment by school administrators than their heterosexual counterparts. As with the racial disparities in school suspensions and expulsions, these higher rates of punishment do not correlate to higher rates of misbehaviour among gay and transgender youth. What the research suggests is that gay and transgender youth actually face harsher sanctions by school administrators even when committing similar offences.

Surely bias and discrimination among teachers, staff, and administrators contributes to the unfair treatment of gay and transgender youth in schools. Adults in schools often draw assumptions of guilt based on a student's physical characteristics, demeanour, dress, or mannerisms, deeming those deviating from an accepted gender norm to be agitators. Such assumptions are not only misguided, but biased against gay and transgender students who do not fall within rigid stereotypes of expression. Moreover, studies reveal that gay and transgender youth are often the victims, rather than the aggressors in school conflicts, which stem from bullying and harassment. Consider, for example, a gender nonconforming girl exhibiting masculine traits, who is disciplined for fighting but may be defending herself from peers' taunts. Yet more often than not, school administrators will consider her the aggressor based solely on her physical demeanour and will suspend or expel her despite the defensive nature of her actions.

For many students, suspension and expulsion are the first steps toward time behind bars. This is equally true for gay and transgender youth. Black boys and gender nonconforming girls similarly experience disproportionately harsh punishments and juvenile justice system referrals in schools, but the latter are rendered all but invisible because sexual orientation and gender identity are not included in the federal school discipline data cited earlier in this report. A first step in addressing the unfair punishment of gay and transgender youth in schools is to expand the research and collection of school discipline data to include gay and transgender youth, which will help policymakers and practitioners alike better understand the problem and formulate more supportive school discipline policies.

Unfair criminalisation by the system

Once in the juvenile justice system, gay and transgender youth are too often denied basic civil rights, wrongly categorised as sexually deviant simply because of their sexual orientation, gender identity, or gender non-conformity, and even labeled as sex offenders. They are also subjected to the biases and discrimination of law enforcement agents, judges, and other justice system officials that leave them vulnerable to abuse and neglect.

Classification as sex offenders

Gay and transgender youth who end up in the justice system are at-risk of being labeled as sex offenders, regardless of whether they have actually committed a sexual crime. Gay and transgender youth "are more likely to be prosecuted for age-appropriate consensual sexual activity" than their heterosexual counterparts – a lopsided application of the law, which has devastating consequences for gay and transgender youth who would be required to register as sex offenders in 29 states if convicted. The stigma of being a registered sex offender could haunt them for the rest of their lives, negatively impacting their future employment and life opportunities and causing significant psychological distress.

Many gay and transgender youth charged with non-sexual offences are also unfairly treated as sex offenders and ordered by the court to undergo sex offender treatment programs or sex offence risk assessments simply because of their sexual orientation or gender identity. This misguided categorisation by the courts has led gay and transgender youth, innocent of violent crimes or sex offences, to be placed in restrictive punitive settings for high-risk youth and to be given longer stays in out-of-home placements. These restrictive settings not only hinder rehabilitation efforts, they perpetuate the stigma that being gay or transgender is wrong. Additionally, extended stays in out-of-home placements prevent gay and transgender youth from reconnecting with their families, a critical step proven to stabilise their lives and reduce their risk of returning to the system. These unfair practices make gay and transgender youth susceptible to discrimination and harmful treatment while in the system.

Detention as a default

In most incidences juveniles who have been arrested or detained will only be released from custody under the supervision of a parent or guardian. Without someone to claim them, youth can be left to languish in detention centres with youth convicted of crimes, even if they have not been. Gay and transgender youth are most at-risk of detainment by default by the juvenile justice system as they are more likely to be estranged from their families and lack parental support, which leaves them to fend for themselves. As a consequence, these youth are subjected to criminal incarceration while they await foster or group home placements.

Segregation and isolation of gay and transgender youth

From the moment gay and transgender youth enter a detention facility they are at risk of being inappropriately classified and housed. Transgender youth, for example, are often placed according to their birth sex rather than by their gender identity in an effort to force transgender youth to conform to societal norms. Doing so can be psychologically devastating and leave them vulnerable to physical and sexual abuse. Additionally, youth facility staff often view them as threatening or sexually predatory, harmful stereotypes that taint placement decisions and influence the treatment of transgender youth.

Some facilities will automatically segregate gay and transgender youth or place them in solitary confinement for their "own safety," but this isolation perpetuates the stigmatisation of gay and transgender youth, casts them as sexually deviant, and signals that they might be of threat to other youth.

According to the American Psychiatric Association, isolation "is a form of punishment and is likely to produce lasting psychiatric symptoms." Unwarranted segregation deprives gay and transgender youth of educational, recreational, and programming opportunities that they are otherwise entitled to receive, punishing them unfairly and at a particularly vulnerable time in their adolescent development.

Physical, sexual, and emotional abuse

A 2007 study funded by the California Department of Corrections and Rehabilitation found an astounding 67 percent of gay or transgender men have been sexually assaulted by another inmate – a rate 15 times higher than the overall inmate population. Another study found that sexual assaults that occur are not just isolated events, but that 30 percent of all inmates have endured six or more sexual assaults.

Gay and transgender youth are particularly at risk for physical, sexual, and emotional abuse while in detention, by both staff and other youth. Eighty percent of those surveyed by the Equity Project believed a lack of safety in dentition was a serious problem. Some reports suggest that staff have turned a blind eye to incidents of rape and abuse against gay and transgender youth, confusing gay and transgender identity as an invitation for sex. Gay and transgender youth are not only subjected to abuse by their peers but by staff as well, particularly in the facilities that lack training and policies that promote inclusiveness and rely on biases rather than on best practices in treatment and placement decisions. This type of environment allows physical, sexual, and emotional abuse toward gay and transgender youth to happen without so much as a second thought and leaves them with nowhere to turn for help.

Unsafe reparative or conversion therapy

Gay and transgender youth have been subjected to reparative or conversion therapy to change their sexual orientation by both social workers and the courts, even though so-called reparative or conversion therapy has been condemned by every major health organisation, including the American Medical Association, American Psychological Association, and the American Academy of Child and Adolescent Psychiatry.

Sadly, the juvenile justice system is rife with examples of misguided interventions. One judge hospitalised a gay youth to stop his same-sex attraction, while another judge, with the parent's approval, had a young lesbian who was caught in a sexual act with another girl placed in a private hospital to be "treated and diagnosed for this behaviour." These examples may be the extreme, but instances such as a 15-year-old boy being given a women's lingerie catalogue with the purpose of teaching him "appropriate" sexual desires and a male-to-female transgender youth, who was detained in a boy's facility, being placed on "treatment plan" to "help with gender confusion and appropriate gender identity," are more common examples of unsafe reparative therapy.

The inclination to change a youth's sexual orientation or gender identity or force him or her to conform "social norms" hinders general mental health and causes severe psychological distress. This type of "counselling and other services are virtually worthless [for gay and transgender youth] because they either ignore or criminalise the youth's sexuality."

Conclusion

Gay and transgender youth are pipelined into the juvenile justice system at disproportionate rates, often stripped of their basic dignity and civil rights, and treated in a harmful and discriminatory manner once in the system. The current policies and practices of schools and the juvenile justice system overlook gay and transgender youth and perpetuate stigma and bias that can lead to their unwarranted criminalisation and unfair treatment.

Helping Kids in Bad Situations (Excerpt)

Rachel Coleman

If you grew up in a bad or less-than-ideal family and/or homeschooling environment, what are things that people around you could have done to help you and make your life better, more tolerable, etc.?

Compliment the child to the parents in front of the child. Even if the parents shoot down the compliment, it might be one of the kindest things the child has heard about themselves in years.

Let them overhear you offer to include them in your own family events/outings. Even if the parents refuse, it might offer the child hope for the future and give them a self-esteem boost.

Give them opportunities, however small, to express their own feelings or thoughts. Tell them it's ok to have feelings and thoughts, especially if they're super repressed.

Encourage them to dream of careers. Encourage them to dream of careers beyond gender role ideals by remarking on what they're good at. They'll remember it for years and years.

Attribute their successes and their great personality traits to them, and them alone. None of this "your parents must have raised you right!" or "you must have great parents" or "parents did a good job on this one!" Let the kids know they deserve praise for their own accomplishments. They are not their parents' puppets or pet dogs.

If a parent tells you they're being harsh or strict with their children, don't praise them for doing so. You don't necessarily need to assume they're wrong but you should always keep in mind that the parent you're talking to is a potential abuser.

If they are stressed out about family, do your psychoanalysing silently. It is very likely they're being gaslighted at home and otherwise mentally/emotionally abused. Process in your own head. If you suspect something, ask around how to appropriately intervene.

Let them know it's never wrong to question. Truth will stand up under scrutiny. Question down to the foundations, and when you get to a wall of assumptions or tenets or axioms you can't get past, ask yourself why. Question your beliefs and question the reasons for your beliefs. Question authority. That's not a statement of rebellion, it's a search for truth. Truth will always prevail, and if/when your beliefs come out whole on the other side, you'll be that much stronger in holding them, because the hard questions are behind you.

Accept them. Even if they are different, even if they seem a bit odd, shower them with acceptance. They need acceptance, not judgement.

Love them. Listen to them like they matter because they might not get much of that. Simple little gestures like telling them it's okay to be sad or saying 'you can do it!' 'I believe in you' or 'I am proud of you' can stick in their mind for years.

Remember to distinguish between the children and their parents. Strive to distinguish between religious homeschooling parents and religiously home-schooled kids, rather than negatively lumping them all together as "religious home-schoolers."

Challenge them. They'll probably disagree with you, but it opens you up as someone who they might be able to ask questions they don't already know the right answers for. It gives them permission to consider alternative view points, just knowing that someone they respect can have good reasons to think in a different way than the conservative noise machine.

Encourage them, period. Let them know it gets better. I wish someone had told me that I would be able to make it on my own both mentally and physically because I was strong and capable. Give them hope that there is life beyond the prison they are in and that with enough determination and planning you are fully capable of escaping. Let them know that the life they have outside of their parents' home is so much more beautiful and amazing than they can imagine and that although the road is hard it is worth every effort it takes to get there so don't stop trying.

When appropriate and welcomed, show them safe physical affection. If they aren't uncomfortable with it (always ask first) give them hugs and pats on the back and warmth.

Teach them about consent. It would be really helpful if you discussed things like consent and that it really is ok if you say no.

Teach how to establish boundaries. Encourage them to be careful of mentors who try to treat you like their child. We have broken relationships with our parents, so we crave these bonds, but it's often the first red flag for someone who will try to control and spiritually abuse you.

Help them with resources to succeed. Help or show them how to find the right resources and make good choices in housing, employment, and whatever else might be necessary to get out.

Stand up for them against their family. One thing I wish someone had done was stand up for me.

If you're going to help them in a drastic way, actually be prepared. If you offer a way out, be sure you have all the ducks in a row, because they likely have very little resources at their fingertips and cannot truly function as an adult "outside". Think of them as being raised in "The Village" and finally being outside for the first time. They are going to need a safety net.

Don't give up on them. Stick around. If you sense that anything might be wrong, stick around and find out what it is and what you can do. Even if the family situation makes you uncomfortable, even if the parents hate you and creep you out. Stay in the child's life. It will take a long time for them to come to trust you, but once they do you can be an invaluable lifeline.

NO!

AGAINST ADULT SUPREMACY
Issue 7

Documents and Depression

Kris Anne Bonifacio

Joaquin Luna's dream was simple. He wanted to become a civil engineer. But the Texas student's undocumented status limited his options for the future. Left without hope, the 18-year-old shot himself the day after Thanksgiving last year. In his goodbye letters, Luna expressed despair. In one letter addressed to Jesus Christ, he wrote that he had "no point of existence in this cruel world... I've realised that I have no chance in becoming a civil engineer the way I've always dreamed of here... so I'm planning on going to you and helping you construct a new temple in heaven."

Luna was one of the more than 2 million undocumented children and young adults living in the United States. The inability for them to legally obtain a social security number makes it a struggle to get a driver's licence, apply to college and find a job. Young people like Luna are already at a heightened risk of having anxiety disorders, that often go untreated, according to the National Institute of Mental Health. But for undocumented youth, the risks are even greater due to uncertainty over their future, fear of getting arrested and deported, and social stigma about being undocumented. "Being undocumented means instability, uncertainty," says Fanny Lopez-Martinez, an undocumented 23-year-old graduate student at the University of Chicago. "You have no future. You can't plan. You can't envision what you want to do. You feel locked in a box. And it's hard to come to terms with the fact that you're going to be like this for you don't know how many years."

Clinical Research

According to Josefina Alvarez, a professor on Latino mental health at the Adler School of Professional Psychology in Chicago who works with immigrant community organisations, evidence about the mental health consequences of being undocumented are beginning to emerge out of case studies with immigrant children and families. "Feeling insecure and uncertain about your life and your future has serious mental health consequences and may lead to anxiety and depression," Alvarez says. "Feeling stigmatised and unwanted can also have a negative impact on self-esteem and may lead to depression and other negative behaviours."

In a 2008 study done by the Carolina Population Centre at UNC-Chapel Hill, 31% of Latino adolescents in North Carolina showed signs of sub-clinical or clinical anxiety and 18% showed signs of depression. The study did not distinguish between those who are here legally and those who are undocumented, but the demographics of those surveyed reflect that 93% of the children were not U.S. citizens. The study also looked at the participants' usage of mental health services and found that only

4% of those surveyed had received any mental health services in their lifetime. Undocumented immigrants are already at a disadvantage due to the structural barriers to accessing these services, such as lack of health insurance, cost of services and language barriers.

Paralysing Fear

Fear of authorities and fear of deportation isn't just a barrier to seeking mental health care. It can often be the very cause of anxiety and depression for undocumented immigrants. In 2010, 19-year-old undocumented Brazilian Gustavo Rezende hung himself behind his Marlborough, Mass., home, reportedly worried about his court hearing after being arrested on misdemeanour charges for driving under the influence and driving without a licence. Rezende's family and friends said he was afraid of being deported back to a country he barely knew.

In a case earlier this year, 22-year-old Yanelli Hernandez attempted suicide twice while being detained at Butler County Jail in Ohio. Hernandez had been arrested on a DUI charge and was awaiting deportation. Her case became the cause célèbre for many immigration groups, including National Immigrant Youth Alliance (NIYA) and the Chicago-based Immigrant Youth Justice League (IYJL). Activists demanded that Hernandez be released from detention so she could receive treatment for depression, but Immigration and Customs Enforcement officials announced in late January that she was deported to Mexico. Saavedra, who is a friend of Hernandez's and organises with NIYA, experienced the conditions inside a detention facility first hand when he infiltrated the Broward Transition Centre in Florida in July. Saavedra and another NIYA activist, Viridiana Martinez, intentionally turned themselves in at Port Everglades in order to raise awareness about the detention and deportation proceedings are like.

"The wait while you're inside [the detention centre] is huge mentally," Saavedra says. "It was taxing. The centre is nowhere near their families and these people don't know their legal rights. They're about to be deported to countries where they have no resources." Saavedra says that though the detention centre was very similar to a motel, the psychological effects of being imprisoned take a toll on the undocumented immigrants, especially the minors.

Furthermore, detention and deportation often causes family separation, something that Velazquillo personally experienced. In 2010, her brother Erick was driving home from the gym in North Carolina when a cop pulled him over for driving with his high beams on. He was arrested and charged for driving without a licence and spent three days in jail. He posted a bond and was released, but for almost a year, his future remained uncertain as he faced the prospect of deportation back to Mexico.

Velazquillo and her family worked with NC DREAM Team to publicise her brother's case. After a judge granted her brother a reprieve, ICE officials decided in August 2011 to let him stay in the country.

"For those who find themselves or their loved ones in detention, it causes a lot of distress," Velazquillo says. "You're separated from your family, and it's hard to get in touch with them to try to get information about what's going on. The financial aspect is also a huge burden, having to post a bond for them to be released. And the effect it has on children in the family, it's hard to explain to them what's going on."

Keeping Secrets

Even those who manage to avoid arrest and deportation still deal with the daily worries of keeping their status a secret. Yaxal Sobrevilla, a Chicago resident and organiser for IYJL, says that while her parents were open about their immigration status within their family, her mother told her she had to be careful about whom she talked to about being undocumented.

Furthermore, simple tasks that citizens and legal residents sometimes take for granted become a source of frustration, such as getting a driver's licence. "What were supposed to be minimal privileges, such as getting a driver's licence, become such an obstacle," Sobrevilla says. "I became dependent on my parents and friends to get me places. Although they were, for the most part, willing to drive me around, it made me feel like such a burden."

For Saavedra, the constant lying and keeping secrets took a toll on his mental health. Saavedra said that as he came closer to graduating from college, the pressure about his immigration status and uncertain future caused a lot of stress. "The timeline for me was getting shorter, so I started feeling really depressed during my junior year of college," Saavedra says. "For the sake of my mental health, I decided it was time to tell people the truth about my immigration status."

After College

In a study conducted last year by University of Chicago professor Roberto Gonzales, only 31 of the 150 undocumented immigrants interviewed received a bachelor's degree or more. Of those 31, none were able to pursue their chosen careers after graduation. And though all of the 150 respondents were educated in the United States, they ended up in the same jobs their parents had, such as working in construction, cleaning services and restaurants.

Carla Navoa, a 23-year-old undocumented Filipina who studies at University of

Illinois at Chicago, says that while her immigration status inspired her to work hard in school, she found out later that she wouldn't be able to achieve her dream of becoming a teacher. "In high school, knowing that I was undocumented made me work harder in school to prove I was just as good as other students and the sacrifices my parents made coming here were worth it," Navoa says. "But in my junior year in college, I found that I couldn't apply for a teacher's certificate. I had a serious breakdown and had a lot of mental issues, and I had to leave school for a while to work through that."

In an incident similar to Luna's, Chicago resident Benjamin Pintor committed suicide on Thanksgiving weekend in 2010 because, friends and family say, his undocumented status left him without many options. Dr. Martinez says that undocumented youth have a tendency to take it upon themselves to help their family rise above their immigration status.

"They take on a lot of responsibility, in some ways self-imposed, that they have to be the one to lift up and advance their family," Martinez says. "It's common in undocumented families, a lot of whom are low on the socio-economic scale. They know that education is the key to a good quality of life, but when the opportunity to succeed is taken away, it takes a severe toll on their mental health."

Undocumented and Unafraid

One bright spot is that young activists are feeling empowered by the DREAMers movement and many of them say that organising and getting involved has helped them cope with depression and anxiety. "For me, coming out and being outspoken about how urgently the immigration system needs to be fixed is so necessary," Sobrevilla says. "It was hurting me more not being able to try to change my situation." Sobrevilla says that groups like IYJL and NIYA provide a support network for many undocumented youth. That network is particularly comforting for undocumented young adults, as they risk getting arrested and deported by coming out about their immigration status.

The University of Chicago's Lopez-Martinez says she found comfort in attending an IYJL meeting and hearing the stories of undocumented youth just like her. She says she first heard about the group from two of her college friends. "They told me that there's a group of students just like us," Lopez-Martinez says. "They're undocumented, they're young and they want to make a difference. IYJL is a place to talk about your feelings, what it means to be undocumented. That's very empowering, to know that you're not alone and that many other youth just like you are going through the same thing."

Velazquillo and other organisers from NIYA decided to use the healing power of a support system to help other undocumented youth across the country. They started Undocuhealth, a blog that deals specifically with the mental health needs of undocumented immigrants. "We wanted a place where we could talk about these issues because they are not being addressed," Velazquillo says. "We want to be able to provide resources for those who need it."

But ultimately, the lack of action on immigration reform continues to be taxing for undocumented youth. Though there was a lot of buzz after the election on the increasing electoral power of Hispanics and the pressure they can levy on politicians, immigration, in the immediate future, has taken a backseat to the fiscal cliff discussions in Washington. "Continuing to delay a solution to the problems related to undocumented immigrants adds to the stress these young people feel," Alvarez says. "If they see that we, as a society, can't find a solution to this problem, they will become more discouraged and hopeless."

Saavedra says that he is hopeful he and other activists can increase understanding and awareness among Americans about undocumented youth. "I hope our work humanises DREAMers instead of having people think of us as 'illegal' or 'border crossers,'" Saavedra says. "People need to recognise that we can suffer from depression just like they can." Alvarez agrees that humanising the issue would help address the problem. "Immigration policy has real mental health consequences," she says. "It's not just about dealing with those who have broken the law and securing the borders. There are real human beings that are going to be affected by our immigration policies."

Zero Tolerance: Childfree and Bigotry

Henry A. Giroux

There are mounting ideological, institutional, and political pressures among conservatives, liberals, and other advocates of corporate culture to remove youth from the inventory of ethical and political concerns that legitimise and provide individual rights and social provisions for members of a democratic society. One consequence is that there is growing support among the American public for policies, at all levels of government, that abandon young people, especially youth of colour, to the dictates of a repressive penal state that increasingly addresses social problems through the police, courts, and prison system. As a result, the state has been hollowed out, largely abandoning its support for child protection, healthcare for the poor, and social services for the aged. Public goods are now disparaged in the name of privatisation, and those public forums in which association and debate thrive are being replaced by what Paul Gilroy calls an "info-tainment telesector" industry driven by dictates of the marketplace. As the public sector is remade in the image of the market, commercial values replace social values and the spectacle of politics gives way to the politics of the spectacle.

In the summer of 2000, The New York Times Sunday Magazine ran two major stories on youth within a three-week period between the latter part of July and the beginning of August. The stories are important because they signify not only how youth fare in the politics of representation but also what identifications are made available for them to locate themselves in public discourse. The first article, "The Backlash Against Children" by Lisa Belkin, was a feature story forecasted on the magazine's cover with a visually disturbing, albeit familiar, close up of a young boy's face. The boy's mouth is wide open in a distorted manner, and he appears to be in the throes of a tantrum. The image conjures up the ambiguities adults feel in the presence of screaming children, especially when they appear in public places, such as R-rated movies or up-scale restaurants, where their presence is seen as an intrusion on adult life. The other full-page image that follows the opening text is even more grotesque, portraying a young boy dressed in a jacket and tie with chocolate cake smeared all over his face. His hands, covered with the gooey confection, reach out towards the viewer, capturing the child's mischievous attempt to grab some hapless person by the lapels and add a bit of culinary dash to his or her wardrobe.

According to Belkin, a new movement is on the rise in American culture, one founded by individuals who don't have children, militantly describing themselves as "child free," and who view the presence of young people as an intrusion on their rights. Belkin charts this growing phenomenon with the precision of an obsessed accountant. She commences with an ethnographic account of 31-year-old, California software computer consultant Jason Gill, who is looking for a new place to live because the couple who have moved in next door to him have a new baby and he can hear "every wail and whimper." Even more calamitous for the yuppie consultant, the fence he replaced to prevent another neighbour's children from peering through at him is now used by the kids as a soccer goal, "often while Gill is trying to read a book or have a quiet glass of wine." But Belkin doesn't limit her analysis to such anecdotal evidence, she also points to the emergence of national movements such as an organisation called No Kidding!, which sets up social events only for those who remain childless. She reports that No Kidding! had only 2 chapters in 1995 but has 47 today. In addition, she comments on the countless number of online "child free" sites with names like "Brats!" and a growing number of hotels that do not allow children under 18 unless they are paying guests.

Of course, many parents and non-parents alike desire, at least for a short time, a reprieve from the often chaotic space of children, but Belkin takes such ambivalences to new heights. Her real ambition has very little to do with providing a space for adult catharsis. Rather it is to give public voice to a political and financial agenda captured by Elinor Burkett's The Baby Boon: How Family-Friendly America Cheats the Childless – an agenda designed to expose and rewrite government policies that relegate "the Childless to second-class citizens." Included in Burkett's laundry list of targets are: the federal tax code and its dependent deductions, dependent care credits, child tax credits among "dozens of bills designed to lighten the tax burden of parents" and, "most absurd of all" an executive order prohibiting discrimination against parents in all areas of federal employment. Her position is straightforward enough: to end "fancy" benefits (i.e., on-site child-care and health insurance for dependents) that privilege parents at the expense of the childless and to bar discrimination on the basis of family status. "Why not make it illegal to presuppose that a non-parent is free to work the night shift or presuppose that non-parents are more able to work on Christmas than parents?" Burkett demands. Indeed, why should the government provide any safety nets for the nation's children at all?

Belkin modifies her sympathetic encounter with the child-free worldview by interviewing Sylvia Ann Hewlett, a Harvard educated economist and nationally known spokesperson for protecting the rights of parents, and the founder of the National Parenting Association. Hewlett argues that parents have become yet another victimised group who are being portrayed by the media as the enemy. Hewlett translates her concerns into a call for parents to organise in order to wield more economic and political power. Hewlett's comments occupy a minor commentary in the text that overwhelmingly privileges the voices of those individuals and groups that view children and young people as a burden, a personal irritant, rather than a social good.

The notion that children should be understood as a crucial social resource who present for any healthy society important ethical and political considerations about the quality of public life, the allocation of social provisions, and the role of the state as a guardian of public interests appears to be lost in Belkin's article. Instead, Belkin focuses on youth exclusively as a private consideration rather than as part of a broader public discussion about democracy and social justice. She participates in an attack on youth that must be understood within the context of neoliberalism and hyper capitalism in which the language of the social, community, democracy, and solidarity are subordinated to the ethos of self-interest and self-preservation in the relentless pursuit of private satisfactions and pleasures. In this sense, the backlash against children that Belkin attempts to chronicle are symptomatic of an attack on public life, on the very legitimacy of those non-commercial values that are critical to defending a just and substantive democratic society.

The second article to appear in The New York Times Sunday Magazine is titled "Among the Mooks" by RJ Smith. According to the author, there is an emerging group of poor white males called "mooks" whose cultural style is fashioned out of an interest in fusing the transgressive languages, sensibilities, and styles that cut across and connect the worlds of rap and heavy metal music, ultra-violent sports such as professional wrestling, and the misogyny rampant in the subculture of pornography. For Smith, the kids who inhabit this cultural landscape are losers from broken families, working-class fatalities whose anger and unexamined bitterness translates into bad manners, anti-social music, and uncensored rage.

Smith appears uninterested in contextualising the larger forces and conditions that gives rise to this matrix of cultural phenomena – deindustrialization, economic restructuring, domestic militarisation, poverty, joblessness. The youth portrayed in Smith's account live in a historical, political, and economic vacuum. Moreover, the teens represented by Smith have little recourse to adults who try to understand and help them navigate a complex and rapidly changing cultural landscape in which they must attempt to locate and define themselves. Along with the absence of adult protection and guidance, there is a lack of serious critique and social vision in dealing with the limits of youth culture. No questions are raised about the relationship between the popular forms teens inhabit and the ongoing commercialisation and commodification of youth culture. There is no understanding in Smith's analysis of how market driven politics and established forms of power increasingly eliminate non-commodified social domains through which young people might learn an oppositional language for challenging those adult ideologies and institutional forces that both demonise them and limit their sense of dignity and capacity for political agency.

Of course, vulgarity, pathology, and violence are not limited to the spaces inhabited by the hyper-masculine worlds of gangsta rap, porn, extreme sports, and professional wrestling. But Smith ignores all of this because he is much too interested in depicting today's teens, and popular culture in general, as the embodiment of moral decay and bad cultural values. Smith suggests that poor white kids are nothing more than semi-Nazis with a lot of pent up rage. There are no victims in his analysis, as social disorder is reduced to individualised pathology, and any appeal to injustice is viewed as mere whining. Smith is too intent in reinforcing images of demonisation and ignorance that resonate comfortably with right-wing moral panics about youth culture. He succeeds, in part, by focusing on the icons of this movement in terms that move between caricature and scapegoating. For instance, The Insane Posse is singled out for appearing on cable-access porn shows; the group Limp Bizkit is accused of using their music to precipitate a gang rape at the recent Woodstock melee; and the performer Kid Rock is defined in racially coded terms as a "vanilla version of a blackploitation pimp" whose concerts inspire fans to commit vandalism and prompts teenage girls to "pull off their tops as the boys whoop." It gets worse.

At one level, "mooks" are portrayed as poor, working class, white kids who have seized upon the most crude aspects of popular culture in order to provide an outlet for their rage. But for Smith, the distinctive form this culture takes with its appropriation of the transgressive symbolism of rap music, porn, and wrestling does not entirely explain its descent into pathology and bad taste. Rather, Smith charges that black youth culture is largely responsible for the self-destructive, angst-ridden journey that poor white male youth are making through the cultural land mines of hyper-masculinity, unbridled violence, "ghetto" discourse, erotic fantasy, and drugs. Smith points an accusing finger at the black "underclass," and the recent explosion of hip hop which allegedly offers poor white kids both an imaginary alternative to their trailer park boredom and a vast array of transgressive resources which they proceed to fashion through their own lived experiences and interests. Relying on common racist assumptions about black urban life, Smith argues that black youth culture offers white youth a wide-screen movie of ghetto life, relishing the details, relating the intricacy of topics like drug dealing, brawling, pimping, and black-on-black crime. Rap makes these things seem sexy, and makes life on the street seem as thrilling as a Playstation game. Pimping and gangbanging equal rebellion, especially for white kids who aren't going to get pulled over for driving while black, let alone die in a hail of bullets (as Tupac and B.I.G. both did).

Trading substantive analysis for right-wing cliches, Smith is indifferent to both the complexity of rap as well as the "wide array of complex cultural forms" that characterise black urban culture. Smith alleges that the problem of white youth is rooted in the seductive lure of a black youth, marked by criminality, violent hyper-masculinity, welfare fraud, drug abuse, and unchecked misogyny. Smith unapologetically relies upon this analysis of black youth culture to portray poor white youth as dangerous and hip-hop culture as the source of that danger. Whatever his intentions, Smith's analysis contributes to the growing assumption that young people are at best a social nuisance and at worse a danger to social order.

These articles reflect and perpetuate in dramatically different ways not only the ongoing demonisation of young people, but also the growing refusal within the larger society to understand the problems of youth (and especially youth of colour) as symptomatic of the crisis of democratic politics itself.

As the state is divested of its capacity to regulate social services and limit the power of capital, those public spheres that traditionally served to empower individuals and groups to strike a balance between "the individual's liberty from interference and the citizen's right to interfere" are dismantled. At the same time, it becomes more difficult for citizens to put limits on the power of neo-liberalism to shape daily life – particularly as corporate economic power is feverishly consolidated on a transnational level. Nor can they prevent the assault on the state as it is being forced to abandon its social role as the guardian of public interests. The result is a state increasingly reduced to its policing functions, and a public sector reduced to a replica of the market. As neoliberalism increases its grip over all aspects of cultural and economic life, the autonomy once afforded to the worlds of cinema, publishing, and media production begins to erode.

Public schools are increasingly defined as a source of profit rather than a public good. Through talk shows, film, music, and cable television, for example, the media promote a growing political apathy and cynicism by providing a steady stream of daily representations and spectacles in which abuse becomes the primary vehicle for registering human interaction. At the same time, dominant media such as the New York Times condemn the current cultural landscape – represented in their account through reality television, professional wrestling, gross-out blockbuster films, and the beat-driven boasts and retorts of hip-hop – as aggressively evoking a vision of humanity marked by a "pure Darwinism" in which "the messages of popular culture are becoming more brutally competitive."

Unfortunately, for mainstream media commentators in general, the emergence of such representations and values is about the lack of civility and has little to do with considerations of youth bashing, racism, corporate power, and politics. In this sense, witness to degradation now becomes the governing feature of community and social life. Most importantly, what critics take up as a "youth problem" is really a problem about the corruption of politics, the shrivelling up of public spaces and resources for young people, the de-politicisation of large segments of the population, and the emergence of a corporate and media culture that is defined through an unadulterated "authoritarian form of kinship that is masculinist, intolerant and militaristic."

At issue here is how we understand the ways youth produce and engage popular culture at a time in history when depravation is read as depravity. How do we comprehend the choices young people are making under circumstances in which they have become the object of policies that signals a shift from investing in their future to assuming they have no future? Certainly not a future in which they can depend on adult society for either compassion or support.

"Normalising" Intersex Youth

Hida Viloria

People who promote nonconsensual genital surgeries and/or hormone therapy for intersex infants and children – often called "corrective" or "normalising" treatment – believe intersex children will grow up to be adults who fall short of social norms. However, these beliefs are purely speculation because they have not taken the time to speak with intersex adults like myself who did not undergo surgery, or to do follow-up studies on the children whose bodies they irrevocably changed. Doctors simply assumed that our bodies are not desirable, and that non-consensual treatments would help us and/or our families. In my personal experience, and from the experiences that countless of intersex adults have shared, this couldn't be further from the truth.

Doctors decided, back in the late 1950's, that they knew how to make intersex bodies better. Although dozens of intersex adults who were subjected to these "corrective" procedures have been speaking out for almost two decades about how harmful these "treatments" were for them, the medical establishment has still not recommended that they be postponed until the child is old enough to decide for themselves if they'd like to change the genitals they were born with. Although other humans are given this right (with the exception of circumcision), most intersex infants today, sadly, are not.

One of the reasons these surgeries persist is similar to the reason circumcision does: people get used to whatever "look" is popular and want their children to have it, to "fit in." However, the bigger reason is that some people still assume that, because our biological sex is not standardly male or female, our social gender won't be either. It is this fear of an androgynous, non-binary social gender role that drives recommendations for surgery, for some believe it will lead to children and adults who "stick out," or suffer psychological difficulties.

I have found, in talking to dozens of intersex adults, that these fears are unfounded and incorrect, but, as a recent New York Times article illustrates, they persist:

> There haven't been any studies that would support doing nothing," says Larry Baskin, Grumbach's protégé and current chief of paediatric urology at the University of California, San Francisco. "That would be an experiment: don't do anything and see what happens when the kid's a teenager. That could be good, and that could also be worse than trying some intervention." In Baskin's view, being intersex is a congenital anomaly that deserves to be corrected like any other. "If you have a child born with a cleft lip or cleft

palate or an extra digit or a webbed neck, I don't know any family that wouldn't want that repaired," he told me. "Who would say, 'You know what, let's wait until Johnny is 20 years old and let him decide?'"

Contrary to Dr. Baskin's statement, there have been studies that would support doing nothing. In fact, one of only two studies in existence about intersex adults, performed in 1952 by Dr. John Money for his dissertation at Harvard, showed that intersex adults who had not been medically tampered with showed less incidence of psycho-pathology than non-intersex adults. In other words, intersexuals were found to be psychologically healthier and better adjusted than non-intersexuals.

The other study, performed recently in England, found that even when adult intersexuals had voluntarily employed surgery to "normalise" their bodies, the results were ineffective and harmful. The surgeries were unable to provide "normal" bodies and created physical problems, such as tremendous physical pain, which made their lives more difficult than before.

Dr. Baskin claims it would be an "experiment" to "do nothing" to an intersex infant or child. However, changing a healthy body via modern medical science in order to try to make it "better" than what nature created is what seems an experiment. His view that ambiguous genitals are akin to a cleft lip that any parent would want to correct before adulthood is astoundingly simplistic and inaccurate. The function and psychosocial significance and impact of genitals is much more complex and significant than that of a cleft or uncleft lip. He misses the points that adult intersexuals and their advocates have made about how the surgeries left them sexually damaged and/or impaired and often very psychologically confused about their true identity.

However good the intentions may be, surgeries done on infants to "correct" their sex or their sexual organs have been shown repeatedly to be unsuccessful. Children do not need these organs to look any particular way until they become sexually active later, and as we have often seen, it is impossible to determine how an infant or child will want to express themselves sexually as an adult. Because we can not tell how masculine, feminine or androgynous a baby will later want to be, "picking" how to "make" their body appear is basically a crap-shoot. Why would you want to run that kind of irrevocable risk on your child's future fulfilment? What if you and the doctors made the wrong choice, one your child was ultimately so miserable with as to be suicidal, as we see in so many cases of "corrective" medical treatment.

In thinking about children and their development and experiences, many adults forget, or perhaps do not realise, that prejudices and stigma are learned. Children do not believe, for example, that black and brown people are dangerous, poor, unintelligent, or inferior until they learn these beliefs from an adult. Even in those instances, some children reject these learned beliefs in favour of their own by adulthood or throughout it.

Because no one ever said a word about my genitals being "wrong" in some way, and I wasn't operated on or given hormones to "correct" anything, I was able to form my own beliefs about my body and my identity, and those ideas were positive. As I mentioned in 2002 on ABS's 20/20, the first time I saw another girl's genitals in a locker room at age eleven, my first thought was "she's missing something." There was no reason for me to assume anything was wrong with my body and so I did not. Such is the case for others who escaped "medical normalisation."

In 1998 I interviewed three intersex adults for my undergraduate thesis at U.C. Berkeley entitled, "Experience Versus Theory: The Testimonies of Adult Intersexuals on the Medical Management of Intersexuality." These adults, like myself, had not undergone surgical or hormonal treatment of their intersex conditions. The interviews revealed that, as children, they did not experience the trauma and confusion that doctors and others often presume they will, despite having very ambiguous genitalia and very unusual social circumstances to navigate through. Further, as adults, they were all in long-term, committed, seemingly happy, healthy relationships. They appeared mentally healthy, were gainfully employed, and had friends and a social life. Basically, they seemed just as happy and successful as any other group of people I've known.

One of the doctors who supports "corrective" surgery said to me once during a debate on the issue, "People can't even accept people of different colours sometimes, how can we expect them to accept a third sex?" My answer to him was, "By that reasoning, if you could make everybody white would you do that too?"

Even if people do not, out of ignorance and/or bigotry, accept a group, eliminating that group of people, or the characteristics that make them different, is a poor solution to ending discrimination. If doctors or others in power had been able to do that with other minority groups in the past, we would have a much different society today. Our society would be similar to Adolf Hitler's vision of a homogenous race deplete of people of colour, gays, and anyone else considered different by the group in power. Fortunately, Hitler was stopped before he could fully realise his dream, and Jewish people and others he considered inferior did not suffer total extinction. However, thousands suffered beforehand, just as thousands of intersex people have suffered since "normalisation" began.

Outdated and unfounded bigotries towards intersex people have caused them decades of suffering. It is sometimes shocking to me and to the people I inform about this that these attitudes still exist. Then I remember that many humans are threatened by minority groups, by those who are different from them. They react with fear, rather than curiosity, and fear, as we know, sometimes leads people to hurt those they find threatening.

It's time to stop the intersex gendercide. To let go of old notions that came out of the 1950's (weren't African-Americans forced to use different drinking fountains back then, etcetera…?), to stop playing God on intersex children's bodies, and to accept intersex people as equals. Every person and particularly, parent, alive has the power to do this right now, and, I believe, the heart to want to.

Parenting Versus Protesting?

Kirsten Anderberg

Is it irresponsible to take children to political protests? Some argue it is a good experience for children to participate, first-hand, in political organising, marches, protests, and the making of history. I am glad my mother took me, as a child, to civil rights protests, and actions against the Vietnam War, during the 1960s and 1970s. I do not believe textbooks can convey the feeling one gets when surrounded by riot police, while trying to peacefully demonstrate. I am glad I took my son to protests of the Gulf War in the 1990s, and the Iraq War in 2003. I feel it was part of his education to see non-violent free speech and riot police clash on his own city streets, while with his mom for safety. But could I really guarantee my son's safety anywhere that riot police were present? Some argue that children should not be taken onto the front lines of American political change. But as an activist single mother, I could not just sit home, not protest wars, simply because I had a child. And children are supposedly our hope for the future. Thus it seems essential to include them in our political struggles, if we want the issues to live longer than us. Are certain protests acceptable for children to attend, but not others? How does one determine which protest activities are appropriate for our children? How does a politically active parent balance their own needs to protest a war, for instance, with the responsibilities of parenting?

I surveyed a group of activists on this topic, from different parts of America; from Chicago, New York City, and Seattle, as well as from Wisconsin, Maryland, California, and Colorado; and also from England and Canada. More in the group self-identified as anarcho-feminists than the other categories cited, which included radical leftists, anarchist parent of colour, anarchist, Green Party member, progressive humanist atheist, and others. Seven of the 12 people interviewed are street medics, and 10 of those surveyed are parents. And only two of those surveyed say they had parents who took them to political protests. So, basically, this article is written from the viewpoint of first-generation (except for two), politically-active, parents and street medics. Yet even within this somewhat politically-homogenous group, the opinions on this topic of kids at protests differ.

When asked if it is irresponsible to take children to protests, the overwhelming response from those surveyed was it depended on the nature of the protest. Several respondents felt protests that directly affected children's services, such as funding cuts at hospitals that treat children, or midwifery rights protests, warranted the strategic use of children at the protests. But many feel it is positive to involve children in a broad spectrum of political issues. For example, at the FTAA protests in Miami in November 2003, there was a Baby Bloc of mothers with children who marched together. One parent surveyed said, "I think it is not only safe, but necessary, to take children to (most) protests. As activists, and as parents bringing up the next generation, we need to show our children that when things are going wrong, it is our responsibility to voice our dissent." Another respondent said taking kids to protests was a good idea because "children need to know that their parents hold certain views, and that these views are not unique to their parents…" Some said it would be nice if the community could work together so that some parents can be medics and legal observers, while others could centre solely on children at protests. Another mother surveyed said she had quit being politically active, then her adult daughter (who she used to take to protests as a child), asked her to go to a protest, and now she is protesting again. That went full circle!

A distinction was made by some regarding direct actions and marches/demonstrations. Many felt large, permitted, labor union marches, for example, were safer than direct actions against corporations, like some of the FTAA or WTO protest actions. The former was seen as non-confrontational and the latter as confrontational. One street medic said, "I had to treat an 8-month old boy for tear gas/pepper spray in Quebec during the FTAA protests there and I don't want to EVER, EVER, EVER have to do that again!" Yes, we all agree we do not want that to EVER happen, and that is why we need to talk about this topic seriously. Protests are not your typical family event, and we all know that. One respondent said protests are as safe for kids as they are for anyone else, "in other words, usually safe, often not, and usually hard to know in advance." Some felt that large gatherings of people in any context, presented a danger to children, in general, and that protests were no different. One person said, "You could argue because there is sometimes trouble at soccer matches (in the UK), it would be irresponsible to take children to soccer matches, but 100,000s go and get looked after by their parents."

"I do not think it is 'irresponsible' to take children to protests. I think it is irresponsible for police departments, fellow protesters, and others, to not recognise that children have a legitimate right to be at protests. At the Feb. 15th anti-war march in New York City, several police officers made snide comments that we were being irresponsible mothers by taking our children to the march. However, there is something very, very wrong with our society if children do not belong and cannot be kept safe at marches for peace," says one activist I surveyed. Two other people surveyed said, "I think that the police presence needs to be responsive to the fact that there are regularly kids in the crowd," and "If the reality is that kids are regularly SEEN at protests, then the response from police might change." And these are good points. If we can get police to behave as if there are children in their midst at all protests, perhaps they can rein in some of their random violence, and free speech would be safer for all in America.

Most of the activists I surveyed felt if you were politically aware enough to protest for political causes, you should be astute enough to do proper research on a protest before bringing a child. There seemed a consensus that parents needed to know who called the demonstration, what the political issues involved are, who would attend, what the agenda of the protest is, if the protest is permitted, what tactics are expected both by protesters and police in response, etc. All agreed "Safe Places" cannot be guaranteed, and one medic surveyed wondered aloud if the community should begin having kid-friendly non-violent action trainings. The parents surveyed felt you should have a clearly defined contingency plan with children, "from bathroom breaks to police attacks," including what to do if separated. Suggested basic supplies to take to protests with kids included sunscreen, extra diapers, food, water, and proper layers of clothing. Some commented paying attention to weather reports was also beneficial, as a kid wet in pouring rain at a protest, or frying hot in sun, will not be fun, and thus proper weather protection is an issue as well. A basic knowledge of street first aid would be nice too, if you live somewhere you can get access to that, such as Boston or Portland. Other advice included "always be aware of where you are, the mood of the crowd, the mood of the kids (and other adults if in a group), and the mood of the police." Many felt the best way to go for parents, kids and protest were small affinity groups, where parents and children could collectively take care of one another. And although these are all good tips for parents and children, these are basics for adults too.

NO!

AGAINST ADULT SUPREMACY

Issue 8

The Sound of Our Movement Growing

Victoria Law

Last week I was part of Queering Abolition, a panel discussion on queer and trans prison advocacy and abolition. One of my co-panelists was Susan Rosenberg, a former political prisoner who spent 16 years in prison before her sentence was commuted by outgoing President Bill Clinton. The panel was in the auditorium of the City University of New York Graduate Centre. Being on the panel was exciting – not just because I was part of a dialogue around prison advocacy and abolition that centred on trans people, but also because it reminded me of how far I'd come and how much community and movement support have enabled me.

I first saw Susan Rosenberg in that same auditorium about 12 years ago. She had been released from prison the year before and was part of a day-long conference on incarceration. My daughter was not quite two years old and, like many political events – both then and now – there was no child care. The organisers told me that I was welcome to bring my child and so I did.

She had a fantastic time. My daughter, after nursing for a bit and sitting in my lap for an even shorter bit, wriggled out of my arms and explored the back rows of the auditorium. The seats were like those in the movie theatre, springing up when no weight was applied. She was entranced with these seats, pulling them down and letting them flip back up with a clatter. She did this again and again, much to the amusement of the handful of 20-somethings around us. I kept one eye on her and one eye on the stage where, far below, Susan Rosenberg, Laura Whitehorn and two other important people in the prison movement talked about women and incarceration. When the audience erupted into applause, my daughter stopped and applauded along. "Yaaaay!" she cheered, as she clapped her tiny hands together over and over.

Partway through the next panel, she grew bored with the back row and began making her way down the aisle. I let her get about 10 feet away from me before grabbing her and carrying her back. She did this several times, growing more and more confident navigating the shallow slope. Then, she began to run towards the stage and the stairs leading to the stage, steps that are oh-so-alluring in the eyes of a not-quite two-year-old. By then, only a sliver of my attention was on the discussion on-stage; most of it was on my daughter and trying to keep her from disrupting the conference. So, we left.

Twelve years later, I was back in that same room – not as a harried and under-supported parent this time, but as a panelist. Unlike the last time, as I set foot in the auditorium, the organisers of Queering Abolition (Black and Pink – NYC, which supports queer and trans people inside prisons) offered child care. And it also made me think about all the ways, between those two events and those 12 years, that people in various movements and communities stepped up to support me as a mother in their midst, enabling me to learn, grow and continue to be part of social justice organising. Without their support, I might have kept on being the person who left discussions and events until I grew tired of even trying.

But I'm lucky. There are so many people who have recently become parents or primary caregivers who don't have that kind of support – or people in their lives who understand the need for support and are willing to help meet that need. We parents know that we need support if we're going to continue being part of political organising, but it's overwhelming and exhausting to continually ask our supposed comrades if they can accommodate our new needs. It's even more overwhelming and exhausting when the answer is no.

In 2003, I met China Martens, a mother in Baltimore who would become my co-conspirator for what we called the "all-ages child care revolution." What we realised, early on, is that, rather than trying to get parents to take on the additional responsibility of building their support networks, it's much more effective to talk to people who do not have caregiving responsibilities and make them understand the importance of supporting parents and caregivers' participation. People without children (or other caregiving responsibilities) have more time to help out, to plan support strategies and to advocate for family-friendly movement spaces and events. It shouldn't always fall on those most directly affected (and exhausted) to have to create these spaces on their own. That's a pretty sure way to push them away from organising work.

Here are some ways that helped and can easily be applied to your own organising work. They don't require a huge amount of resources, but do demonstrate a commitment to creating movements that accommodate all ages.

Provide child care

Child care doesn't need to be elaborate. It does need to be in a room that is clean and safe, meaning that there are no hazards for a small child. Ideally two (or more) people should be doing child care so that, if an emergency arises, no children are left alone.

Child care does require a commitment from the organisers that it is a priority and should not be left until the last minute. It should also be clearly announced on all outreach and publicity. Otherwise, parents assume that there is no child care and will stay home.

If you don't have a rapport with kids, find other ways to help

Be the one to come in early, clean the room and make sure there are no choking hazards, exposed electrical outlets, plastic bags or sharp objects. Crawl on the floor and look at the room as if you were a baby. What do you see there that might be dangerous? Not sure what constitutes a choking hazard? If it seems like it would fit through a toilet paper tube, get it out of there!

Offer to be the one on call if an emergency arises and ferry information to the appropriate person. If a child suddenly misses their caregiver or doesn't feel well, be the person to locate the caregiver and make sure they get to the room quickly.

Have food

The organisers of Queering Abolition served dinner (a vegan and gluten-free dinner at that), and made sure to announce that fact on all of their publicity.

For parents, having food at an evening meeting or event may be the deciding factor as to whether they attend or whether they hustle their child(ren) home after school and fix them supper. (Even people without children will appreciate not having to choose between eating dinner and attending a meeting or event.)

Be prepared to have children in the room

This might sound like it contradicts the first point, but it doesn't. Even when you provide child care, some children don't want to be so far from their caregivers (and vice versa). Be prepared to have children in the meeting or event space. If you're the facilitator or a speaker, make an announcement about children's presence beforehand so that parents don't feel obliged to leave the room once their child(ren) start making noise. When he notices children in the room, Jason Lydon of Black and Pink Boston announces, "Children's noise is the sound of our movement growing." I've taken to saying that too and, when I do, I've noticed that not only do parents visibly relax, but others in the room don't give them the side-eye.

Have toys and activities for kids to do. When my daughter turned two, a fellow volunteer at ABC No Rio, a community arts centre, bought her a bag of wooden blocks, which we kept there. We also kept a basket of toys for her so that whenever she came with me or her dad, she would have a variety of things to do. Similarly, the office of Women on the Rise telling HerStory, or WORTH, an advocacy organisation of formerly incarcerated women, had a crib, children's books and toys.

Be the person who gets down on the floor and plays with the kid in the room

Children, particularly young children, don't like being left to play by themselves, even if they are in the middle of the room. Be the person who gets down on the floor to colour with them or build a fabulous structure out of blocks. You can still keep an ear on the discussion — trust me, I know from years of experience

— while also allowing the parent or caregiver to participate more fully.

This also applies to spaces where organising grows: At WORTH, when a staff member had a baby, she brought him to the office regularly and everyone took responsibility for him. They held him so that she could have two hands free to meet her responsibilities. They fed him when he was hungry. They changed his diaper. And, when he began to toddle around, they followed him and made sure he didn't hurt himself or wreak too much havoc on the office.

Supporting the all-ages revolution doesn't end when the meeting or event comes to a close. You can incorporate these into your everyday life – and make a new friend in the process!

Doing something a child might enjoy? Invite that kid along!

Do you have a plot in a garden? Do you love to skateboard or bike? Do you bake cookies, make giant puppets or quilt? Invite a kid to join you. It may be slow-going at first to teach a three-year-old how to safely wield a needle or not to rub glue or paint in their hair, but they learn quickly. In the meantime, you're giving them an opportunity to experience something new while also giving their caregiver a probably much-needed break.

Start to develop relationships with caregivers and children in your movements and communities

It can start with inviting them over to have dinner (or lunch or brunch). Get to know them – and let them get to know you. Asking for help from people who are virtually strangers can be difficult but, as they grow to know you better, caregivers and kids will feel easier letting you know what they need, as well as what doesn't work for them. And you'll get to know them and figure out ways that you and those around you can accommodate their needs so that they can stay involved.

This is far from an exhaustive list. There are many different ways to help build an all-ages revolution. My co-conspirator China and I put together *Don't Leave Your Friends Behind* originally as a zine series and, two years ago, as an edited anthology, to include the many different ways that caregivers, kids and others in their community have worked to create all-ages movements.

Religion and Trauma

Marlene Winell

Children learn very early to repress independent thinking and not to trust their own feelings. For truth, believers rely on external authority – scripture and religious leaders. With the consequences of disbelief so severe, leaders are able to demand acceptance of far-fetched claims at the expense of personal observation or scientific evidence. The culture rewards individuals who contribute in religious ways. Proselytising is generally expected, even for children. Obedience is the highest value and personal development truncated.

Clearly, psychological problems can develop long before the additional trauma of leaving the fold. I'll use the example of Bible-based fundamentalisms. True to the definition of trauma, survivors of these report feelings of terror, helplessness, and horror in facing death and injury – the horror of Jesus' death (along with other atrocities in the Bible), the terror of hell for oneself and everyone else, and the helplessness of being a frail human in a wicked world, a tiny player in an overwhelming cosmic drama.

Toxic Teachings

There are different churches in this category with beliefs and practices that vary but core doctrines are consistent. All of the major authoritarian religions have enormous psychological control because they are based on fear, which is the most primitive and powerful human emotion. Secondly, they emphasise shame; humans are bad and need redemption. So the basic meme complex passed on to each generation of children is that you need religion in order to survive and in order to be acceptable.

Eternal Punishment

The first key doctrine is eternal damnation (or annihilation) for all unbelievers. This is the terrifying backdrop for the salvation message presented to all newcomers and all children born into the faith. The Bible is quoted, including the words of Jesus, to paint a horrifying picture of hell as a lake of fire, a fire of eternal torture impossible to quench despite any pleading. Mormons describe a hell of "outer darkness" that is cold and just as terrifying. Jehovah's Witnesses threaten the horror of dying forever at Armageddon and missing out on Paradise. Small children can obviously visualise these things while not having the brain capacity to evaluate the message. Moreover, the powerful social context makes rejecting these teachings impossible. Children are completely at the mercy of religious adults.

The salvation formula is offered as a solution, of course, but for many, it is not enough to ward off anxiety. How does one really know? And what about losing one's salvation? Many adults remember trying to get "saved" multiple times, even hundreds of times, because of unrelenting fear.

> I feel like much of my life was lived in fear. I am reading all I can to continue to find peace from what I've been taught. I still fear and I am 65.

> I feel little hope, because I don't know how it is remotely possible for me to ever let go of my fear of hell. If I give up my belief system, I'll go to hell. Even though my whole life has been so unhappy in the church – it has brought me nothing but turmoil and heartbreak and disappointment and unanswered questions and dissatisfaction.

"Left behind" Terror

Another horrible fear is about missing the "rapture" when Jesus returns. I have heard many people recount memories of searching for parents and going into sheer panic about being left alone in an evil world. Given that abandonment is a primary human fear, this experience can be unforgettably terrifying. Some report this as a recurring trauma every time they couldn't find a parent right away.

> During my freshman year in college, I started having nightmares. In my dreams, the rapture would happen and I would be left behind, or worse, sent to hell. Several times I woke up just before I was tossed into the flames, my mouth open, ready to scream. My mind was crying out, "Please, Jesus! Forgive me! I'm sorry I wasn't good enough! I'm sorry!

> After twenty-seven years of trying to live a perfect life, I failed… I was ashamed of myself all day long. My mind battling with itself with no relief… I always believed everything that I was taught but I thought that I was not approved by God. I thought that basically I, too, would die at Armageddon.

Surrounded by Threat

Believers simply cannot feel safe in the world if they take to heart the teaching about evil everywhere. In the fundamentalist worldview, "the World" is a fallen place, dangerously ruled by Satan and his minions until Jesus comes back and God puts everything right. Meanwhile it's a battleground for spiritual warfare and children are taught to be very afraid of anything that is not Christian. Much of "the World" is condemned at church, and parents try to control secular influences through private and home schooling. Children grow up terrified of everything outside the religious subculture, most of which is simply unfamiliar.

> I was raised on fire and brimstone, speaking in tongues, believing the world was a dangerous and evil place, full of temptation and sinners seeking to destroy me/drag me down.

Some groups place more emphasis on literal teachings about demons, and believers learn to be afraid of evil spirits lurking everywhere. Being saved is a "covering" and one must put on the "whole armour of God" to go about ordinary life. A frequently quoted verse with a terrifying image is I Peter 5:8, "Be sober, be vigilant; because your adversary the devil, as a roaring lion, walketh about, seeking whom he may devour."

Self as Bad

Second to the doctrine of hell, the other most toxic teaching in fundamentalist churches is that of "original sin." Human depravity is a constant theme of fundamentalist theology and no matter what is said about the saving grace of Jesus, children (and adults) internalise feelings of being evil and inadequate. Most of these churches also believe in demons quite literally, some to the point of using exorcism on children who misbehave. One former believer called it "bait-and-switch theology – telling me I was saved only to insist that I was barely worth saving."

> I've spent literally years injuring myself, cutting and burning my arms, taking overdoses and starving myself, to punish myself so that God doesn't have to punish me. It's taken me years to feel deserving of anything good.

Believers can be understood to be in the crazy-making situation of a double bind – having heavy personal responsibility to adhere to religious rules but not having the ability to do so. Never is God blamed for not answering prayer or empowering the faithful as promised.

I spent most of my life trying to please an angry God and feeling like a complete failure. I didn't pray enough, read enough, love enough, etc.

To think you are good or wise or strong or loving or capable on your own is considered pride and the worst sin of all in this religious worldview. You are expected to derive those qualities from God, who is perfect. Anything good you do is credited to God and anything bad is your fault. You are expected to be like Him and follow His perfect will. But what if it doesn't work? Fundamentalist Christianity promises to solve all kinds of personal problems and when it does not, it is the individual that bears the paralysing guilt of not measuring up.

I have tried to use this brand of Christianity to free myself from the depression and addictions that I have struggled with from childhood, and have done all the things that "Christianity" demanded I do. I have fasted, prayed, abstained from secular things, tithed, received the spirit, baptised in the spirit, read the Bible, memorised Scripture, etc. etc. None of it has worked or given me any lasting solution... I have become so desperate at times, that I have wanted to take my own life.

Demon Possession

A special form of abuse occurs when children are actually accused of being demon possessed. This can happen when children misbehave, parents are incompetent, or children's behaviour is misinterpreted in spiritual ways, often with the help of clergy. I have heard many stories of this kind of labelling, which is of course the ultimate in both shame and fear. Forced exorcisms are also all too common, even in this modern day, and certainly qualify as trauma, lasting into adulthood.

> When your parents exorcised you and said you had "unclean" spirits that was very very wrong. To believe a child can have demons just shows how seriously deluded your parents really were. You have spent your whole life being scared... being scared of your dad, of God, of hell, the rapture, the end of the world, and death as well as the dark.

Cycle of Abuse

A believer can never be good enough and goes through a cycle of sin, guilt, and salvation similar to the cycle of abuse in domestic violence. When they say they have a "personal relationship" with God, they are referring to one of total dominance and submission, and they are convinced that they should be grateful for this kind of "love." Like an authoritarian husband, this deity is an all-powerful, ruling male whose word is law. The sincere follower "repents" and "rededicates," which produces a temporary reprieve of anxiety and perhaps a period of positive affect. This intermittent reinforcement is enough to keep the cycle of abuse in place. Like a devoted wife, the most sincere believers get damaged the most.

> I prayed endlessly to be delivered from those temptations. I beat my fists into my pillow in agony. I used every ounce of faith I could muster to overcome this problem. "Lead me not into temptation, but deliver me from evil" just didn't seem to be working with me. Of course, I blamed it on myself and thought there was something wrong with me. I thought I was perverted. I felt evil inside. I hated myself.

I do not want to give up my faith in Christ or God but I have NEVER been able to hold onto my own decisions or to make them on my benefit without IMMENSE PAIN re: God's will which I was supposed to seek out but could not find.

Don't Think, Don't Feel

Fundamentalist theology is also damaging to intellectual development in that it explicitly warns against trusting one's own mind while requiring belief in far-fetched claims. Believers are not allowed to question dogma without endangering themselves. Critical thinking skills are under-valued. Emotions and intuitions are also considered suspect so children learn not to trust their own feelings. With external authority the only permissible guide, they grow up losing touch with inner instincts so necessary for decision making and moral development.

> Fundamentalism makes people crazy. It is a mixture of beliefs that do not make sense, causing the brain to keep trying to understand what cannot be logical.

> I really don't have much experience of decision making at all. I never made any plans for my adult life since I was brought up to believe that the end of the world would come.

> I suppressed a lot of my emotions, I developed cognitive difficulties and my thinking became increasingly unclear. My whole being turned from a rather vibrant, positive person to one that's passive and dull.

Abuses of Power

Added to these toxic aspects of theology are practices in the church and religious families that are damaging. Physical, sexual, and emotional harm is inflicted in families and churches because authoritarianism goes unchecked. Too many secrets are kept. Sexual repression in the religion also contributes to child abuse. The sanctioned patriarchal power structure allows abusive practices towards women and children. Severe condemnation of homosexuality takes an enormous toll as well, including suicide.

> I had so many pent up emotions and thoughts that were never acknowledged… Instead of protecting me from a horrible man, they forced me to deny my feelings and obey him, no matter what. It's no wonder I developed an eating disorder.

So while the religious community can appear to offer a safe environment, the pressures to conform, adhere to impossible requirements, and submit to abuses of power can cause great suffering, which is often hidden and thus more miserable.

Ageism is an LGBT Issue

Kathleen Nicole O'Neal

In the LGBT community, we rightly spend a lot of time discussing (if not exactly acting on) the problems facing the youngest members of our community. Suicide, harassment in schools, bias-motivated crimes, rejection at home (sometimes leading to homelessness), obstacles to trans-related and sexual healthcare, religiously motivated bigotry in local communities, and general feelings of hopelessness and malaise have become classic examples of the way heterosexism impacts our young people.

We are quick to look at these dynamics and express outrage over the role that heterosexism, homophobia, transphobia, and biphobia play in the lives of young LGBT people. With the advent of the "It Gets Better" project, bemoaning the way in which our society hurls abuse at LGBT youth has become something of a cliché.

It is a positive step in the right direction that LGBT people and their supporters are finally paying attention to the toll bigotry takes on youth. However, our analysis rarely goes deep enough to begin to unpack the intersectional role that ageism plays in these tragedies. As long as we refuse to take into account the way that ageist social structures unnecessarily inhibit the liberty, equality, and pursuit of happiness of our youngest LGBT people, our analysis of the problem will be toothless and incomplete.

Not long after I came out as bisexual, I became involved in the youth rights movement. Because young people are basically treated as parental property until they turn 18 years old, are confined in schools not of their choosing for most of their waking hours, and have limited mobility due to their impotence at the hands of law and custom, almost every avenue available to LGBT adults to improve their lots is closed to them.

This is neither natural nor inevitable – it is a function of the way our government and society relates to young people. It is ultimately harmful to all youth, but LGBT youth often suffer the most. And no matter how many same-sex couples are able to marry or how many anti-discrimination ordinances are passed, these problems will remain until we get serious about the fact that ageism is an LGBT issue.

Were LGBT youth persecuted in their schools able to choose to educate themselves elsewhere; were our young people able to emancipate themselves from problematic home situations; were young people able to invoke legal rights against parents who send them to facilities for "troubled teens" due to their sexual orientation and/or gender identity, we would not see the same degree of problems that we do among young LGBT people – even if a significant segment of society never supported our equality.

When Constance McMillan bravely endured her prom fiasco we shook our collective heads and asked why the school would not let her bring her date to prom. Instead we should have shaken our heads and wondered why she was forced to attend school among such a den of vipers to begin with. When we tell our youth "it gets better" we should be asking ourselves "Why do we feel it has to be so bad for them now?" and we should also be saying that "We can do better."

LGBT rights advocates must become youth rights advocates too. For all our talk of intersectionality and challenging privilege, we almost never seriously discuss – let alone plan our activism around – the ways in which ageism intersects with heterosexism to make life harder than need be for so many LGBT young people. Until we get serious about confronting the political, social, economic, and cultural ways in which our society oppresses all young people, LGBT youth will be hit hardest of all.

NO!

ISSUE 9

AGAINST ADULT SUPREMACY

Ageism: A Pillar of Ableism

Kathleen Nicole O'Neal

Several years back I began reading and learning about disability rights issues. As is the case with my interest in LGBT, women's, people of colour, social justice, youth, and other issues, I was particularly drawn to the highly theoretical critical work that many disability rights theorists have been producing since the late twentieth century. One viewpoint I found repeatedly represented in this body of work (and which I have also heard expressed multiple times by my friends with disabilities) is that one of the primary pillars of disability oppression is the way in which people with disabilities, regardless of age, are treated as if they were forever children. My friend and fellow youth and disability rights advocate Matt Stafford has written about the ways in which parents and others use the institution of guardianship in order to exert undue influence in the lives of people with disabilities who have passed the age of majority. Another friend who is a youth and disability rights advocate has spoken with me about how the doctors they work with will refuse to talk respectfully and directly to them about their medical issues despite the fact that my friend has no cognitive impairments and even recently graduated from law school.

Disability rights advocates have long sought greater rights and autonomy for all people with disabilities, including individuals with cognitive and communication impairments. They have challenged our entire society – especially the institutions set up by the non-disabled to manage people with disabilities – to view disabled persons as being as deserving of autonomy and dignity as everyone else no matter what mental or physical limitations or differences they may possess. In doing so they have not only greatly improved the lives of disabled people, they have also laid the theoretical groundwork for a compelling defence of youth liberation.

Disability is a complicated issue. There are various types of disabilities and there are various frameworks for understanding the rights of disabled people and even disability itself. However, every serious advocate of disability rights will agree that centring the autonomy of disabled people is important and that all too many people believe that an inability on the part of disabled people to function according to the standards of non-disabled individuals justifies their lifelong infantilisation. Of course, the reason that many people feel comfortable with denying rights and autonomy to persons with disabilities on these grounds is that we already have a widespread precedent within our society of using this as a pretence to deny rights and autonomy to children.

The implicit assumption behind the actions and belief system of every judge that casually turns over guardianship of a person with cognitive disabilities to another adult, of every parent who believes they have an undisputed right to make medical decisions for a disabled adult son or daughter, and of every legislator who defends the corralling of disabled individuals into oppressive and even abusive institutional settings are not only ableist (although they are that): they are also profoundly ageist.

The way our society treats minors has set the precedent for what we believe is the ideal way to relate to those whom we perceive (rightly or wrongly) as lacking the capacities of the average adult human being. We deny them bodily autonomy. We ignore their needs and preferences in the realm of education. We segregate them in various institutions where they are rarely permitted to interact in a meaningful way with the rest of the world. We deny them the right to their sexuality, either alone or partnered. We turn their decision-making authority over to various institutions and family members without asking them what they prefer in the matters which affect them most. We deny them opportunities for meaningful work. Finally, we expect them to react with gratitude for the nearly endless oppression they live under because first and foremost we view them as a burden who should feel fortunate that anyone wishes to fool with them at all. No wonder so many people believe that relating to disabled individuals this way is the best that can be done for them. It is the only way our society believes that we can relate to minors. Thus nearly universal acceptance of the oppression of youth opens the door to tolerance and even admiration of the oppression of disabled people of all ages. Of course, no one calls it oppression even though by any reasonable definition it is.

It is important for disability rights advocates to recognise the link between youth and disability oppression. Ageism does much of ableism's heavy lifting and it is important to recognise that in order to combat the pernicious influence that ableism plays in the lives of disabled individuals. It is also important for youth rights advocates to recognise that support for youth liberation logically necessitates support for the disability rights movement. Allowing anyone in our society to be denied liberty, justice, and equality sets a precedent whereby doing this to any other group of individuals becomes much more widely accepted. We best protect youth and people with disabilities when we protect their rights and not when we pretend to protect them from themselves.

The Child and Its Enemies

Emma Goldman

Is the child to be considered as an individuality, or as an object to be moulded according to the whims and fancies of those about it? This seems to me to be the most important question to be answered by parents and educators. And whether the child is to grow from within, whether all that craves expression will be permitted to come forth toward the light of day; or whether it is to be kneaded like dough through external forces, depends upon the proper answer to this vital question.

The longing of the best and noblest of our times makes for the strongest individualities. Every sensitive being abhors the idea of being treated as a mere machine or as a mere parrot of conventionality and respectability, the human being craves recognition of his kind.

It must be borne in mind that it is through the channel of the child that the development of the mature man must go, and that the present ideas of the educating or training of the latter in the school and the family – even the family of the liberal or radical – are such as to stifle the natural growth of the child.

Every institution of our day, the family, the State, our moral codes, sees in every strong, beautiful, uncompromising personality a deadly enemy; therefore every effort is being made to cramp human emotion and originality of thought in the individual into a straight-jacket from its earliest infancy; or to shape every human being according to one pattern; not into a well-rounded individuality, but into a patient work-slave, professional automaton, tax-paying citizen, or righteous moralist. If one, nevertheless, meets with real spontaneity (which, by the way, is a rare treat,) it is not due to our method of rearing or educating the child: the personality often asserts itself, regardless of official and family barriers. Such a discovery should be celebrated as an unusual event, since the obstacles placed in the way of growth and development of character are so numerous that it must be considered a miracle if it retains its strength and beauty and survives the various attempts at crippling that which is most essential to it.

Indeed, he who has freed himself from the fetters of the thoughtlessness and stupidity of the commonplace; he who can stand without moral crutches, without the approval of public opinion – private laziness, Friedrich Nietzsche called it – may well intone a high and voluminous song of independence and freedom; he has gained the right to it through fierce and fiery battles. These battles already begin at the most delicate age.

The child shows its individual tendencies in its plays, in its questions, in its association with people and things. But it has to struggle with everlasting external interference in its world of thought and emotion. It must not express itself in harmony with its nature, with its growing personality. It must become a thing, an object. Its questions are met with narrow, conventional, ridiculous replies, mostly based on falsehoods; and, when, with large, wondering, innocent eyes, it wishes to behold the wonders of the world, those about it quickly lock the windows and doors, and keep the delicate human plant in a hothouse atmosphere, where it can neither breathe nor grow freely.

Zola, in his novel "Fecundity," maintains that large sections of people have declared death to the child, have conspired against the birth of the child – a very horrible picture indeed, yet the conspiracy entered into by civilisation against the growth and making of character seems to me far more terrible and disastrous because of the slow and gradual destruction of its latent qualities and traits and the stupefying and crippling effect thereof upon its social well-being.

Since every effort in our educational life seems to be directed toward making of the child a being foreign to itself, it must of necessity produce individuals foreign to one another, and in everlasting antagonism with each other.

The ideal of the average pedagogist is not a complete, well-rounded, original being; rather does he seek that the result of his art of pedagogy shall be automatons of flesh and blood, to best fit into the treadmill of society and the emptiness and dulness of our lives. Every home, school, college and university stands for dry, cold utilitarianism, over-flooding the brain of the pupil with a tremendous amount of ideas, handed down from generations past. "Facts and data," as they are called, constitute a lot of information, well enough perhaps to maintain every form of authority and to create much awe for the importance of possession, but only a great handicap to a true understanding of the human soul and its place in the world.

Truths dead and forgotten long ago, conceptions of the world and its people, covered with mould, even during the times of our grandmothers, are being hammered into the heads of our young generation. Eternal change, thousandfold variations, continual innovation are the essence of life. Professional pedagogy knows nothing of it, the systems of education are being arranged into files, classified and numbered. They lack the strong fertile seed which, falling on rich soil, enables them to grow to great heights, they are worn and incapable of awakening spontaneity of character. Instructors and teachers, with dead souls, operate with dead values. Quantity is forced to take the place of quality. The consequences thereof are inevitable.

In whatever direction one turns, eagerly searching for human beings who do not measure ideas and emotions with the yardstick of expediency, one is confronted with the products, the herd-like drilling instead of the result of spontaneous and innate characteristics working themselves out in freedom.

"No traces now I see

Whatever of a spirit's agency.

'Tis drilling, nothing more."

These words of Faust fit our methods of pedagogy perfectly. Take, for instance, the way history is being taught in our schools. See how the events of the world become like a cheap puppet show, where a few wire-pullers are supposed to have directed the course of development of the entire human race.

And the history of our own nation! Was it not chosen by Providence to become the leading nation on earth? And does it not tower mountain high over other nations? Is it not the gem of the ocean? Is it not incomparably virtuous, ideal and brave? The result of such ridiculous teaching is a dull, shallow patriotism, blind to its own limitations, with bull-like stubbornness, utterly incapable of judging of the capacities of other nations. This is the way the spirit of youth is emasculated, deadened through an over-estimation of one's own value. No wonder public opinion can be so easily manufactured.

"Predigested food" should be inscribed over every hall of learning as a warning to all who do not wish to lose their own personalities and their original sense of judgment, who, instead, would be content with a large amount of empty and shallow shells. This may suffice as a recognition of the manifold hindrances placed in the way of an independent mental development of the child.

Equally numerous, and not less important, are the difficulties that confront the emotional life of the young. Must not one suppose that parents should be united to children by the most tender and delicate chords? One should suppose it; yet, sad as it may be, it is, nevertheless, true, that parents are the first to destroy the inner riches of their children.

The Scriptures tell us that God created Man in His own image, which has by no means proven a success. Parents follow the bad example of their heavenly master; they use every effort to shape and mould the child according to their image. They tenaciously cling to the idea that the child is merely part of themselves – an idea as false as it is injurious, and which only increases the misunderstanding of the soul of the child, of the necessary consequences of enslavement and subordination thereof.

As soon as the first rays of consciousness illuminate the mind and heart of the child, it instinctively begins to compare its own personality with the personality of those about it. How many hard and cold stone cliffs meet its large wondering gaze? Soon enough it is confronted with the painful reality that it is here only to serve as inanimate matter for parents and guardians, whose authority alone gives it shape and form.

The terrible struggle of the thinking man and woman against political, social and moral conventions owes its origin to the family, where the child is ever compelled to battle against the internal and external use of force. The categorical imperatives: You shall! you must! this is right! that is wrong! this is true! that is false! shower like a violent rain upon the unsophisticated head of the young being and impress upon its sensibilities that it has to bow before the long established and hard notions of thoughts and emotions. Yet the latent qualities and instincts seek to assert their own peculiar methods of seeking the foundation of things, of distinguishing between what is commonly called wrong, true or false. It is bent upon going its own way, since it is composed of the same nerves, muscles and blood, even as those who assume to direct its destiny. I fail to understand how parents hope that their children will ever grow up into independent, self-reliant spirits, when they strain every effort to abridge and curtail the various activities of their children, the plus in quality and character, which differentiates their offspring from themselves, and by the virtue of which they are eminently equipped carriers of new, invigorating ideas. A young delicate tree, that is being clipped and cut by the gardener in order to give it an artificial form, will never reach the majestic height and the beauty as when allowed to grow in nature and freedom.

When the child reaches adolescence, it meets, added to the home and school restrictions, with a vast amount of hard traditions of social morality. The cravings of love and sex are met with absolute ignorance by the majority of parents, who consider it as something indecent and improper, something disgraceful, almost criminal, to be suppressed and fought like some terrible disease. The love and tender feelings in the young plant are turned into vulgarity and coarseness through the stupidity of those surrounding it, so that everything fine and beautiful is either crushed altogether or hidden in the innermost depths, as a great sin, that dares not face the light.

What is more astonishing is the fact that parents will strip themselves of everything, will sacrifice everything for the physical well-being of their child, will wake nights and stand in fear and agony before some physical ailment of their beloved one; but will remain cold and indifferent, without the slightest understanding before the soul cravings and the yearnings of their child, neither hearing nor wishing to hear the loud knocking of the young spirit that demands recognition. On the contrary, they will stifle the beautiful voice of spring, of a new life of beauty and splendour of love; they will put the long lean finger of authority upon the tender throat and not allow vent to the silvery song of the individual growth, of the beauty of character, of the strength of love and human relation, which alone make life worth living.

And yet these parents imagine that they mean best for the child, and for aught I know, some really do; but their best means absolute death and decay to the bud in the making. After all, they are but imitating their own masters in State, commercial, social and moral affairs, by forcibly suppressing every independent attempt to analyse the ills of society and every sincere effort toward the abolition of these ills; never able to grasp the eternal truth that every method they employ serves as the greatest impetus to bring forth a greater longing for freedom and a deeper zeal to fight for it.

That compulsion is bound to awaken resistance, every parent and teacher ought to know. Great surprise is being expressed over the fact that the majority of children of radical parents are either altogether opposed to the ideas of the latter, many of them moving along the old antiquated paths, or that they are indifferent to the new thoughts and teachings of social regeneration. And yet there is nothing unusual in that. Radical parents, though emancipated from the belief of ownership in the human soul, still cling tenaciously to the notion that they own the child, and that they have the right to exercise their authority over it. So they set out to mould and form the child according to their own conception of what is right and wrong, forcing their ideas upon it with the same vehemence that the average Catholic parent uses. And, with the latter, they hold out the necessity before the young "to do as I tell you and not as I do." But the impressionable mind of the child realises early enough that the lives of their parents are in contradiction to the ideas they represent; that, like the good Christian who fervently prays on Sunday, yet continues to break the Lord's commands the rest of the week, the radical parent arraigns God, priesthood, church, government, domestic authority, yet continues to adjust himself to the condition he abhors. Just so, the Free-thought parent can proudly boast that his son of four will recognise the picture of Thomas Paine or Ingersoll, or that he knows that the idea of God is stupid. Or that the Social Democratic father can point to his little girl of six and say, "Who wrote the Capital, dearie?" "Karl Marx, pa!" Or that the Anarchistic mother can make it known that her daughter's name is Louise Michel, Sophia Perovskaya, or that she can recite the revolutionary poems of Herwegh, Freiligrath, or Shelley, and that she will point out the faces of Spencer, Bakunin or Moses Harmon almost anywhere.

These are by no means exaggerations; they are sad facts that I have met with in my experience with radical parents. What are the results of such methods of biasing the mind? The following is the consequence, and not very infrequent, either. The child, being fed on one-sided, set and fixed ideas, soon grows weary of re-hashing the beliefs of its parents, and it sets out in quest of new sensations, no matter how inferior and shallow the new experience may be, the human mind cannot endure sameness and monotony. So it happens that that boy or girl, over-fed on Thomas Paine, will land in the arms of the Church, or they will vote for imperialism only to escape the drag of economic determinism and scientific socialism, or that they open a shirt-waist factory and cling to their right of accumulating property, only to find relief from the old-fashioned communism of their father. Or that the girl will marry the next best man, provided he can make a living, only to run away from the everlasting talk on variety.

Such a condition of affairs may be very painful to the parents who wish their children to follow in their path, yet I look upon them as very refreshing and encouraging psychological forces. They are the greatest guarantee that the independent mind, at least, will always resist every external and foreign force exercised over the human heart and head.

Some will ask, what about weak natures, must they not be protected? Yes, but to be able to do that, it will be necessary to realise that education of children is not synonymous with herd-like drilling and training. If education should really mean anything at all, it must insist upon the free growth and development of the innate forces and tendencies of the child. In this way alone can we hope for the free individual and eventually also for a free community, which shall make interference and coercion of human growth impossible.

Exploitation and Moral Management

Jeremy Weiland

Child exploitation is an evil that has plagued humanity throughout its history. Social awareness of child welfare and consensus on its definition is relatively recent but on the rise. Following this trend, many in Congress work continuously to address this issue, creating new legislative prerogatives for the State to interdict predators and protect children.

How, then, do we reconcile these goals with the case of Mark Foley, a Congressman recently caught engaging in sexually explicit conversations with a minor? Perhaps those who seek to protect us from the nameless, faceless criminals out there have completely misunderstood the problem. The body empowered with enacting nationwide laws, creating criteria for punishing people, and directing the full power of the State contains the very corruption it seeks to root out among us.

It makes one wonder: whom can we trust?

As an anarchist promoting the abolition of this governmental body, it seems reasonable to me that Congress would be as prone to the evils and weaknesses of human experience as any of us. That is precisely the reason they are worthy of ruling neither me nor anybody in this country. We are all fallible, equally capable of deceit and depravity – but also nobility and prudence. We learn whom to trust and whom to avoid not by decrees from on high but by building relationships.

Society is the answer to our problems: the fashioning of markets, communities, networks, and organisations on a voluntary basis, allowing people the freedom to experiment, innovate, band together, and part ways based on their own interests and judgment. We defend our families by allying ourselves with our neighbours, hiring agents among a proven pool of open competitors, and sharing information and advice. Protecting children is best accomplished by the people who understand the stakes: parents and communities.

Of course, bad things happen – whether or not you have the power to pass laws. This brings us to a question anarchists are often asked: how would we prevent x, y, or z from happening without the state? What mechanisms exist to guarantee outcomes acceptable to all? How do we "balance" the sheer volume of competing interests in the world without some empowered and managing body? And in the case of child exploitation: how do we ensure our children's safety from depraved individuals?

These are all good questions whose answers normal people seek. Unfortunately, they're rarely asked honestly in politics. Rather, they are posed as rhetorical preludes to some new control placed on society. Instead of looking at the problem as one of complex interpersonal and community dynamics, with a host of causes and possible solutions, we are encouraged to see the problem as a one-dimensional, simple omission: evil originates from a lack of sufficient governance.

The answer from government is always to cripple ourselves for our own good. By making society less complex, less adaptive, and less empowered, we are easier to manage in a top-down fashion and, therefore, more predictable and homogeneous. Through stricter oversight and prohibitions handed down by Congress we can start to rediscover our virtue, at least as Congress defines it.

But the irony is that Congress doesn't have virtue figured out, either.

The Foley scandal demonstrates the impotence of authority to effect moral management of society. Those who make laws on our behalf are just as flawed as we are. Their officialdom grants them no special insight into human nature. Their power doesn't convey the ability to discipline society — or themselves. When we ask for leadership from above, a guarantee of safety and order, we surrender our consciences to the unworthy. Government will forever attempt to deliver on unreachable guarantees of safety and moral health by instituting more controls on us.

Indeed, reports indicate that politicians from both parties may have known of the problem and yet did nothing to stop it. Think about it: the most powerful body in the Nation, ignoring a case of exploitation they can address immediately without resorting to political manoeuvring or deliberation. Then ask yourself: is any of this about the children?

Think about Foley the next time a law is passed that takes away more of our liberty and freedom "for our own good" or to "protect the children". He demonstrates the truth of politics: virtue is not a matter of coercive laws and enlightened governance. We must place our faith and trust in ourselves, cooperatively building the solutions we seek rather than hoping they will be forced upon us.

Working Moms & the Battle for Play

Aya de Leon

Lately, I've been reading non-fiction books about over-worked moms. Really, I listen to them in audio format as I do overworked mom things like housework and schlepping my kid to and from pre-school. First I read *Maxed Out: American Moms on the Brink* by Katrina Alcorn and now it's *Overwhelmed: Work, Love and Play When No One Has the Time* by Brigid Schulte. They catalog how moms are drowning in the demands that we be perfect workers and perfect mothers.

In *Overwhelmed*, I felt validated by the chapters on overwhelm and inequality. I felt vindicated by the section where she reveals the gender bias in the leisure researchers' methods. Her message is clear: we, as working moms, are being squeezed by a US society that demands perfection from both workers and mothers. Working motherhood sits at the intersection of various oppressive structures in the society. Decades of anti-feminist backlash have engineered the myth that our children will suffer if we work outside the home. From flawed studies to commercials to peer pressure from "helicopter moms," countless daily messages reinforce mothers' anxiety that only our perfectly attentive presence 24/7 will ensure our children's well-being. Yet meanwhile the economy demands two incomes for families to keep up with rising cost of living. Economic insecurity and mistreatment of workers keeps everyone anxious and determined to be the perfect worker in order to keep their jobs and ensure their economic survival. This fear-based pressure intensifies for parents and in times of economic recession. And (unlike many European societies) the US refuses to organise structures to support families in general and working families in particular. So we working mothers live in the centre of this dual pressure, using our sheer will and overwork to ensure our economic survival and our children's well-being.

I loved these books! But when Schulte got to the chapter on play, it got hard to keep listening. In the play chapter, she pushed her readers to look at the places where we, as working moms, routinely collaborate with the oppression and deny ourselves joy in the pursuit of perfection in these other two areas.

I didn't want to look at that. I have lowered the joy bar to be satisfied with the joy of accomplishment and the satisfaction of crossing something off the to-do list. I have settled for creating a spark of delight in my daughter's eyes. My own spark is only reflected light these days. In this context, it was downright painful to think about my own joy and play and delight. Because it feels like one more thing to do. And I couldn't imagine how I can make it happen.

But fortunately for me, I hit the heart of the play chapter while I was camping in the redwood forest. Somehow, surrounded by trees that are a few hundred feet high, anything seems possible. Some of the biggest trees have serious burn scars, but they have continued to grow and thrive anyway, their tops are lush and green in the far above distance. The burns are scars from a fire they survived and kept growing.

So I claim parenting through my kid's early years has been a fiery time I survived but now I'm ready to thrive. To that end, my biggest project this summer is reclaiming play. Miniature golf. Waterslides. Karaoke. I have a whole list. And it's not gonna be easy. I've been home five days and have only managed to do one thing on my list: order the platform shoes off the internet.

It's hard to prioritise play. As mothers go to work, and our small children cry and don't want us to leave, many of us comfort ourselves with the notion that it's important for kids to see their moms engaged in the world. And many studies bear this out, that there are advantages to having working moms. Particularly if we have daughters, working moms can model women's engagement and influence in the larger world.

As a teacher and performer and writer, I have modelled this easily for my daughter. The area of play is the biggest place where my life is lacking. This is the place where I want to model for my daughter that adult women get to have fun, too. Particularly as a black woman, this goal is a crucial contradiction to the historical legacy that we are workhorses in this country. Previous generations of black women have worked ourselves ragged to ensure our children could have a better life. They had to. The conditions were that hard. But I have a chance to do it differently, so I plan to. My goal is not only to run around like a crazy person to make sure my daughter has a good life, but to set up my life that I'm modelling a good life for her. And that needs to include play.

12 Helpful Ideas for Caregivers

Benjamin Fife

Alicia Lieberman and Patricia Van Horn of the UCSF Child Trauma Research program have written extensively on the topic of psychotherapeutic treatments that support development in young children impacted by early trauma and loss. They contributed a very thoughtful chapter to the 2009 third edition of the Handbook of Infant Mental Health, where they described a model of working with young children and their parents which they called Child Parent Psychotherapy. CPP is a relationship based model that combines an array of other approaches to work with young children and their parents. Like earlier models developed from the 1980s onward CPP uses joint child-parent therapy sessions to promote healthy child development. Lieberman and Van Horn organise their treatment model on the premise that long term mental health and resilience is supported when attachment relationships can meet infants', toddlers' and preschoolers' basic needs for "care, protection, and culturally sanctioned patterns of affect modulation, interpersonal relatedness and learning." One thing I love about this model is that it provides 12 easy to understand, and useful guidelines for understanding and interpreting young children's behaviours in the context of their attachment relationship.

While the authors use the term parents when describing these guidelines, I've paraphrased their guidelines here and use the term caregivers instead. I make this change in language because I think that caregivers more accurately reflects that children often have significant attachment relationships with people who are not their biological or legal parents and that both distress and resilience can be born of these relationships. I intend caregivers here to be a term that includes parents while also including the attachment relationships young children have with non-parental adults in and outside of the family that can be so key to development.

Young children's crying and clinging are attempts to communicate an immediate need for their caregivers to be close and to be caring.

Young children's distress at separations is an expression of the fear of losing their caregiver or caregivers.

Young children fear their caregiver's disapproval and want to please their caregivers.

Young children fear being hurt and fear losing parts of their bodies.

Young children imitate their caregiver's behaviours because they,

a) want to be like their caregivers and, b) assume that their caregiver's behaviour is a model to emulate.

Young children feel responsible and blame themselves when their caregivers are upset, whatever the 'real' reason is for the upset.

Young children are convinced that their caregivers know everything and are always right.

Young children need clear consistent limits put on dangerous or culturally inappropriate behaviours in order to feel safe and protected.

Young children use the word "no" to establish their autonomy and to practice being and feeling autonomous.

Memory starts when babies are born. Babies and young children remember experiences before they can speak about them.

Children need their caregiver's support and help in order to learn to express strong emotions without harming themselves or others.

Conflicts between children and their caregivers are inevitable because children and caregivers can and should have different developmental needs. Conflicts between children and their caregivers can be resolved in ways that promote trust and support development.

NO!

ISSUE 10

AGAINST
ADULT
SUPREMACY

Why is the Child Crying? Slavery, Settler Colonialism, and the Ontological Misfortune of Childhood (Excerpt)

Toby Rollo

Conceptions of early human life differ across cultures. Childhood, like infancy, is in part a social construct comprised by a set of ideas and imaginaries which organise how we think and act in relation to young human beings. What we commonly think of as childhood is a distinctly European social category. For early western thinkers, the absence of language in the young suggested that they were more animal than human. In the western philosophical idiom, fully-human Man is a rational animal precisely because he has been forced to transcend his "childhood animality" through discipline, education, and violence. Although rooted in ancient views of humanity, the view of children as animals is still prevalent today, as we see in philosopher Georges Bataille's quip: "What are children if not animals becoming human?". In classical thought, the figure of the child was considered the bridge or missing link between reason and instinct, human and animal, heaven and earth, spirit and body, order and chaos. The distinctive convergence of life (bios) with reason and language (logos) was defined over and against the mere life of the child. Human improvement is attained through the violent inculcation of logos. The violence that is required to usher us out of childhood is a moral imperative so any interference with the civilising of children constitutes a moral tragedy.

To obstruct the telos of humanity is to suffer the chaos of cognitive disability, criminality or madness. Madness, as Foucault once observed, "is childhood". Indeed, it is necessary for dominant cultures to assert the irrationality and criminality of childhood in order to position the adult as sane and lawful. The denigrating construction of youth as childhood exists in order to confirm the agency, freedom, and humanity of the adult. To be located in childhood is to lack agency, and therefore to be fixed as a fungible object for use by those with agency, adults, in accordance with adult epistemologies. I refer to this antipathy toward children and childhood as misopedy. The term is a partial cognate of more familiar terms such as misogyny (antipathy towards women and femininity) and misanthropy (antipathy toward human beings and sociality).

This childhood/human binary has been the primary model for positioning Europeans over and against non-Europeans. The relationship between misopedy and the oppression of non-Europeans is not a contingent analogy, but rather, a structuring principle at work in almost all western attempts to define itself over and against an Other. Feminist scholar Anne McClintock describes the relationship in terms of the projection of an image:

Because the subordination of woman to man and child to adult were deemed natural facts, other forms of social hierarchy could be depicted in familiar terms to guarantee social difference as a category of nature… Projecting the family image onto national and imperial progress enabled what was often murderously violent change to be legitimised as the progressive unfolding of natural decree. Imperial intervention could thus be figured as a linear, non-revolutionary progression that naturally contained hierarchy within unity: paternal fathers ruling benignly over immature children.

We should note, however, that adult power over children is not just a rhetorical trope whereby the "image" of the bestial child is used only to "depict" the natural subjugation of animalian others. Rather, the child/human binary is the model or organising principle upon which these modes of subjugation are structured. There is a homologous relationship between the domination of children and most other modern systems of domination: they share a common root and structure in the veneration of speech and reason. To understand the relation of misopedy to empire, colonialism and slavery, it is important to understand how the childhood/human binary emerged. Beginning in the classical period of Greek and Roman civilisation, and probably before, children were used as labourers and slaves whose productivity was central to the formation of a leisure class that could then cultivate cultural institutions related to religion, art, philosophy, politics and science. Ancient thinkers (the main beneficiaries of such labour) associated human toil with necessity and the absence of autonomy, a degraded condition for which the child stood as the perennial archetype. Vulnerability and physical dependency were lamented as indicative of some defect of character or constitution. Children were positioned as the natural embodiment of the defect. In the writing from antiquity, then, we encounter deep resentment for the miserable helplessness of the newborn and the dependence of young children. Only through violence and discipline could the bestial child emerge from the world of labour and play that is common to all animals into the world of language and reason (logos) achieved only by human beings (and epitomised in the philosopher).

Before the age of reason, children were understood as non-persons. Aristotle argued that slaves, women, and children are naturally excluded from political life on the grounds that they possessed deficient forms of logos. Most young boys and girls lived in conditions of servitude, slavery, or abandonment. Servitude is a natural condition, in Aristotle's account, for those who cannot organise their own lives. But although there was debate even among classical thinkers over the validity of slavery, as well as over the equality of the sexes (and even of animals) the natural servitude and subordination of children was self-evident and never debated. At best, children were the living tools of adults. At worst, they were animals. In either case, the bodies of children were the property of adults.

Contemporary thinkers tend to project the Romantic vision of childhood reverence back into the classical period. Philosopher Giorgio Agamben has asserted that the child's life of play is not a kind of bare life created by the imposition of sovereignty, but a self-contained form of life: "the child is a paradigm of a life that is absolutely inseparable from its form, an absolute form-of-life [forma-di-vita] without remainder." He concludes that "the child is never bare life [nuda vita], that it is never possible to isolate in a child something like bare life or biological life." While this may be accurate with respect to the phenomenological register (i.e., with respect to the way young human beings engage with and experience the world), at least for very young children, it is not an accurate political ontology. European conceptions of sovereignty have been direct and explicit expressions of the relegation of children to the status of Other. Even during the Romantic period, when poets and philosophers associated childhood with innocence and bucolic nostalgia, the animality of children was the object sentimentalisation. The lesson here is that the experience of oppression does not always or even necessarily reflect the motivations behind oppression. The phenomenology of subjugation is sometimes an untrustworthy window into the etiology of domination.

Treat Children Like Adults

Brian Davis

Our son started talking early and one of his first tricks was to parrot what we said and how we said it. I know that it sounds cute – and it was in the beginning – but mostly it was maddening. We quickly realised that traditional parenting is really, really condescending. Don't believe me? Try this experiment with your significant other:

Give seemingly arbitrary orders without any context or reasoning ("Don't touch that.")

Ignore feedback ("Do you want to go to the park? No? Well, we're going to the park anyway.")

Ask rhetorical questions in a passive-aggressive fashion ("Do big boys cry?")

Respond to frustration with more orders ("Stop pouting.")

Deny autonomy at every opportunity ("Let me do that for you. You'll hurt yourself.")

Impose arbitrary punishments ("Keep that up, and I'm taking away your car keys.") Be serious about it, just as if you were talking to a child. If, after a week of this treatment, you and your significant other haven't had at least one bitter argument, then you are either extremely lucky or already mired in a dysfunctional relationship.

So, how do you parent a child without treating them like a child? Here are some tricks that have worked for us:

Explain Yourself

Kids ask "Why?" so much because they genuinely want to learn. At some point, they stop asking, and it's generally because we stop giving them real answers.

When a child questions your instructions, it's a great opportunity to teach. When you explain the reasons and context behind a rule, you're giving the child the tools to build their own moral framework, to fill in the blanks between the rules they know and the ones they don't. This is fundamental to learning. Offering an explanation is also a great opportunity for your own reflection. If you don't have a good reason for a rule ("Stop making faces."), it's probably a crappy rule and you're probably taking yourself too seriously.

Ask Them Questions

Play this game: See how long of a conversation you can have with your child by only asking questions. At first you'll be surprised at how much they talk. Then you'll be surprised at how beautifully complex their minds actually are. And then you'll be surprised at how rewarding it is to really get to know your own kid.

As for the child, they will love the fact that you care enough to ask about their day, about their feelings, about their preferences – about all the trivial little things that loom large in a child's mind. Asking questions is the single strongest signal you can send that you're listening, that you love them, and that you care what they think.

Give Them Options

A lot of a child's frustration stems from having no choice in anything. A lot of your frustration stems from having to make lots of tiny, trivial decisions every day that drain your mental batteries. Delegate some of those decisions to your child and you can solve both problems at once. Your child gets to feel like an important, contributing member of the family because they got to pick out which beans to eat tonight. You get to make one less decision. Win-win.

This, more than any other trick, nips conflict in the bud. The child owns the decision now. They have no injustice to protest. Our son eats all his vegetables because he picks out which ones to buy.

Give Them Space

Speaking as an American, we tend to be too controlling of our kids, denying them the right to have their own initiative and to make their own mistakes. A child has to fall a lot before they learn to walk. And they have to trip a lot before they learn to run. By giving them the space to trip and fall – to experiment and to fail – you're helping them learn faster.

Now, that doesn't mean you should just let your kid wander into traffic in order to learn the importance of looking both ways before crossing, but we parents tend to confuse inconvenience for danger. A good rule of thumb is to ask yourself this: "If my child screws this up, will it cost more than $20 to fix, hurt more than a scraped knee, or take longer than an hour to clean up?" (Adjust according to your financial/emotional/time budget.)

Practice Defensive Parenting

Remove sources of conflict before conflict arises and both parent and child will be much happier. In our case, that meant moving valuables up high, getting rid of lots of sharp stuff, and plastering the bottom 3 feet of our walls with butcher paper. Our son gets to draw on the walls without, you know, ruining our walls.

We also got duplicates of things we couldn't replace or remove. He has his own books, his own pens, his own wallet. That way he doesn't go around "borrowing" ours all the time.

Ask For Help

Kids want to help. By doing everything for them, we infantilise them and lull them into a state of dependency. It's great, as a parent, to feel needed, but it's also exhausting.

Free yourself. Ask for help washing dishes. Ask for help cracking eggs. Ask for help moving the furniture.

As they get older, ask for help with things that are just at or above their developmental level. It challenges them and it gives them a powerful sense of belonging. Remember the first time your parents let you park the car? Remember how exhilarating that felt? That's how a 3-year-old feels when you ask them to help you sweep the floor. Give them that gift as often as you can. You'll be surprised how much they'll want to help. In the end, treating a kid like a person prevents a parent from needing "discipline" at all.

Punishment, deprivation, praise, criticism, distraction, and a lot of the other things people have recommended don't actually do much to teach your child good behaviour. More often than not, they teach children to be retributive, praise-seeking, or distracted.

Ultimately, parenting is not about control. Kids aren't irrational beasts out to deprive you of patience and silence. They're little people in need of understanding and a helping hand. And when they get what they need they're usually pretty spectacular.

It takes practice and time to change your habits, but after a couple of months you'll be amazed at how self-policing your kid is. Good luck.

On Torture: The Truth That Lies Within (Excerpt)

Arthur Silber

Children who become too aware of things are punished for it and internalise the coercion to such an extent that as adults they give up the search for awareness. But because some people cannot renounce this search in spite of coercion, there is justifiable hope that regardless of the ever-increasing application of technology to the field of psychological knowledge, Kafka's vision of the penal colony with its efficient scientifically-minded persecutors and their passive victims is valid only for certain areas of our life and perhaps not forever. For the human soul is virtually indestructible, and its ability to rise from the ashes remains as long as the body draws breath. – Alice Miller, For Your Own Good

I have read extensively in my life, and Alice Miller is the most profoundly courageous writer in the world today to my knowledge. She writes unflinchingly and with a gaze that never turns away from what it perceives, no matter how horrifying it may be. Miller describes the untold cruelties that are inflicted on the most innocent and defenceless of victims – infants and very young children. Almost all of us accept these cruelties to one degree or another. I am not speaking only of the obvious cruelties, of corporal punishment and similar barbarities – although we should never forget that the great majority of parents believe that spanking is sometimes necessary. I will begin to trace the connections here at the outset: just as Charles Krauthammer maintains that we are "morally compelled" to utilise torture in rare circumstances in the name of our own survival, so most parents believe that physical violence is sometimes morally "required" if their children are to be taught to be "civilised."

Let us try to be as brave as Alice Miller: what we mean by "civilised" when we speak in this way, is that children must be taught to obey. If the principle of obedience is instilled in children from earliest infancy, and if parents further teach their children that physical violence is the means of commanding obedience, why do we wonder that some adults will torture those who have been rendered helpless and delivered into their control? They are merely re-enacting what their parents taught them.

But we refuse to see this. We will not acknowledge what has been done to us. Miller continues in her work, because she understands better than anyone that these issues must be understood if the horrors are to be stopped. But she has met with fierce resistance every step of the way. In a similar way, although on an immensely more modest scale, I have found that many readers who agree with me on many issues – and many readers who may have followed this series so far, nodding their heads in confirmation at every point in my argument – will stop here. They will not acknowledge these particular truths, because they are too threatening.

This is because there is a necessary corollary to the obedience we are taught: the idealisation of the authority figures in our lives. As children, we dare not question what our parents do: we depend on them for life itself. To comprehend fully what is being done to us would be unbearable, and it might literally kill us. So we must believe that, whatever our parents do, they do it "for our own good." To believe otherwise is the forbidden thought. So we must deny our own pain when we are young; such denial is necessary if we are to survive at that stage in our lives.

But if we maintain the denial when we become adults, it spreads throughout our lives. When such modes of thought are established in our psychologies, they cannot be isolated or contained. We deny our own pain – so we must deny the pain of others. If we acknowledge their pain fully and allow ourselves to realise what it means, it will necessarily call up our own wounds. But this remains intolerable and forbidden. In extreme cases, we must dehumanise other human beings: they become "the other," the less-than-human. By using such devices, we make inflicting untold agonies on another person possible: if they are not even human, it doesn't matter if we torture them. This is always how we create hell on earth.

I said I was not referring only to the obvious cruelties inflicted on children by physical violence. Just as important, and often of much greater significance, are the psychological agonies to which parents subject their children. How often do we hear parents say to a child who will not follow an order: "Why are you making me so unhappy? You don't want to make your mother unhappy and sad, do you, darling? Now just do what I say." We should recognise this for what it is: emotional blackmail. The unstated threat – but the threat that is deeply felt by the child, even if he is not able to understand it – is that the parent's love will be withdrawn unless the child obeys. Since the child knows that his life depends on that love, the threat is a terrifying one. Such blows are delivered countless times every day, by millions of parents around the world.

This knowledge is inaccessible to the majority of adults. We are taught to obey, and we learn to idealise our parents. We tell ourselves they did the best they could, or they couldn't help it. In one sense, that is true: they raise their children as they were raised. They learned obedience very well, and they do to their own children what was done to them. But most of us cannot leave this truth at this point: to maintain the veneration of our parents, we must insist that they in fact were right – that they did it "for our own good." That is where the great danger lies.

When the idealisation of the authority figure spreads once we become adults, it can encompass additional authority figures. There are two primary such figures: God – who may have been there from the beginning, if the child is raised in a very religious household where God is the ultimate authority, and the parents only speak on His behalf – and country. When one's nation becomes such an authority figure, there are subsidiary ones as well: the nation's leaders, and the nation's military.

Many of today's hawks exhibit the kind of denial to which I refer in an extreme form: because they will not acknowledge any of this, they must insist that the U.S. military could never commit such atrocities. It must all be a vicious lie. As I explain in [When the Demons Come], this was the ultimate root of the hatred heaped on John Kerry: he dared to speak the truth about what had happened in Vietnam. For the deniers, this is the one crime for which no forgiveness is possible. As I wrote about this kind of denier (Rich Lowry and Andrew Sullivan were the particular writers to whom I was responding, but the same is true of many millions of additional people):

With no effort at all, you could multiply examples such as these a thousandfold, every single day. In this manner, defenders of our current foreign policy wipe out of existence all the facts, all the costs, all the deaths, and anything else that might bring into question what is an absolute of their faith: the United States is right, what we have done and are doing in Iraq is right, our military is right, we are inherently unable to make mistakes, and the authorities must not be questioned.

These are the victims described by Miller – now grown into adulthood, continuing their denial, with additional authority figures added to the ones they first had. Besides the original parent, they now revere our government and our military and, beyond a certain point, nothing they do is to be challenged… to do so would bring into question these individuals' entire false sense of self, it would undermine their worldview completely, and it represents a threat that cannot be allowed to come too close. As always, what is dispensable in all this are facts, untold national wealth, reputation and prestige, and above all, the lives of human beings.

As I have said before, it is in this manner that horrors are unleashed upon the world. And if this mentality is carried far enough, you will finally end up with the kind of thinking, and the kind of psychology, that lies behind the journal entry from World War II (written by a German soldier) that I quoted in the previous part of this essay:

"On a roundabout way to have lunch I witnessed the public shooting of twenty-eight Poles on the edge of a playing field. Thousands line the streets and the river. A ghastly pile of corpses, all in all horrifying and ugly and yet a sight that leaves me altogether cold. The men who were shot had ambushed two soldiers and a German civilian and killed them. An exemplary modern folk-drama." 1/27/44

If you never allowed your authentic self to develop (or your parents never allowed you to develop one), if you denied and continue to deny the reality of your own pain, then you will deny the pain of others, even as the corpses pile up – and you will be prepared to believe anything.

And the horrors continue, beyond all human reckoning – and without end.

In When the Demons Come, I also offered a brief summary of my own of Miller's central thesis:

By demanding obedience above all from a child (whether by physical punishment, by psychological means, or through some combination of both), parents forbid the child from fostering an authentic sense of self. Because children are completely dependent on their parents, they dare not question their parents' goodness, or their "good intentions." As a result, when children are punished, even if they are punished for no reason or for a reason that makes no sense, they blame themselves and believe that the fault lies within them. In this way, the idealisation of the authority figure is allowed to continue. In addition, the child cannot allow himself to experience fully his own pain, because that, too, might lead to questioning of his parents.

In this manner, the child is prevented from developing a genuine, authentic sense of self. As he grows older, this deadening of his soul desensitises the child to the pain of others. Eventually, the maturing adult will seek to express his repressed anger on external targets, since he has never been allowed to experience and express it in ways that would not be destructive. By such means, the cycle of violence is continued into another generation (using "violence" in the broadest sense). One of the additional consequences is that the adult, who has never developed an authentic self, can easily transfer his idealisation of his parents to a new authority figure. As Miller says:

"This perfect adaptation to society's norms – in other words, to what is called 'healthy normality' – carries with it the danger that such a person can be used for practically any purpose. It is not a loss of autonomy that occurs here, because this autonomy never existed, but a switching of values, which in themselves are of no importance anyway for the person in question as long as his whole value system is dominated by the principle of obedience. He has never gone beyond the stage of idealising his parents with their demands for unquestioning obedience; this idealisation can easily be transferred to a Fuhrer or to an ideology."

NO!

Issue 11
AGAINST
ADULT
SUPREMACY

Playground Anarchy?

Before we can answer this question, we must ask: what is play? Play is the antithesis of work. Work is the art of an exploitative science. It tugs at the reigns of capital, conducting its movements, speed and flow, carrying with it the hearse of companionship. It tramples our natural sociality, but binds us in a common hatred. Play is the revitalisation of life, of our dreams and our desires. It is the rejection of the necessary non-freedom promoted, produced, and projected by work. It is releasing human floods of bodily desire across the barriers of separation created by work. Play is unmediated joy.

Anarchy is a condition: that of being without rule. Anarchy is the absence of, and the rejection of the notions that give rise to the legitimisation of authority. It is unmediated freedom. Freedom to shape our lives as we see fit, to make our own decisions outside the realm of politics, where biological life is exposed to death, and to appropriate the means of existence from the chokehold of industrial civilisation and its arsenal of economies, experts, and militaries.

Playground Anarchy is a conception: an understanding of what it is to experience life as play while simultaneously realising its anti-authoritarian implications. Further, it can be considered the absolute embrace of a peculiar yet collective singularity: that of our inner-child. Further still, Playground Anarchy may be best described as the destruction of the great appendage known as chronological history and the creation of an always and all-at-once present appropriation of the past, during which we move from our shared affectivity to a shared direction.

We, its practitioners, recognise that upon entering adulthood (a.k.a. the realm of work, material overproduction, commodity fetishism, etc.) an individual can own nothing but their own labour power, surrendering all other autonomous projects. It becomes painfully evident that we gradually and incontrovertibly lose our real sense of selves. Diametrically, we recognise that in our experiences during the years of our youth, life had been actualised. In childhood, life was all that it could be, and all that it is currently not: adventure, exploration, discovery, learning, loving, sharing, bonding, and growing. This recognition is explicated not only in the theoretical writings of Marx or the classical literary contributions of Salinger, but universally: in every individual's perceived need, even if it is expressed through the great irony of consumerism, to escape from the world of work, and thus, the logic of capital.

Yet, as anarchists we desire more than a pathetic dislodging from the dominion of capital. We are not interested in securing such matters of temporality: rather, we seek an eternal and unmediated freedom, which is to be materialised through a life (re)structured by play. Under capitalism, play has become yet another potentially affirming activity separated from everyday life.

True to its own perverse logic, capitalism designs, manufactures, and sells "parks" to communities – designated areas where our play is premeditated and established within assigned parameters. We are allotted a time and a place to play, so long as it does not threaten the sanctity of the work week, the monetary system at large, or the rigid social order it permeates. These are (often successful) efforts to maintain normalcy. When the clock strikes three, we flood the lot, and things appear to be going along as usual – running the way that they "should" be. Thus, it is only when we make our play total, outside of the increasing limitations of capital, that we destroy the constructs of work and leisure, of production and consumption, while simultaneously re-territorialising the space we inhabit through the liberation of our desires.

In a similar fashion, the standing mode of production – being an insatiable beast which finds sustenance only in merciless commodification – has adopted the technique of reifying our common nostalgia. While they rob us of life by exploiting us to wage slavery on the one hand, they expect us to believe that we can buy it all back in films, books, costumes and theme park tickets. We choose, as a response to the great lie we have been fed, to shove dirt in the mouth of such a courteous oppressor, in all of their offerings and claims of opportunity.

In Playground Anarchy we will henceforth begin to take back the images they exploit and credit themselves with – those images that we, their unwanted children, gave life to in worlds outside of work. The genuinely positive social relations (those of cooperation, sharing, and aiding) prevalent in childhood are to be made distinct from the spectacle's vulgar interpretation/presentation: synthetic friendships, stories that applaud hierarchy and heroism, and adventures that only amount to transparent celluloid. We seek to collectively live out our dreams, while they seek to keep us stationary and entertained with a cheap imitation thereof.

We call for the immediate dismantling of all borders, boundaries, and restrictions. We will leap over every fence. No longer will we accept the painful familiarity of their predictable realm of play. We will watch possibilities explode, like the gunpowder and dust of their spectacular images, yet ours will be so immense that they shade the night sky permanently.

In attempts to liberate seized playgrounds with locked fences, relentlessly stencil four-square courts up and down city streets, and to occupy abandoned homes, factories and universities, we give content to our particular form of subversion. Whether your experience is in sprinting through a cemetery after dusk, opening a fire hydrant on a hot summer day, or exploring a decaying manufacturing plant, we urge you to rediscover the child within you – to release it at once, and in every direction. Use your imaginations, pack some candy, go outside, find each other, and enact the most bodily of revolts. The playground is open.

Preschool to Prison
Sonali Kolhatkar

Although African-Americans constitute only 13 percent of all Americans, nearly half of all prison inmates in the U.S. are black. This startling statistic has led the United Nations Human Rights Committee to publicly criticise the U.S. for its treatment of African-Americans. A number of recent studies and reports paint a damning picture of how American society dehumanises blacks starting from early childhood.

Racial justice activists and prison abolition groups have long argued that the "school-to-prison" pipeline funnels young black kids into the criminal justice system, with higher rates of school suspension and arrest compared with non-black kids for the same infractions. More than 20 years ago, Smith College professor Ann Arnett Ferguson wrote a groundbreaking book based on her three-year study of how black boys in particular are perceived differently starting in school. In "Bad Boys: Public Schools in the Making of Black Masculinity," Ferguson laid out the ways in which educators and administrators funnelled black male students into the juvenile justice system based on perceived differences between them and other students. Today this trend continues with record numbers of suspensions as a result of "zero-tolerance" school policies and the increasing presence of campus police officers who arrest students for insubordination, fights and other types of behaviour that might be considered normal "acting out" in school-aged children. In fact, black youth are far more likely to be suspended from school than any other race. They also face disproportionate expulsion and arrest rates, and once children enter the juvenile justice system they are far more likely to be incarcerated as adults.

Even the Justice Department under President Obama has understood what a serious problem this is, issuing a set of new guidelines earlier this year to curb discriminatory suspension in schools. But it turns out that negative disciplinary actions affect African-American children starting as early as age 3. The U.S. Department of Education just released a comprehensive study of public schools, revealing in a report that black children face discrimination even in preschool. (That preschool-aged children are suspended at all is hugely disturbing.) Data from the 2011-12 year show that although black children make up only 18 percent of preschoolers, 42 percent of them were suspended at least once and 48 percent were suspended multiple times.

Consistent with this educational data and taking into account broader demographic, family and economic data for children of various races, broken down by state, is a newer study released this week by the Annie E. Casey Foundation that found African-American children are on the lowest end of nearly every measured index including proficiency in math and reading, high school graduation, poverty and parental education. The report, titled Race for Results, plainly says, "The index scores for African-American children should be considered a national crisis."

Two other studies published recently offer specific evidence of how black children are so disadvantaged at an early age. One research project, published in the Journal of Personality and Social Psychology, examined how college students and police officers estimated the ages of children who they were told had committed crimes. Both groups studied by UCLA professor Phillip Goff and collaborators were more likely to overestimate the ages of black children compared with nonblack ones, implying that black children were seen as "significantly less innocent" than others. The authors wrote:

> We expected… that individuals would perceive Black boys as being more responsible for their actions and as being more appropriate targets for police violence. We find support for these hypotheses… and converging evidence that Black boys are seen as older and less innocent and that they prompt a less essential conception of childhood than do their White same-age peers.

Another study by researchers at UC Riverside found that teachers tended to be more likely to evaluate black children negatively than nonblack ones who were engaged in pretend play. Psychology professor Tuppett M. Yates, who led the study, observed 171 preschool-aged children interacting with stuffed toys and other props and evaluated them for how imaginative and creative they were. In an interview on Uprising, Yates told me that all the children, regardless of race, were "similarly imaginative and similarly expressive," but when their teachers evaluated those same children at a later time, there was a discriminatory effect. Yates explained, "For white children, imaginative and expressive players were rated very positively [by teachers] but the reverse was true for black children. Imaginative and expressive black children were perceived as less ready for school, as less accepted by their peers, and as greater sources of conflict and tension."

Although it is clear that negative behaviours were magnified through "race-coloured glasses," according to Yates, her study of children engaged in pretend play found that "there is also potentially a systematic devaluing of positive attributes among black children." This made her concerned about how "very early on, some kids are being educated towards innovation and leadership and others may be educated towards more menial or concrete social positions." Reflecting on the 2001 book Bad Boys and how little seems to have changed since then, Yates affirmed that author Ferguson's assertion that black children are given a "hidden curriculum" is still true now. She told me, "Our data suggests that that hidden curriculum may be persisting today and that it's starting much earlier than we ever could have anticipated." She noted her deep concern that "we're actually reproducing inequality generation after generation."

When I asked her to comment on the Goff study showing police estimates of black children as older than they are, Yates agreed that it appears as though "the same objective data are being interpreted differently as a function of race." Ferguson also apparently noted this trend, calling it an "adultification" of black boys. Yates recounted an example from Ferguson's work in which "when a white student fails to return their library book, they're seen as forgetful and when a black student fails to return a library book, terms like 'thief' or 'looter' were used."

Studies such as these consistently show that African-Americans have the deck stacked against them starting in early childhood through adulthood. Taken together, they make a strong case for the existence of a "preschool-to-prison" pipeline and the systematic dehumanisation that black children face in American society. Yates summarised, "Across these different studies, black children are viewed differently. They are consequently given less access to the kinds of structural avenues required to advance in our society and ultimately they become less valued in our culture," and are ultimately "fast tracked to the margins."

Daily Beast staff writer Jamelle Bouie, writing about black preschoolers being disproportionately suspended, provocatively asked, "Are Black Students Unruly? Or is America Just Racist?" Yates gave me the obvious answer saying, "We know that [discrimination] exists. It's the most parsimonious explanation for these kinds of persistent inequalities." But perhaps there is also an element of justifiable unruliness involved. Yates offered that "black children – rightfully so – are more likely to disengage from their educational milieus and potentially rebel against them because these systems are at best failing to support them, and at worst channeling them into this pipeline towards negative ends."

She indicted American society as a whole, saying, "Our educational system, our economic system, our judicial system, all of these are converging to reproduce these kinds of inequalities and perpetuate the criminalisation of blacks in our culture." Although Attorney General Eric Holder's push to reform mandatory minimum sentences that disproportionately incarcerate African-Americans is indeed laudable, strong action is needed now to address the early childhood barriers facing black kids. The preschool-to-prison pipeline needs to be dismantled from its starting point rather than simply its endpoint. Ultimately, "change," Yates said, "is really going to require effort at all levels such as individual teachers, superintendents, police officers, attorneys general and even in the media."

Fight Ableism. Fight Child Abuse.

s.e. smith

The internet was abuzz last week with the Hillary Adams case; a young woman bravely videotaped her father beating her as a teen, and uploaded the video to YouTube several years later, sparking an international discussion about child abuse. It's a horrible video to watch, made more chilling when you realise the level of planning and thought that must have gone into it.

Fighting child abuse is challenging on so many levels because it can be hard to identify the victims, especially when they are too terrified to speak. It's telling that Adams didn't come out about her abuse until she was in a safe environment, outside her home, many years later. Clearly she lives with the memories not just of what she experienced, but the systems that failed her and allowed that abuse to continue, because people thought her dad was a good guy, a stand-up kind of fellow, reputable, because he was a judge.

In the ample analysis of the video and discussions about how Adams' father should be punished, one element of the case has been minimally examined: Hillary is disabled. She has cerebral palsy. This is a key aspect of the story that shouldn't be left out, because it's central to a larger discussion. You cannot talk about child abuse without addressing, specifically, the abuse of children with disabilities. A UNICEF report in 2005 stressed that any action on child abuse needs to fully integrate children with disabilities. Disability-specific interventions are critical because of the disability-specific issues children experience globally, and 10% of the world's children are disabled or will become disabled by age 19, which makes them a non-trivial population.

> A child born with a disability or a child who becomes disabled may be directly subject to physical violence, or sexual, emotional or verbal abuse in the home, the community, institutional settings or in the workplace. A disabled child is more likely to face violence and abuse at birth and this increased risk for violence reappears throughout the life span. This violence compounds already existing social, educational and economic marginalisation that limits the lives and opportunities of these children. For example, disabled children are far less likely than their non-disabled peers to be included in the social, economic and cultural life of their communities; only a small percentage of these children will ever attend school; a third of all street children are disabled children. Disabled children living in remote and rural areas may be at increased risk.

Disability radically increases the chance that you will experience violence, sexual assault, and physical abuse in your home. A study in 2000 indicated that disabled children experience physical abuse in the home at a rate 3.8 times higher than that of their non-disabled peers. It's actually extremely hard to get accurate statistics because so few regions collect data, or collect incomplete data that is difficult to extrapolate. This lack of interest in even determining the extent of the problem illustrates, starkly, how little interest there is in addressing the issue. When abuse of disabled children is reported, it's often ignored.

This is the result of social attitudes about people with disabilities, particularly disabled children. Disability becomes a value judgment, and people with disabilities are found lacking. Less valuable. Less important. Casual abuse of disabled children isn't just rampant, it's socially acceptable. 'Caregivers' argue that they need to be able to discipline their children, that raising a disabled child is inherently harder. In abuse and neglect cases, the media often portrays the abuser sympathetically. Parents who murder their disabled children get the kid glove treatment because having a disabled child is viewed as a tragedy, and it's sometimes suggested that killing disabled children is a 'mercy.'

People in a position to act may be slow to intervene in cases of child abuse involving children with disabilities, and the cost of that slowness can be devastating. When disabled children are taken from abusive environments, they may be placed in newly abusive environments, either in foster care or institutions. The number of disabled children living in institutions is alarmingly high, and institutional environments are not necessarily safe for children. The same abuses people experience in the home – rape, physical abuse, emotional abuse – may transfer into 'care homes.' And yet, there is a collective silence on these topics.

Cases of neglect and abuse of disabled children are in the news every week. Children are starved to death, exposed in the woods to die, beaten to death, kept in filthy conditions, repeatedly abused, or simply neglected to death. These stories are heartbreaking not just because they involve real people and real lives, but because they illustrate how little society cares about disabled children. Opportunities for intervention slip past, and often, when cases finally do attract attention, sympathy rests with the parents. They must have been driven to it. It was too hard for them. They had no choice. There were 'extenuating circumstances.'

Ableism kills. It kills children who live brief, violent, miserable lives and it kills adults subject to many of the same kinds of abuses. And yes, ableism contributes to the lack of social support for parents of children with disabilities, many of whom struggle to meet the needs of their children in a society that's busy slashing social services.

All parents need respite care, but parents of disabled children have a much harder time getting it, and may be balancing expensive medical conditions and other factors on top of the stresses of parenting. Parenting is stressful and it's hard regardless of disability status. It's difficult to go it alone, without social support. It's hard when you and your children are being bullied because of disability and your pleas for help go unaddressed because you're not considered a full member of society.

But that doesn't mean that the abuses endured by disabled children are justified, or that society as a whole is doing the right thing by standing by while children die. Hillary Adams got lucky: she escaped her father and built a new life for herself. She boldly spoke out about the case to raise awareness of the issue. And it's excellent to see people talking about child abuse and what happens when people in positions of authority, like judges, are allowed to get away with abusive behaviour. But it's also disappointing to see that few people are specifically tying this case in with disability, and talking about the disability implications here, because they are important, and they should be centred in conversations about the case.

Hillary Adams defies social narratives about disability, which is often perceived as a state of helplessness and inability to act with autonomy. She demonstrated ingenuity and enterprising behaviour, two things people with disabilities are not supposed to do, when she taped her father abusing her. She communicated on her own terms, another thing we are not supposed to do, when she posted the video and started talking about it. This makes it easier to ignore the disability aspect of the case, to treat Adams as exceptional and focus just on the abuse.

But abuse doesn't happen in a vacuum, and the fact that Hillary has CP matters. Which means that it should be part of the discussion. Because any conversation about ending child abuse must include disabled children. Not just because they are children too and thus are part of the picture, but because they are particularly vulnerable to abuse and because there are disability-specific issues that must be addressed at the same time we fight child abuse as a whole.

Fighting ableism fights child abuse, because fighting ableism gets at the core of the attitudes that treat disabled children as disposable objects rather than human beings, as legitimate targets of abuse rather than victims. This is why 'intersectionality' sometimes feels like an inadequate word; it's not just that disability intersects with child abuse, but that it's a core intertwined issue that cannot be ignored without leaving children out in the cold.

Abolish CPS

Carlos Morales

Standing in an office while two kids beg me to go back to their home, I begin retreating back into my inner-child. I imagine how I would have felt if I was seven years old and a Child Protective Services (CPS) investigator told me I couldn't stay with my mom anymore. Their mother had committed the crime of respecting the children's desire to play outside. Paperwork has already been checked by the supervisor, the judge has backed it, and now I have to find a placement. I put them in my car and we drive. The tears continue, my guilt is overwhelming, and I grant them over to a temporary shelter. Two court proceedings, tens of thousands of dollars out of the mother's pocket, and five bottles of ADHD medications for the kids later, the mom is given back her children. All because she let them play outside.

Guilt is what led me to where I am today. Guilt for kidnapping children for the state, and guilt for being an anti-drug warrior. It has led me to become a child advocate, an author of a book on the subject, and an anti-reformer. There is no reforming CPS, and there is no reforming the government. The entirety of government's power comes from its promise of reform. No one believes the government is perfect, but nearly everyone believes it can be changed to benefit them. When you see the tears of children begging for their mother, when you see children drugged because the government gives incentives for doing so, and when children die in part because of your actions as a CPS drone, you stop believing in reform. I fell for political hope. I had faith I could be the good guy working for the state – that I would be different. We all imagine that we'll be the hero in our story, but I was not. My faith is gone and reason has replaced it. The state is a religion and the political reformers are keeping the faith strong. The only way out is complete abolition.

There are over 400,000 children in Child Protective Services care in America. Eighty percent of those cases are not for physical or sexual abuse, but rather parental negligence. Negligence can mean the child is playing outside, is too fat, doesn't like school, or – as in forty percent of cases – is for the parent using marijuana.

Perhaps CPS's biggest problem is its evidentiary standard. CPS cases can be based on something that happened years ago and not even something that a witness saw firsthand. The agency uses evidence that is based on a memory of a story that a witness overheard years ago. How's that for reliability? The investigator is actually told not to record the information taken during interviews word for word. Instead, they're instructed to take notes and to use their judgment in entering the notes into a database in narrative form. In other words, the investigator creates a story based on their own memory of another person's memory, which person may not have even seen the alleged abuse. Fantastic. This third (or even fourth) hand story is considered evidence strong enough for life-altering legal action. All of this is done despite an array of information documenting CPS's extreme faultiness. Yet, CPS maintains a massive budget subsidised by the very parents they terrorise. This is the nature of government. Abolitionism is the only ethical stance in the face of a coercive agency like Child Protective Services.

NO!

Issue 12

**AGAINST
ADULT
SUPREMACY**

The Psychological Dimension of Revolution (Excerpt)

Ashanti Alston

I had a typical upbringing where the inner-city was Niggertown with all the customs and traditions of racism, sexism and powerlessness. You come into this kind of world ignorant but increasingly learning about people, society, roles and duties. You recognise the supreme authority of the Whites, of the rich and "God," of the police in the streets. Of the preachers and teachers in the churches and schools, and of the parents and older folks in the home and neighbourhood.

Though my first authority figures were my parents (and older brothers and sisters) I soon found out that beyond the world of home, there were others in authoritarian positions over me. But whatever or whoever the authority, the cultural lesson that tied it all together was the one that began in the home: "Respect and obey your parents! Do as we say. we know how to raise you." Disrespect and disobedience was not to be tolerated. Funny, you didn't like it as a child, yet you found yourself following the same customs and traditions when you were in the role as parent, as an authority. It made your life as a child miserable in many respects with the roles and chores, the dos and don'ts and all. But, it was said to be necessary if you were going to fit in and make it in this society.

No child just automatically conforms to such authoritarian raising, such methods. There is naturally rebellion and resistance. But you are just a child, weak and dependent upon those around you to "prepare" you for the real world. So what can you do but eventually submit, conform to their social designs? I am certain that I had to learn through this process of instilling fear in me, to cement each lesson in my soul. Not like I got it much, but I didn't like to get my butt whooped, didn't like to be shouted at, threatened, ordered to stay in the house away from friends and games and all. They were upset with my natural wild zest for life and mostly, all of their measures were designed to restrict it, that "wild zest." I didn't know but it was obvious that I had ongoing choices to make to please them, whether I liked it or not. Mama knows best, Papa knows best… but I didn't know a damn thing! Hell, I guess that I was just supposed to go along with the programme. It was no question that when I did, it brought more rewards than punishment, and when faced with a choice between the two, man, you get tired of punishment! Without ever fully understanding why, you come to realise that the things you truly want, desire to do, think, say, feel… have got to be repressed, hidden and if done at all, done on the sly. Just can't be you. Why?

Once those customs and traditions become a part of a person they form a psychological mask quite unknowingly to the person. You come to don that mask reluctantly, as your every physical, mental and emotional fibre resists. But once its fastened on your face, on your soul, it functions just like your heart pumps blood, lungs air, or stomach digests food. You forget about, or repress the memories of, the traumatic experiences which created the mask, and go on through life not even realising that it governs, influences, pulls and jerks your every physical, emotional and intellectual activity. It effectively cuts you off from being in direct touch with your true feelings, with your spontaneous contact with the outside world, with friends, with your energy, and with your curiosity about life in general.

Poor child has no idea that its dependency upon those who raise him/her is gonna cost him/her that natural, playful, soulful zest for life; its psychic and biological health and development twisted and suffocated by a series of traumatic experiences designed and invoked in the name of God and the American way and good child-rearing practices to produce powerless, dependent, fearful, self-enslaving, law-abiding citizens (first- and second-class). It's sad that parents don't see the real damage they inflect on their children in their rearing methods, but the end-result always shows in the inability of people in general to govern their own lives without an authoritarian figure hovering over them; it shows in their apathy, hopelessness and feelings of insignificance.

After the coup d'etat of the family institution over the natural freedom and aliveness of the child, that child is trained into an adulthood in which it will continue to repress freedom (its full human developmental capacities) and continue the whole process anew in its offspring. What was done to your parents in childhood, they did to you, and you, in turn, do it to your children. And so on, never thinking about the harmful consequences of blindly carrying on traditions which distort our humanity. It is here, though, and in this way of words and behaviour, that the sexism, racism, capitalism, the religious, intellectual and moral belief systems, as well as the lying, dishonesty, irresponsibility, emotional denial, liberalism, manipulation, egotism, slavishness, etc., are taught and passed on.

In sociology the process itself is called "socialisation" or "enculturation." The object is to "civilise" the child and keep everyone bound to the traps of tradition and belief. But what it amounts to is a vast suppression of the force or fire of life within the child or population in general, because it is that "fire" which rebels against any kind of oppressive socialisation which is not in harmony with the free development of a human being's potential for healthy, satisfying love, work and knowledge. What is wanted is a well-behaved, obedient, productive person who will not disturb nor question the established authoritarian order, but will merely carry on as proscribed and arranged for generations.

Generally, there is one brief period in the human development cycle where we are, relatively, free: when the culture has not yet restricted, twisted, or distorted the natural, spontaneous living expressions of a thinking, feeling and doing human being. This period is from birth to 3, 4 or 5 years old. The child is "born free". This is when our emotional, physical and mental energies are most delightfully burning, most alive, vibrant, responsive, honest, curious, sensuous, logical, rational and crazy. You fear not new things or people; you fear not adventure or trying new activities; you don't become stuck in anxieties or depressive moods; nor worry about what others think about you. You are open, receptive and geared to nothing else but life itself and all its pleasure and struggle. You are just a wellspring of energy to love, to learn and to act.

Every day, every minute and every experience in the life of a child is one of curiosity and a powerful drive to learn... about things, people, self. Those eyes are bright, observant. Those hands and arms, legs and feet are moving and touching, reaching. The child, every child, is a natural explorer! Eyes, mouth, ears, hands, senses. Not only does s/he learn and do from seeing, hearing, touching, feeling, tasting the objects of its surrounding reality, they also learn about themselves and the use of the capacities of eyes, ears, hands, legs, feet, tongue, muscles, sexual organs, thinking and feeling and the whole "humanimal" range. In other words, they are on the road – naturally – to self-discovery, in its totality and on his/her own terms. Self and surroundings are one.

These days or years of "born freedom" are not going to last long in our culture. Our society is not geared nor interested in nurturing human development on the basis of natural freedom. It is geared to develop us on the basis of authority – class, race, sex, age, etc. The need to obey, rather than the need to be, is the over-riding concern. This is what makes "childhood" as we had it imposed on us, an oppressive institution. Good ol' western, U.S. childrearing is an innocent appearing, good intentioned fire extinguisher used to put out a fine, sweet, bright and wildly burning human flame, in the person of an uncivilised, unadulterated child. And let it be said again and again, so that there'll be no misunderstanding: The ground-breakers, the spirit-breakers or foundation builders of this pillar of psychological loyalty to the social system is the family. Parents, brothers, sisters and other relevant figures tied to your immediate surroundings.

It is not that the child must not be taught or raised: it is the why's and how's and what actual characteristics are being produced in us by our addiction to the traditions and beliefs that keep them alive. We are born into a society which has been in existence for several hundred years, complete with its own established way of life, life philosophy and institutions for perpetuating its existence via education and other political power institutions. Its basic ways and beliefs, as in terms of sexual and class relationships – the why's and how's – have roots going back 6 to 10 thousand years.

One insignificant, tiny baby, coming into the world knowing nothing of it and at the complete mercy of other people to care for it, cannot contend with society's tremendous and awesome cultural forces.

Whether conscious of it or not, the person accustomed to, and receptive to, the society's authoritarian beliefs and traditions, does not normally challenge her/himself to affirm those "anti-social" deeply-felt feelings or longings for unadulterated life. The beliefs and traditions do not challenge the person to consciously allow his/her sexual, emotional, intellectual and physical seeds to develop in a more natural, less culturally oppressive way. And it is rare the person who will allow the rebel fire of life within to be channeled into the human developmental forms that are indicative of personal and social freedom, consciousness, responsibility and happiness. It is even rarer the person who will know how to follow the faintest or strongest inklings and desires to be free or change the circumstances of life as s/he knows or has known it.

The reason why even revolutionaries – or sincere-meaning people who get involved with movements – cannot change their social circumstances is because they do not recognise, or just deny, the existence of powerful unconscious, self-enslaving emotional habits, thought patterns and defence-mechanisms within them that overwhelms the best and most righteous of intentions and endeavours to change society. This is the inner social dynamic of the mask whose function it is to frustrate and repress the vast potential of each and every human being to be free and wholly alive.

It starts with such seemingly meaningless things as feeding and teaching the child to "cooperate"; cleaning or bathing and teaching the child to be still and "cooperate"; peepee-ing and doodoo-ing and potty-training the child; teaching the child one perspective of life – yours; teaching sexism, racism and other shit whose message is to be "loyal" to Authority. It is here that the saying "action speaks louder than words" is relevant. The overt and subtle messages come across to the memory more through people's actions, their behaviour. For example, parents don't sit a child down and actually say, "You are the inferior one because of your age, sex, and race." It is given from the daily behaviour of parents and significant others. Again, it is not that the child must not be raised or taught – it is the why and how behind it.

The infant can naturally signal hunger and should have her hunger satisfied then. But Mama, many times, ignores this and forces the baby to comply with what's convenient for Mama, or with some so-called scientifically worked out time schedule for feeding. When this happens the baby is being put through some heavy trauma. The baby is not "scientific" nor so rigid. S/he is an organism of natural rhythm and needs, of harmonious instincts and pure feelings. The authoritarian manner of forcing a child to comply, to conform, to submit to a rigid schedule instead of its natural rhythm and signaling, or to force him/her to eat when they're not hungry, or to strap a child to a high-chair and let him sit there until he "learns" how to eat civilised, is cruel punishment. But even in this example, it is done supposedly on the child's behalf – for the child's own good.

To teach us to repress ourselves in the name of respect and obedience to authority (parents, preachers, teachers, principals, police, politicians, etc) dehumanises us. If a child is forbidden to express his/her feelings, explore her/his potentials, s/he will never be able to unfold freely in a rich and joyous life, or in a life of revolution dreaming, creating, destroying, healing, contesting, renewing; the social repression and its learned self-repression is going to negatively affect his/her concept of self and her/his ability to relate positively to self, others and environment with a sense of freedom and responsibility through love, work and critical reflection. The reactions to those traumatic or fearful events in one's earlier life has armoured one's psychological make-up against the natural, the instinctual. Our self-concept is, and has been, continually bombarded with negative experiences and subliminal messages which leave us with the feelings of insignificance, self-hatred, helplessness, powerlessness, and lifelessness. The way we learn to cope with it is by the masquerade.

We'll be able to understand, in greater depth, the problems that block revolution in this country when we are more willing and daring to learn about the psychological dimension, or that dynamic aspect of the mask. It is what one perceptive activist referred to as "self-inflicting psychological oppression." It arose from a discussion of the ways in which people in general, and activists, in spite of their high self-opinions, perpetuate the very society oppressing them by holding on to the ideas, opinions, beliefs, addictions, attitudes, gestures, relationships and established traditions that make this national life powerful and workable for the rich and already powerful. To understand this, to make an honest attempt to understand this, you must step out of the obsession with the masses, or with proving studiousness and loyalty to a particular ideology or belief. For this, you must start by examining your own damn self!

Harmful to Minors

Liz Highleyman

Few issues cause as much consternation as the sexual lives of young people, a fact made abundantly clear to author Judith Levine and the University of Minnesota Press upon publication of *Harmful to Minors: The Perils of Protecting Children from Sex*. In the furore over the book, most commentators have missed Levine's main point: "Sex is not ipso facto harmful to minors." In fact, "America's drive to protect kids from sex is protecting them from nothing. Instead, often it is harming them."

Despite what critics contend, *Harmful to Minors* is not about paedophilia. It tackles a wide range of issues including censorship, statutory rape laws, abstinence-only sex education, abortion, gender, AIDS, and child welfare. The latter issue, which raises questions beyond sexuality about how our society provides for its neediest children, is "the most important one in the book," Levine told AlterNet, and "the real reason the Right is against me." But the inflammatory issue of child-adult sex continues to draw the headlines.

Why does the proposition that youth deserves sexual autonomy, pleasure, and privacy seem so radical? In the 1970s, the sexual revolution was in full swing and the idea that children and teens were sexual beings was accepted, at least among progressives. Books such as Heidi Handman and Peter Brennan's "Sex Handbook: Information and Help for Minors" and Sol Gordon's "You!" showed respect for young people and their ability to make their own sexual decisions.

For the past two decades, though, the religious right has been winning the war against comprehensive sex education, access to abortion and contraception, and the sexual autonomy of young people. By the late 1980s, Gordon had shifted his advice toward parents with "Raising a Child Conservatively in a Sexually Permissive World," and child pornography laws made it illegal to even possess a copy of "Show Me!," an award-winning sex education book for children.

What happened? Levine does not place all the blame on the Right, acknowledging the role cultural feminists played in imposing a regime of overwhelming sexual protectionism. "The Right won, but the mainstream let it," she says. "Comprehensive sex educators had the upper hand in the 1970s, and starting in the 1980s, they allowed their enemies to seize more and more territory, until the Right controlled the law, the language, and the cultural consensus." Add to this the fact that the sexual liberationists of yesterday are parents today, facing all the typical parental fears. As the joke goes, a conservative is a liberal with a teenage daughter. Many people feel a pervasive sense of dread about children and sex, but as Levine notes, things are not appreciably worse now than they were in the past. Children's exposure to sexual images is hardly new, and research indicates that rates of teen sexual activity are not "galloping upward."

As Levine documents throughout the book with copious studies and reviews of news sources, fears of rampant paedophilia, child abduction, ritual abuse, and Internet sexual predators are at best exaggerated, at worst completely unsupported by evidence. For example, studies commissioned by Congress show that between 50 and 150 children are kidnapped and murdered by strangers each year, yet in a Mayo Clinic survey three-quarters of parents said they are afraid their children will be abducted. And a 1994 U.S. government report analysing over 12,000 accusations of Satanic ritual abuse found "not a single case where there was clear corroborating evidence."

Nevertheless, parents are nervous – even squeamish – about their children's and teens' sexuality, often seeking to deny their offspring the sexual freedoms they themselves demanded at the same age. Physician Victor Strasburger has even penned a paean to hypocrisy entitled "Getting Your Kids to Say 'No' in the '90s When You Said 'Yes' in the '60s." In the past two decades youthful sexual desire has become widely pathologised. As Levine notes, "It's as if (parents) cannot imagine that their kids seek sex for the same reasons they do: They like or love the person they are having it with. It gives them a sense of beauty, worthiness, happiness, or power. And it feels good."

The panic surrounding youthful sexuality can perhaps best be compared to the war on drugs: Both are based on ideology rather than science, and no amount of evidence can change the minds of true believers. Both mask underlying social agendas in which concern for children is used to control the behaviour of adults. And both engender problems of credibility as young people reject exhortations to "do as I say, not as I did." Many adults recognise that they made mistakes in their youth and understandably wish to spare children similar missteps, especially in the age of AIDS. Yet too often, Levine contends, censorship and abstinence-only sex education are really an effort to hold back children's coming of age, offering parents an illusory "freedom from watching their kids grow up."

But denying young people knowledge about sex will not help them become responsible sexual citizens. As Levine notes, children today know about IPOs and the hole in the ozone layer, just as they know about abortion and sadomasochism. Parents cannot block out all uncomfortable knowledge. In order "to give children a fighting chance in navigating the sexual world," Levine says, "adults need to saturate it with accurate, realistic information and abundant, varied images and narratives of love and sex."

If a person truly has the good of young people in mind, one would hope he or she would be interested in what research has to reveal. *Harmful to Minors* offers a plethora of findings, from studies showing that exposure to sexually explicit images does not harm children, to evidence that teens' sexual relationships with adults are not uniformly devastating, to research on the ineffectiveness of abstinence-only education in delaying sexual activity. But more crucial than research is listening to what children and teens have to say about their own experiences, honestly acknowledging our own experiences at those ages, and applying a healthy dose of common sense. While we are constantly reminded of the importance of believing young people's allegations of coercion and abuse, too often we give considerably less credence to their avowals of consent and pleasure.

Most of us came across sexual images in our youth, and most of us did not turn out to be sexual monsters. Further, there is no evidence that cultures in which explicit sexual imagery is prevalent (such as Denmark or the Netherlands) produce more sexual pathology than those in which such material is forbidden; in fact, there are indications that quite the opposite is the case. In the explosive realm of adult-youth sex, many teens say that such relationships can be consensual and positive. And more than a few of us remember having such positive sexual relationships with adults when we ourselves were teens.

"Teens often seek out sex with older people, and they do so for understandable reasons: an older person makes them feel sexy and grown up, protected and special," writes Levine. "Often the sex is better than it would be with a peer who has as little skill as they do. For some teens, a romance with an older person can feel more like salvation than victimisation." Romantic heartbreak – and plain old bad sex – are just as likely with same-age peers as with older partners. Within the gay community, especially, one often hears fond reminiscences of youthful sexual relationships with adults. For many gay men, a teenage relationship with an older man was their release from a homophobic family and peers and their introduction to a supportive community.

As lesbian syndicated columnist Paula Martinac recently wrote, the differences of opinion between gay men and lesbians regarding adult-youth sexuality represent an ongoing rift within the gay community. Mainstream gay and lesbian groups understandably wish to disassociate themselves from sordid accusations of paedophilia – and correctly point out that the vast majority of child sexual abuse is perpetrated by heterosexual men – but they cannot so easily distance the community from its long history of gay icons who have spoken and written positively about adult-teen relationships.

As for abstinence-only education, young people in Western European countries where children receive comprehensive sex education and where sex is treated as a normal and healthy part of life do not experience more sex-related pathology. Quite the contrary, according to The Surgeon General's Call to Action to Promote Sexual Health and Responsible Sexual Behaviour published last year by the Department of Health and Human Services, other Western countries have lower rates of teen pregnancy, abortion, sexually transmitted disease, AIDS, rape, incest and child abuse than the U.S.

Levine has taken considerable heat for holding up as a "good model" the Netherlands' age of consent law, under which young people ages 12-16 can legally consent to sex with older people who are not parents or authority figures, but under which charges can be brought if teens or their parents (with the Approval of the Council for the Protection of Children) believe the young person is being exploited. But her support for the Dutch law cannot be taken out of the context of that country's social welfare system and relaxed cultural attitudes about sex. "In the Netherlands, children are respected as citizens with rights like everyone else, to housing, health care, good day care, school, and college," Levine told AlterNet. "They get sexuality education from the get-go, condoms are available in vending machines everywhere, abortion is free from the national health service, their parents receive generous parental leave and, if they choose to stay home longer with the kids, social welfare benefits to subsidise that important work. While protecting children, the Dutch (and other Europeans) do not infantilise them."

The child welfare issue has been all but neglected in the controversy surrounding *Harmful to Minors*. Today in the U.S. the poverty rate stands at over 10 percent, with children making up an increasing proportion of the poor. In the only developed nation that does not provide universal health care, some 11 million children under age 18 are uninsured. A fifth of American women get no prenatal care, and the U.S. infant mortality rate lags behind that of twenty other industrialised countries. And virtually every sex-related problem, from AIDS to incest, is correlated with poverty. It is these conditions, argues Levine – not paedophiles or pornography – that are truly harming young people. "Poor people aren't less moral than rich people," Levine writes, "but poverty, like sex, is a phenomenon rooted in moral priorities, a result of deliberate fiscal and social policies that obstruct the fair distribution of health, education, and wealth in a wealthy country. The result, often, is an unfair distribution of sexual health and happiness, too."

Nevertheless, according to a 1997 Public Agenda survey, Americans persist in defining sex-related problems as moral rather than material, and thus focusing on solutions that are "character building, not situation bettering." Levine's conclusion that "economic security is necessary for sexual safety" aims at the heart of the religious right's agenda of privatisation, parental rights, and consolidation of the authority of the nuclear family over the interests of society and the needs of the younger generation. But such misplaced priorities are nothing new: In the late 19th century, as industrialisation drove children into the factories, moralistic adults worried about saving them from sex. From Levine's point of view, children are not the property of their parents and must be treated as citizens in their own right.

"Legally designating a class of people categorically unable to consent to sexual relations is not the best way to protect children, particularly when 'children' include everyone from birth to eighteen," she writes. Indeed, Levine finds such an idea reminiscent of the now discredited dogma – held by both social conservatives and some feminists – that women, too, were paragons of innocence who did not experience desire, required protection, and were not truly capable of consent. And how, she wonders, has it come to pass that "it is only in the area of violent criminal activity that children (some as young as 11) are considered fully mature"? How can we expect children and teens to learn about healthy sex and relationships if they cannot experiment and explore, with access to increasing information, freedom, and responsibility as they get older?

How can we hope that young people who have received abstinence-only sex education, been shielded from sexually explicit material in the media and on the internet, been deprived of non-sexual touch from adults, and had no opportunity for sexual play with their peers, will magically transform into worldly, responsible, sexually healthy adults upon attaining the age of majority (whatever that happens to be wherever they live)? Experts agree that most young people engage in sex by the end of their teens. Clearly, attempts to prevent sex by withholding knowledge have been ineffectual in achieving that goal, but they have impeded efforts to prevent unwanted pregnancy, AIDS and other problems associated with sexual ignorance.

The idea that young people must never have – or even hear much about – sex makes it difficult to teach them about the differences between consensual and nonconsensual sex, between healthy and exploitative sex, between safe and unsafe sex.

"If sexual expertise is expected of adults, the rudiments must be taught to children," insists Levine. "If educators want to be credible about sexual responsibility, they have to be forthright about sexual joy. If parents want their kids to be happy now and later, it is their duty, and should be their delight, to help them learn to love well, which is to say respectfully of others and themselves, skilfully in body and heart, morally as lovers, friends, and citizens."

I Am Nahid

Nahid W.

I am Nahid
I am the light of the world
I rise out of the black ocean
and become the desire of the nations
I dream
of knowledge for the children of my country
I dream
of equal rights for the women of my nation
I dream of a peaceful land
War and terrorists
invade my dreams,
kill me, cut me apart
but I know that the stars will rise
as I rise out of the black ocean
and become the desire of the nations
I am the light of the world
I am Nahid

Nahid W. was born in a northeastern province of Afghanistan in 1993 but grew up in a neighbouring country as a refugee from the wars.

NO!

ISSUE 13

**AGAINST
ADULT
SUPREMACY**

I will not

I will not

I will not

I will not

I will not

i,ll not

ll not

,ll not

,ill not

Against Parental Rights

Samantha Godwin

Excerpt: academia.edu/19663920/Against_Parental_Rights

There is a significant disjunction between child protectionist theory and rhetoric and the extent of parental powers. The extensive deference to parental preference and discretion seems to have little to do with preserving children's interests and more to do with parental autonomy. We must conclude that only respect for parental autonomy and freedom, rather than child protection, would lead to the belief that parents ought to be granted rights beyond those narrowly derivable from a child's interests. This is true not only of the particular legally recognised parents' rights found in American case law, but also more generally for any conception of parental rights of an independent vitality. This raises normative problems for any version of parental rights independent from children's interests.

When the domain of a person's freedom is thought to extend beyond their body to include the exclusive control of physical things in the world, we think of those things as being their possessions. For example, someone who owns a car is legally at liberty to do with it things that non-owners are not free to do with the car. Car owners are not necessarily at liberty to do everything physically possible to their car—they cannot legally set it on fire in the middle of a city street or drive it past the speed limit while intoxicated. The car's owner is, however, legally permitted to drive it (if licensed) and to exert control over it in ways that other people who are not its owner may not. Car owners can do these things because their car belongs to them. It is their car in the sense of it being a possession and not just having a certain relationship to them.

Restricting what an owner can do with their car, or imposing requirements for car ownership, is thought to restrict the car owner's freedom and autonomy, although such restrictions may be justified in reference to other values. In contrast, if a non-owner is restricted from using the same car without the owner's permission, their freedom is not thought compromised in the same way, because their unauthorised actions are considered theft, conversion, or vandalism. Such actions are beyond what is thought to constitute the domain of the non-owners freedom with regard to someone else's car precisely because it belongs to someone else and does not belong to them.

Parents' prerogatives with regard to their own children that adults do not generally have with regard to someone else's children are construed in a parallel manner. Just as the most basic and general rule of property is that owners may exert exclusive control over that which is their property, the basic attitude of most adults towards children is that it is not right to tell someone how to raise their own child or to try to do it for them. Just as a car thief violates the rights of the owner and not the car, the non-parent acting in deference to parental authority typically understands this deference as respecting the parent.

Relatively few in the political mainstream today speak of parents as the owners of their children, but the implied logic of parental rights suggests a type of ownership or quasi-property interest in children. In many regards, this allocation of powers to parents functions as a sort of ownership, and some (though not all) of the putative legal interests that parents have in their children can be compared to property interests. For example, that the religious education of a particular parent's child is purportedly a matter of that parent's freedom, but the religious education of someone else's child is not, makes sense only if one accepts that in some way children belong to their parents as possessions that the scope of their freedom extends over. The idea that parents can impose on their child what others cannot, because that child is their child and belongs to them, and not to others, amounts to a belief that parents are functionally related to their children as car owners are to their cars. This is of course not to say that quasi-ownership is the only dimension of how parents relate to children legally or socially, but that it is a significant element in the function and legitimacy of parent-child power dynamics.

People often speak in possessive terms about people who are not their children – for example, "my friend," "my niece," "my dentist," "my employer" – without implying a possessory interest to control the friend, niece, dentist, or employer. Parental possessory interests, however, are much more than linguistic conventions. It is never thought to be a matter of an aunt's freedom that she should be able to compel her niece to visit a disliked family friend or to forbid her niece from associating with a child whom she distrusts. To do so would be thought to trespass on the niece's parent's rights to make choices for the niece. This is closely parallel to the way that using someone's chattel property without their permission would be a trespass against the owner's property rights. In both instances the actual interests of the possession in question does not directly enter into the equation – even if the aunt were acting in the niece's best interests, she would have no defence to violating the parents' interests in their child.

John Holt aptly observed that:

> the family was not invented, nor has it evolved, to make children happy or
> to provide a secure emotional and psychological background to grow up in.

If it just so happened that families based on parental domination over children were in fact the optimal legal arrangement for children, it would be a coincidence. Parents generally, and fathers in particular, have held dominion over their children for far longer than the "best interests of the child" rhetoric has been at the fore of legal and political discourse around children. Under ancient Roman law, fathers had the right to kill their children, and in the Massachusetts Bay Colony, children could be put to death for disobeying their parents under laws informed by a belief that children are born in sin and must therefore submit to adult authority.

Rather than viewing children within a protectionist framework, at least prior to the 17th century, children were regarded as the property of their fathers. In the 15th century, it was typical in England for fathers to contract out their children into indentured servitude in other adult's homes from the age of seven or nine until they were between fourteen and eighteen. Widely-cited historian of childhood Philippe Aries noted these arrangements in the Middle Ages were not thought to have anything to do with ensuring children's best interests, welfare, or optimal psychological development. Instead, adults could receive better service from children if they sent their own children to work for other adults while taking in others' children to work for them.

Contemporary parental rights – though no longer expressly articulated as property rights – continue to function much the same although diminished in scope. Unlike in the 17th century, given that it is now seen as morally abhorrent to regard people as chattel, the rhetoric and justificatory framework has changed completely while the scope of parents' pseudo-property rights in their children has been only modestly curtailed. In other words, parental rights were property rights and remain functionally property rights, but it has become so taboo to speak of them as such, so that the way parental power actually functions has become obscure.

Many rights given to parents are especially property-like. Just as coverture laws historically held that a married woman's rights were subsumed into her husband's, such that her property belonged to her husband, in the U.S., parents have a "right to the child's services and earnings" in 47 of 50 states. Barnett and Spradlin have pointed out that being able to order a child to work and then seizing their earnings is in effect a type of economic slavery. The procedure for a child to be rid of parental custody is called emancipation, not coincidentally the term used to describe freeing slaves. Emancipation frequently requires that the parents have effectively abandoned their child or that the child has married with parental permission, reflecting very anachronistic notions of patriarchal property and power.

Although there is no free market in the sale of children, commercial gestational surrogacy is a lawful transaction in some U.S. states (such as California). The official understanding in many states is that surrogates are paid for their services, but in effect surrogates are paid to produce and surrender babies to someone else.

Richard Posner has argued that understanding surrogacy as a form of "baby selling" is mere "argumentation by epithet" and that what a surrogate sells "is not the baby but her parental rights." When one person sells her property to another, the sale legally transfers not the item itself (possession of which might be physically transferred without a sale, through theft or lending), but rather the legal property rights concerning the item.

Property ownership of chattel is not mere possession, but the legal right to control it, use it within the bounds of the law, and exclude others from using it without permission, and it is this bundle of legal rights that is transferred by sale. Likewise, parental rights include the right to control a child and to exclude others from accessing that child. In this regard, arguing that commercial surrogacy sells not children but parental rights makes little sense: selling parental rights is selling the legal right to control a child, just as selling chattel property is selling the legal right to control the chattel property.

Even in states that prohibit surrogacy, parents are permitted other means of transferring rights over their children in a property-like fashion. Parents can "give up a child" for adoption by an adult of their choice, demonstrating a right similar to the right to alienate property through a gift (though not a sale). Children have no parallel right to claim adoption by a preferred potential parent. Parents can even decide who should "inherit" their children if they die while their children are minors by naming guardians in their wills, just as they can name beneficiaries to receive their personal property.

Although it is uncommon to expressly consider children as "property," it is not uncommon to think of children as possessions. Malfrid Grude Flekkoy argued:

> Many adults, some on the basis of teachings of their religion, others in spite of intellectual acceptance of the opposite, feel that they have the same right of possession to the child-product as to other products, or that the ownership right to their child is stronger than other rights of possession, even comparing these rights with the legal rights connected with some other products.

There was substantial discussion in the popular media in 2013 of whether or not children "belong to their parents" after MSNBC news anchor Melissa Harris-Perry stated in a promotional that "we have to break though our private idea that kids belong to their parents or kids belong to their families and recognise that kids belong to whole communities." Although describing children as belonging to the community is also problematic in that it objectifies children as common resources, conservative media figures reacted with outrage of a different sort, believing that children do in fact belong to their parents. More recently, libertarian Senator Rand Paul made this point explicitly by making the statement that "the state doesn't own your children, parents own the children."

That parents' legal interests in children function as property rights does not of course imply that children are property as a matter of law on a formal level. There are also numerous ways in which children's status is not analogous to most forms of property. For example, although parents have some rights to transfer their child to another guardian, most property can be expressly sold, and few forms of property place nearly such substantial legal duties on owners as child custody places on parents. It is also of vital social relevance that while parents are often possessive of their children, they do not tend to conceptualise children literally as property and most would likely find terming them as such objectionable. Children also have legal claims on their parents. Nonetheless, to the extent that parental legal rights are in effect possessory interests or quasi-property rights, this ought to be a basis for regarding them as illegitimate and unwarranted.

athematics

The familiar, hierarchical sequence of math instruction starts with counting, followed by addition and subtraction, then multiplication and division. The computational set expands to include bigger and bigger numbers, and at some point, fractions enter the picture, too. Then in early adolescence, students are introduced to patterns of numbers and letters, in the entirely new subject of algebra. A minority of students then wend their way through geometry, trigonometry and, finally, calculus, which is considered the pinnacle of high-school-level math.

But this progression actually "has nothing to do with how people think, how children grow and learn, or how mathematics is built," says pioneering math educator and curriculum designer Maria Droujkova. She echoes a number of voices from around the world that want to revolutionise the way math is taught, bringing it more in line with these principles. The current sequence is merely an entrenched historical accident that strips much of the fun out of what she describes as the "playful universe" of mathematics, with its more than 60 top-level disciplines, and its manifestations in everything from weaving to building, nature, music and art. Worse, the standard curriculum starts with arithmetic, which Droujkova says is much harder for young children than playful activities based on supposedly more advanced fields of mathematics.

"Calculations kids are forced to do are often so developmentally inappropriate, the experience amounts to torture," she says. They also miss the essential point – that mathematics is fundamentally about patterns and structures, rather than "little manipulations of numbers," as she puts it. It's akin to budding filmmakers learning first about costumes, lighting and other technical aspects, rather than about crafting meaningful stories. This turns many children off to math from an early age. It also prevents many others from learning math as efficiently or deeply as they might otherwise. Droujkova and her colleagues have noticed that most of the adults they meet have "math grief stories," as she describes them. They recall how a single course – or even a single topic, such as fractions – derailed them from the sequential track. She herself has watched more than a few grown-ups "burst out crying during interviews, reliving the anxieties and lost hopes of their young selves."

Droujkova, who earned her PhD in math education in the United States after immigrating here from Ukraine, advocates a more holistic approach she calls "natural math," which she teaches to children as young as toddlers, and their parents. This approach, covered in the book she co-authored with Yelena McManaman, "Moebius Noodles: Adventurous math for the playground crowd," hinges on harnessing students' powerful and surprisingly productive instincts for playful exploration to guide them on a personal journey through the subject. Says Droujkova: "Studies have shown that games or free play are efficient ways for children to learn, and they enjoy them. They also lead the way into the more structured and even more creative work of noticing, remixing and building mathematical patterns."

Finding an appropriate path hinges on appreciating an often-overlooked fact, that "the complexity of the idea and the difficulty of doing it are separate, independent dimensions," she says. "Unfortunately a lot of what little children are offered is simple but hard – primitive ideas that are hard for humans to implement," because they readily tax the limits of working memory, attention, precision and other cognitive functions. Examples of activities that fall into the "simple but hard" quadrant: Building a trench with a spoon (a military punishment that involves many small, repetitive tasks, akin to doing 100 two-digit addition problems on a typical worksheet, as Droujkova points out), or memorising multiplication tables as individual facts rather than patterns. Far better, she says, to start by creating rich and social mathematical experiences that are complex (allowing them to be taken in many different directions) yet easy (making them conducive to immediate play). Activities that fall into this quadrant: building a house with LEGO blocks, doing origami or snowflake cut-outs, or using a pretend "function box" that transforms objects (and can also be used in combination with a second machine to compose functions, or backwards to invert a function, and so on). "You can take any branch of mathematics and find things that are both complex and easy in it," Droujkova says. "My quest, with several colleagues around the world, is to take the treasure of mathematics and find the accessible ways into all of it."

She started with algebra and calculus, because they're "pattern-drafter tools, designer tools, maker tools – they support cool free play." So "Moebius Noodles" includes activities such as making fractals (to foster an appreciation of the ideas of recursion and infinitesimals) and "mirror books" (mirrors that are taped to each other like the covers of a book and can be angled in different ways around an object to introduce the concepts of infinity and transformations). "It's not the subject of calculus as formally taught in college," Droujkova notes. "But before we get there, we want to have hands-on, grounded, metaphoric play. At the free play level, you are learning in a very fundamental way – you really own your concept, mentally, physically, emotionally, culturally." This approach "gives you deep roots, so the canopy of the high abstraction does not wither. What is learned without play is qualitatively different. It helps with test taking and mundane exercises, but it does nothing for logical thinking and problem solving. These things are separate, and you can't get here from there." She doesn't expect children to be able to solve formal equations at age five, but that's okay. "There are levels of understanding," she says. "You don't want to shackle people into a formal understanding too early." After the informal level comes the level where students discuss ideas and notice patterns. Then comes the formal level, where students can use abstract words, graphs, and formulas. But ideally, a playful aspect is retained along the entire journey. "This is what mathematicians do – they play with abstract ideas, but they still play."

Droujkova notes that natural math – whose slogan is "make math your own, to make your own math" – is essentially a "freedom movement." She explains: "We work toward freedom at many levels – the free play of little kids, the agency of families and local groups in organising math activities, the autonomy of artists and makers, and even liberty for us curriculum designers. No single piece of mathematics is right for everyone. People are different, and people need to approach mathematics differently." For example, in a group learning about the properties of rhombuses, an artistically inclined person might prefer to draw a rhombus, a programmer might code one, a philosopher might discuss the essence of rhombi, and an origami master might fold a paper rhombus. Nor does everyone need to learn any particular piece of mathematics, aside from what's essential to function in his or her culture. Many people live to a ripe and happy old age without knowing calculus, for example. "At the same time, the world would be better off with a higher literacy for mathematics, and humanity as a whole needs advanced math to make it through the next 100 years, because there are pretty complex problems we're facing."

Children need to be exposed to a variety of math styles to find the one that suits them best. But they also need to see meaningful (to them) people doing meaningful things with math and enjoying the experience. Math circles, where people help one another, are growing fast and are one way to achieve this. Math know-how (activities and examples) "must come with communities of practice that help newbies make sense of it," Droujkova says. "One does not work without the other." Regardless, if learning is to be as efficient and deep as possible, it's essential that it be done freely. That means giving children a voice in which activities to participate, for how long, and also the level of mastery they want to achieve. ("This is the biggest clash with traditional curriculum development," Droujkova notes.)

Adults must be prepared for those times when a child would rather be doing something other than the planned activity. Says Droujkova: "The role of adults is to inspire, by saying things like, 'Ooh, what a complex shape – have you noticed the curve is made out of straight lines?' Provide math connections with whatever kids are doing. This is hard to do – it requires both pedagogical and math concept knowledge, but it can be learned. And everyone can easily give general support: 'How very interesting, I will investigate more.' You can then look online, or ask on a math circle forum, to find out what it means mathematically." It's also helpful to have a variety of interesting materials on hand and to be okay with the idea of kids taking breaks as needed. Droujkova has noticed that in most groups, there are one or two kids do something else, while the rest do the main activity. (The non-participants still absorb a surprising amount, she adds.)

Pushback has come primarily from two very different (and usually opposing) camps. One is the "let kids be kids" cohort, which worries that legitimising the idea of involving toddlers with algebra and calculus will tempt Tiger Mom types to push their kids into formal abstractions in these subjects at ever younger ages, even though that would completely miss the point. Other critics fall into the "back to basics" camp, which contends that all this play will prevent kids from becoming fluid in traditional calculation skills. Droujkova views these criticisms as indicative of something much bigger: "They reflect rather deep chasms between different philosophies of education, or more broadly, differences in the futures we pave for kids. When we assign a lot of similar exercises, we picture kids in situations that require industrial precision." Giving children logic puzzles or open projects, on the other hand, indicates aspirations of them growing up to become explorers or designers. "It does not work that directly," she concedes, "but these beliefs dictate what mathematics education the grown-ups select or make for the kids."

There are also some who worry about whether this approach is practical for disenfranchised populations. Droujkova says that it can be led by any "somewhat literate" adult; the key is to have the right support network in place. She and her colleagues are striving to empower local networks and enhance accessibility on all fronts: mathematical, cultural and financial. They have made their materials and courses open under Creative Commons, and designed activities that require only readily available materials. "The know-how about making community-centred, open learning available to disenfranchised populations is growing," Droujkova notes, citing experiments by Sugata Mitra and Dave Eggers. Online hubs can connect like-minded community members, and online courses and support are available to parents, teachers and teenagers who want to lead local groups.

Droujkova says one of the biggest challenges has been the mindsets of the grown-ups. Parents are tempted to replay their "bad old days" of math instruction with their kids, she says. With these calculus and algebra games, though, "parents say they get a fresh start. They can experience the joy of mathematical play anew, like babies in a new world."

Towards an Anti-Work Education

Nick Ford

I've discussed Peter Gray before when I reviewed extrinsic and internal goals. As I said there, some of the research that Gray was using seemed shaky at best. Particularly in merely noting the correlation of various negative things that have happened to children in the last few decades with a lack of play. For example, the increase in depression, suicide attempts and so on can just as easily be attributed to better diagnosing mental illness and taking suicide more seriously and measuring the rate of it better. Neither of these things happening more necessarily has to do with a decrease in play even if the two match up on graphs.

Moreover, Gray's field of study, evolutionary psychology (EP), has widely been criticised as a science of "just-so" stories that are reductionist in method, restricting in its conclusions, and largely can't be tested. Now, I'm not an expert on EP and I'm not trying to suggest that the entire field is bunk, as others have. But I just want to stress some amount of caution before we proceed and consider an article Gray wrote back in 2013 on play called The Play Deficit.

Once again, Gray hits on many of my ideological favourite spots. He emphasises play, he advocates youth empowerment, self-directed learned, lauds the Subury Valley School, and in general, praises cooperation and egalitarian relations over authoritarian ones. So there's a lot for me to like about Gray's article. I even like his definition of equality:

> The golden rule of social play is not 'Do unto others as you would have them do unto you.' Rather, it's something much more difficult: 'Do unto others as they would have you do unto them.' To do that, you have to get into other people's minds and see from their points of view. Children practise that all the time in social play. The equality of play is not the equality of sameness. Rather, it is the equality that comes from respecting individual differences and treating each person's needs and wishes as equally important. That's also, I think, the best interpretation of Thomas Jefferson's line that all men are created equal. We're not all equally strong, equally quick-witted, equally healthy; but we are all equally worthy of respect and of having our needs met.

Now, I'm not sure if I agree with such a broad statement that Gray makes at the end. Some people's needs do come from a need to dominate others. Though, to be fair, I'm sure Gray would disagree this is a need that is equally worthy of respect. So perhaps I'm guilty of nitpicking here, which would, admittedly, be nothing new. In any case, the fact that Gray thinks to differentiate separate forms of equality, emphasise individuality over sameness and that a certain sort of respect is due to us in so far as we follow the golden rule of social play is a much better form of equality than I usually see advocated. Despite these admirable qualities of Gray's article he continues to denote possibly spurious correlations:

> The decline in opportunity to play has also been accompanied by a decline in empathy and a rise in narcissism, both of which have been assessed since the late 1970s with standard questionnaires given to normative samples of college students. Empathy refers to the ability and tendency to see from another person's point of view and experience what that person experiences. Narcissism refers to inflated self-regard, coupled with a lack of concern for others and an inability to connect emotionally with others. A decline of empathy and a rise in narcissism are exactly what we would expect to see in children who have little opportunity to play socially. Children can't learn these social skills and values in school, because school is an authoritarian, not a democratic setting. School fosters competition, not co-operation; and children there are not free to quit when others fail to respect their needs and wishes.

So, "normative" samples are a good thing. But not linking to the studies in question isn't. Further, with any college study, it must be kept in mind that college samples don't necessarily reflect general populations. They are often small sample size studies that when not repeated (not applicable here though, to be fair) should be taken with a grain of salt, to say the least. Even when they are repeated, I would still stress that Gray's use of the word "accompanied" is masking the fact that he's only relying on correlations and studies from one portion of population to say this is the case.

And while, yes, you would expect less empathy and more narcissism from people who grow up less and less around others in the form of play there's a few issues with this:

1. An expectation does not equal a causation

2. Just because you expect result A from Thing B doesn't mean Thing B is the only possible thing that could've caused this chain of events. There are other causes that may have have roles or inputs in the chain of events you've been analysing.

3. In this example, we could also expect a rise of narcissism and reduction in empathy from kids being around multi-media (TV, smartphones, the internet, etc.) than around other kids and playing with them. But yet, Gray doesn't seem to make a case that we should limit these things.

Granted, my example in 3. is a superficial correlation at best, but that's my point. It's a struggle for me, because there's much to like about Gray for me, as I've said before. But his methods and citations (even when he does give them, as he did in his

Psychology Today article) just aren't solid enough to build his case on. But let's move on from that and focus on some of his stronger points:

> In another branch of my research I've studied how children learn at a radically alternative school, the Sudbury Valley School. It's called a school, but is as different from what we normally think of as 'school' as you can imagine. The students – who range in age from four to about 19 – are free all day to do whatever they want, as long as they don't break any of the school rules. The rules have nothing to do with learning; they have to do with keeping peace and order.

> …[T]he school has been in existence for 45 years now and has many hundreds of graduates, who are doing just fine in the real world, not because their school taught them anything, but because it allowed them to learn whatever they wanted. And, in line with Groos's theory, what children in our culture want to learn when they are free turns out to be skills that are valued in our culture and that lead to good jobs and satisfying lives. When they play, these students learn to read, calculate, and use computers with the same playful passion with which hunter-gatherer kids learn to hunt and gather. They don't necessarily think of themselves as learning. They think of themselves as just playing, or 'doing things', but in the process they are learning.

> Even more important than specific skills are the attitudes that they learn. They learn to take responsibility for themselves and their community, and they learn that life is fun, even (maybe especially) when it involves doing things that are difficult. I should add that this is not an expensive school; it operates on less than half as much, per student, as the local state schools and far less than most private schools.

I tried to apply to the Sudbury Valley School at one point, to become a staff member. Suffice it say, it didn't work out, but I still hold a big spot in my heart for this school and what they do. Gray's example of Hunter Gatherer's seems too messy and filled with confounding factors.

But having read a few of Sudbury's own books (a requirement if you want to apply to a position there so you can understand their philosophy better) I can say with a better sense of judgment that what Gray says here seems true. Both through the philosophy of the school itself and the books that collect the stories of children who went there. The person Gray mentions, Karl Groos, was one of the first researchers on the subject of play. He developed a theory later called "practice theory of play". That by playing more and more animals become better adaptable to their environment and thus were more easily selected for natural selection in positive ways. I'm not sure how well this translates to humans but Groos apparently was:

> He pointed out that humans, having much more to learn than other species, are the most playful of all animals. Human children, unlike the young of other species, must learn different skills depending on the culture in which they are developing. Therefore, he argued, natural selection in humans favoured a strong drive for children to observe the activities of their elders and incorporate those activities into their play. He suggested that children in every culture, when allowed to play freely, play not only at the skills that are valuable to people everywhere (such as two-legged walking and running), but also at the skills that are specific to their culture (such as shooting bows and arrows or herding cattle).

And so too with Sudbury do children learn play as a form of practice from which to live by and adapt to their environments. There's an interesting way that people justify schools: Test scores. But what good are test scores if you can't exist outside of tests? The "real test", as corny as it may sound, is life itself. It's not the regimented, organised and highly legible experiences of mandatory testing in schools. The tests we face in life are likely to be much more unpredictable and hard to follow then what stares us in the face on our desks. Gray uses China as a particular example:

> In an article entitled 'The Test Chinese Schools Still Fail' in The Wall Street Journal in December 2010, Jiang Xueqin, a prominent Chinese educator, wrote: 'The failings of a rote-memorisation system are well known: lack of social and practical skills, absence of self-discipline and imagination, loss of curiosity and passion for learning. One way we'll know we're succeeding in changing China's schools is when those scores [on standardised tests] come down.' Meanwhile, Yong Zhao, an American education professor who grew up in China and specialises in comparing the Chinese educational system with the system in the US, notes that a common term used in China to refer to graduates is gaofen dineng, meaning 'high scores but low ability'. Because students spend nearly all their time studying, they have little opportunity to be creative, take initiative, or develop physical and social skills: in short, they have little opportunity to play.

I'm tired of the "real world" trope for college students and students. There are plenty of ways that real life (whatever that means) intersects with student life as well. There are ways that student life can be harder than the outside life (consider balancing a job and being a student… many students likely don't have to given college debt) and denying these experiences seems nothing but belittling to me. All of that said, as tired as I am of this trope, the structure of college and anything below it are obviously restricted or liberated in high-minded ways by people who think they know better for others. Self-directed learning, here I agree with Gray quite strongly, better prepares children or anyone for the rough things life can throw at us. And what happens when Sudbury graduates move on to the "real world"?:

> Graduates were continuing to play the activities they had loved as students, with the same joy, passion, and creativity, but now they were making a living at it. There were professional musicians who had played intensively with music when they were students, and computer programmers who had spent most of their time as students playing with computers. One woman, who was the captain of a cruise ship, had spent much of her time as a student playing on the water, first with toy boats and then with real ones. A man who was a sought-after machinist and inventor had spent his childhood playfully building things and taking things apart to see how they worked.

Free play allowed these children to develop themselves into more than capable adults. Adults who can handle not only the faults in our state-capitalist system but come through looking not too shabby, honestly. They find their passions, they explore them and they take them to the end. Maybe that won't guarantee them a career as a CEO or mean they'll not be a bit weirder than other people in some important ways. But it's my hope that that weirdness will spread.

I'm always looking for excuses to mention my favourite anarchist, Voltairine de Cleyre, and her essay Modern Educational Reform is such an excuse.

> The really Ideal School, which would not be a compromise, would be a boarding school built in the country, having a farm attached, and workshops where useful crafts might be learned, in daily connection with intellectual training. It presupposes teachers able to train little children to habits of health, order, and neatness, in the utmost detail, and yet not tyrants or rigid disciplinarians. In free contact with nature, the children would learn to use their limbs as nature meant, feel their intimate relationship with the growing life of other sorts, form a profound respect for work and an estimate of the value of it; wish to become real doers in the world, and not mere gatherers in of other men's products; and with the respect for work, the appreciation of work, the desire to work, will come the pride of the true workman who will know how to maintain his dignity and the dignity of what he does.

Of course, that may sound like what Sudbury is, but it was written many decades before. Voltairine had other things to go off of however, like Fransisco Ferrer and his Modern Schools which serves as the partial basis for the title of her essay.

This leads me to my final point: I think what Gray, Sudbury and Voltairine all suggest here are great foundations for the building of an anti-work education. An education that builds self-reliance, individuality, versatility and generally speaking, a lack of needing others to meet ones needs. A lack of needing masters, gods, managers, bosses, CEOs, systems, societies, teams and anything else that may or may not interfere with the free action of individuals. Having individuals grow up to be self-reliant means they can work for themselves or freely associate with others on whatever basis gives them pleasure and seems most virtuous. They can depart at any time and in that way associations become a form of play itself. A way for people to practice free and voluntary actions that are meaningful to all participants involved, but are also seen as fun. Association becomes less about irrational biases, social signalling and social status. Instead, they become much more about the mutuality and reciprocity of each others individuality being optimised. About their individuality being respected by the actions of those they choose to associate with, for however long that may be.

An anti-work education would be done on this basis. Perhaps it wouldn't need schools and we could go farther into the realm of unschooling. Why shouldn't we dismantle the entire institution of schools itself and let children build their own structures and lead their own lives?

Let them abolish work in their own lives!

NO!

Issue 14

AGAINST ADULT SUPREMACY

The Pedagogy of Religion

Peter Gelderloos

It was my grandfather's memorial service, and the Dutch Reform pastor took a break from talking about God and Heaven to the members of the congregation, in which I, as a dutiful grandson, was unfortunately included for the moment, in order to address the children in the audience, the grand-kids and great grand-kids of the deceased, nearly all of them baptised into the Dutch Reform church or a like-minded denomination, as the apple does not fall far from the tree.

"Now, you all might be wondering," began the pastor in a condescending tone, only slightly more exact in diction and enunciation than that with which he had been addressing the adults, "what all this is about. On Friday, when you found out that Grandpa died, your mommy and your daddy told you that Grandpa had gone to Heaven. They told you that he is leaving us for a while, because God called him up to be with Him in Heaven." His surety of this occurrence seemed about as strong as his conviction regarding my grandfather's posthumous fate. The one being an empirical fact (mommy and daddy either did or they did not explain the death in this fashion) and the other a super-sensory, non-rational statement of faith (Heaven and the soul not being subject to scrutiny or observation), the pastor's narrations were less a conjecture of fact than a reminder of orthodoxy. By trustingly assuming that all parents present used the death as an opportunity to confound young minds into an acceptance of religion, the pastor was also issuing a stern reminder that it was their responsibility to do so, thus talking to the parents as much as he was to the children. The children were not being given the lesson so much as they were the lesson.

"But then when you went to the funeral home on Sunday," he continued, "and saw Grandpa lying there in the coffin, you must have been confused. Didn't mommy and daddy say Grandpa was in Heaven now? Why is he lying here? Well, I'll tell you why. That wasn't Grandpa lying there in the funeral home. It was just his body. You see, the body is just a house for the soul. And when the body dies, that means the soul has gone to heaven. Grandpa is in Heaven now with God, because God called him up, and said: "Hey, it's your time. Come to my side and live with me in Heaven." So Grandpa left his body-house and went to Heaven. But since God made the house, since the house is his creation, and he loves it too, that is why we treat it with respect, dress it up, make it look nice, and put it in a coffin and bury it in the ground. But the soul lives forever, and you and I, we're the souls and our bodies are just a house. The body will die one day, but Christians live forever. When we die, we move out of our body-house to live in the Kingdom of God. It was moving day for Grandpa."

There was a severity underlying the warmth and softness of the pastor's pedantic sermon, as though he were driving home a point that had already been addressed, his words holding the children hostage so as to deliver a message to the rest of us. But I had little more time to think on this theme, as the lady at the piano began cranking out a bunch of dreary hymns about Jesus loving us and dying for us, and we should love Jesus so we can go live with God in the Kingdom of Heaven, etc. I wondered incredulously that these people sat through such repetitions once or twice a week.

On another Sunday several months removed, I awoke to more such hymns by accident when my radio-alarm, normally set to news or music, switched on in time for the broadcast of a local Mennonite church's morning service. An entirely different denomination, but hymns with the exact same hackneyed themes about loving Jesus and going to live with God when we die, as though these white, middle-class parishioners faced lives of utmost agony and oppression that they had to hold their breaths for a life after this one before they could have satisfaction, until that time secure in the knowledge that some invisible leprechaun in the awnings loved them and would protect them from all suffering, except for all the suffering they actually did experience, which, well, was just a test.

Afterwards, the preacher-figure in this congregation brought some children up to the stage, or pulpit, or whatever this particular church had at the front, and interrogated them for the sake of some merry lesson.

"What are some things that make you happy?" asked the preacher.

"Playing with friends," "Sunshine," "Birthdays," came the lisped, falsetto responses.

"Oh, Birthdays, yes. And what are some things that make you angry?" asked the preacher expressively, like some novice actor. The timid responses were inaudible. "Now when something makes you happy or angry," continued the preacher, "who can you talk to about this?" The children seemed uncertain: there were no answers. "Who can you talk to? Who loves you and who takes care of you?"

This answer they knew, and the responses came without hesitation: "My friends." "My parents."

"Yes, your parents. Your parents love you more than anyone!" Once again, this was not a certified fact but the expression of an ideal relationship, and the preacher's confirmation was not extended to the relationship of friend – the difference being, perhaps, that age-group peers cannot provide what parents can: mentoring in the aged hierarchy that comes with religion. "But who else? Do you remember the hymns we just sang? Who else loves you?"

No longer speaking from certain knowledge, instead thinking back to that morning's melodised lesson, the children responded by rote, with the tone of someone who has performed a newly learned trick and expects a reward (I could almost see their tails wagging): "God!"

"Good! That's right!" lavished the preacher. "God loves you more than anyone, even more than your parents! And any time you need to, you can talk to God, because God loves you and He wants to know what you're thinking, He wants to know what is inside your heart. So any time you feel like it, you should talk to God, and tell him what makes you happy, and what makes you angry, even if you're angry at Him." Preparing them for disappointment at such a young age. The sermon continued...

The use of children to explain a moral lesson is worth noting, and I say "use" deliberately. In both instances, children were made the centrepiece of the sermon, and their indoctrination was a sort of play or fable directed at the adults. The children's role as props is made apparent by the totality with which they are ignored before and after their appearance in the lesson plan. That both conversations were pedagogical is plainly demonstrated by the teacher-figure in each case, the one who lectured no less so than the one who entertained a dialogue, a farce clearly intended to lead the children to offer up the "right" answer.

Religion's tautological nature offers some explanation for the priest's use of children to instruct the parents. There are no complex truths in religion to be understood or imparted only by the "mature" mind. Rather, the mind of the believer must be suspended in an "immature" state, in order to accept as profound and unquestionable mysteries the mystifications with which religion dutifully disguises the fully historical moral systems, social relationships and power structures of the status quo. Christianity, for example, is a philosophically simplistic religion (perhaps this is a redundant phrase) and what is required in the believer above all is a childish (Childishness being a socially constructed value and not a trait inherent to children) suspension of disbelief, a never-ending leap of faith even beyond the perennial fantasy of Santa Claus, who at least dispenses some measurable reward in return for the piety he receives. As such, the child, fully trained to admit her ignorance and trust the mythic wisdom of the adult, is the ideal disciple of the church, and the demonstration of the child being taught his lesson is above all a demonstration of the proper behaviour, for all members of the congregation, of a believer before a moral authority figure.

Therefore, the ideal relationship between the constituency and leadership of the church is a fundamentally patriarchal one; that of father and children, or shepherd and sheep, with God as the father and the congregation the children. Not being an active or even present participant, God needs an intermediary: the priest. The priest uses a relationship between himself and the congregation's children to show what must be reproduced between God (represented by himself) and the entire congregation. They are his flock. Other demonstrations of morally sanctioned power (the recent drama in the Catholic church for one) arise from this hierarchical relationship, as a shepherd will do what he must with his sheep.

However, the entire congregation cannot arrest itself, politically, at the level of infantile powerlessness (whereas such a retardation at the intellectual level is far more sustainable over time). The priest alone would not be able to maintain such a tyranny without assistance. Though they do not speak for God, propertied males grow in time to become church elders, in conjunction with contemporaneous systems of hierarchy, though they can do this only so far as they speak with one voice, and offer no rebuttal to the word of God, which is solely the domain of the priest (and accordingly the priest can say nothing unexpected, but must repeat moral lessons by polished rote, like the recitation of a multiplication table). This single-mindedness within the moral hierarchy is not nourished by discourse; it is replicated by inculcation, signified by the programmatic education of children. And since this tired repetition of simplistic truisms allows no room for independent affirmation (as this would also open the door for contradiction or disavowal), it can only renew its validity when it is taught to, and embraced by, new members, and only at the level of childish mysticism are these tautological explanations of morality sufficient; thus the immaturity of the adults, when reflected onto the children, can reaffirm their orthodoxy.

The parents renew their faith vicariously through their children, even as they are instilled with the imperative of indoctrinating them to perpetuate the religious hierarchy. After all, even as they prepare for their real life in Heaven, it is the duty of the God-fearing to multiply, and continue their dominion on earth.

The Problem with Unschooling

Kathleen Nicole O'Neal

The ideas expressed in this post have been germinating in my mind for perhaps a little over a year now. In this post, I aim to provide a constructive critique of many of the assumptions that I see guiding many members of the unschooling community and how I feel that some of these assumptions are problematic not so much for reasons frequently found in the mainstream of education policy and parenting discourse but from a solidly and radically youth rights perspective as well. It is within this spirit that I ask the reader to engage with this post. In other words, the things I find problematic about the ideology of much of the unschooling movement I find problematic mostly on youth rights grounds. I do not find the elements of unschooling ideology I set out to critique problematic because I fear that they are too radically pro-youth liberation or for reasons of political expediency. In fact, in my experience most unschooling parents are far more conservative youth rights advocates, if they are youth rights advocates at all, than I try to be. Rather, I fear that elements of unschooling ideology stand to disempower or even endanger young people in ways that youth rights supporters by definition oppose.

First of all, the idea of unschooling gives parents tremendous control over their children's lives. For all of their problematic aspects, most traditional educational institutions allow young people something of a scope of autonomy (however limited) beyond the reach of their immediate families and they also provide youth with exposure to people of diverse backgrounds and belief systems of the sort whom their parents may not associate with. Unschooling gives parents far more power and control over their children than the traditional division between school and home allots to either parents or school personnel. Unschooling parents have far greater power to surveil their children than they would if the child was spending time away from the parent at school. Furthermore, it is difficult for a young person who spends virtually all of her time around her parents (or those people the parents both know and explicitly endorse the child associating with) to develop a strong sense of independence, identity, and autonomy. Most disturbingly of all, unschooling gives the most dangerous parents even more scope for abuse of their authority whether it involves indoctrinating their child into questionable political or religious beliefs or allowing sexual, emotional, or physical abuse to occur with impunity. With no adults in a child's life besides those handpicked by the parent, it's much easier for serious violations of young people's rights to occur at the hands of the parents themselves.

Secondly, it is important to note that some young people enjoy school and many more would enjoy it were the most oppressive aspects of the traditional K-12 schooling experience done away with. In the contemporary United States, very few young people have any choice in where they go to school and what they study there. Everything from talking without permission (even outside the classroom) to wearing certain items of clothing to using the restroom without permission to carrying necessary medications in one's purse to self-defence of one's person are prohibited for most youth and oftentimes these things result in harsh punishments with little due process. Even in a society in which young people were completely liberated, many youth would choose to attend school for the same reasons many adults pursue careers as scholars. By presenting a version of educational choices in which the options are either unschooling or schooling in its present form, unschooling advocates often demonstrate their inability to imagine a system in which school could be a far better and less oppressive place for the youth that did want to be there. This is concerning for philosophical reasons, but also for practical ones. Many individuals advocating for unschooling refuse to help work towards policies which would make schools more just.

Up until this point, most of my objections towards unschooling could not be said to apply to free schools. While these schools do not follow a set curriculum and simply allow young people to learn and play at their own pace, they provide a scope for youth autonomy outside the parental gaze and could be said to provide a third way between unschooling and traditional schooling. However, the final criticism of unschooling I about about to expound upon could be said to apply equally to free schools and unschooling. In a less direct but still extremely important way, it is a criticism grounded in youth rights concerns and the value of youth autonomy.

I once knew a man who had attended a traditional private school until dropping out and attending a free school in his late teens. While he greatly enjoyed the experience, he once related to me the tale of a young man he had known in his free schooling days who had attended the school from early childhood on. While the man I knew raved about his free schooling experience he told me that his friend felt less positively towards the free schooling philosophy because he could not read until he was twelve years old despite having no learning disabilities or other circumstances which would possibly delay a young person in another sort of schooling environment in acquiring literacy skills. While some might reply "But this young man learned to read eventually!" and be satisfied with that, I myself continue to be concerned about this aspect of unschooling and free schooling.

As a supporter of youth liberation I, like all of us committed to this philosophy, want to create a world in which young people are more free than they currently are to manage their own affairs and participate in important community decision-making. If we are serious about young people having a greater scope of autonomy in voting, making medical decisions, managing their own finances, practicing a religion of their choice (or not), advocating for their rights within the legal system, and participating in other things which a youth liberationist perspective stipulates that young people should be participating in, how are they going to be empowered to do so if many of them are not basically literate or numerate? Traditionally women, people of colour, ethnic minorities, poor people, rural people, immigrants, and people with disabilities have sought greater access to educational institutions because they realised that learning to read, write, add, and subtract would make them less powerless vis a vis more powerful groups and individuals in their lives. Why do we think that not accessing these same institutions and the knowledge they have to offer is going to make an already disempowered group more able to represent their own interests individually and collectively?

I would like to close this piece by saying that I do oppose compulsory education and I believe that unschooling, home schooling, and free schooling are the right choice for many youth. I also believe that these options have both advantages and disadvantages vis a vis the more traditional schooling framework in its contemporary form. However, I think that this is an issue we all need to be thinking and speaking more critically about. When unschooling and free schools are discussed in youth rights circles, they are almost always presented as the paradigmatic educational options that radical youth rights supporters need to rally around. I have even heard of youth who desire to attend more traditional schools spoken of by people in the movement as if they are suffering from some sort of false consciousness or as if, by wanting to learn in a traditional environment, they are somehow consenting to the most abusive and oppressive aspects of traditional K-12 schooling, even though these aspects of schooling usually have very little if anything to do with schools' pedagogic mission. (In most cases I would argue that these oppressive and abusive practices in fact undermine and even subvert schools' pedagogic mission.) I hope that this post starts a dialogue on these important issues within the youth rights movement itself. Young people, like adults, deserve a variety of educational options which respect their dignity and autonomy as well as their unique individual strengths, weaknesses, goals, and desires.

Children of Colour in White Circles

Victoria Law

Siu Loong means "Little Dragon" in Cantonese. But Siu Loong herself isn't Cantonese. She isn't even one hundred percent Chinese. Through me, she can claim to be Hakka, Suzhonese and Shanghainese. From her father, she can claim to be Finnish, Hungarian and Jewish. But she is also an American living among American anarchists, where none of this supposedly matters. Before motherhood became a consideration, I paid little attention to the lack of colour in the New York City anarchist "scene." So what if no one looked like me? Weren't we all struggling for the same thing?

Pregnancy made me sit up and look around at the demographics of the anarchists around me. Yes, I had followed (but not participated) in the short-lived discussion on white privilege in Seattle's protests against the WTO. Yes, I would confront my fellow anarchists about their internalised racism. But I never really went further and questioned why there were so few people of colour – never mind people of colour like me – in the anarchist movement. Motherhood forced me to open my eyes. Before the recommended six weeks of postpartum rest were up, I was up and about on my various projects. Virtually everyone was supportive of my new role as mother and on-call cow. However, I started noticing small things that bothered me about my (mostly white) activist circles. For starters, no one could pronounce my daughter's name correctly. It was pronounced, "Sue Long," "Si Long," "Sue La," any which way except the way it was supposed to be pronounced. If people didn't have trouble making a small circle with their lips to say the word "sou," they couldn't remember that "loong" had two "o"s. One person tried to shorter her name to Suzy. I very firmly put a stop to that.

Before Siu Loong could even remember her environment, I looked at the young children who made up the anarchist scene. Who would she be playing with when she grew old enough to interact with other kids? Most anarchists do not have children. Whether this is a political statement or a personal choice, the face remains that anarchist children are few and far between. On the Lower East Side, the anarchists who choose parenthood and had enough support to remain somewhat involved in the movement tend to be white.

It bothers me that Siu Loong's companions are almost all white. I do not want her growing up in an all-white (or predominantly white) environment. I do not want her to wonder if she is somehow incorrect for not having blond hair and blue eyes as many of her peers do. When I have brought this up with other anarchist parents, they dismiss my concerns. Of course they do not have to worry about whether their child will feel as if she does not belong. Their children, even those who are of mixed parentage, have white skin. They do not have to worry that their child may feel as if she is not as good as her lighter-skinned, lighter-haired friends. They do not have to worry about the fact that our small community sometimes mirrors the racism and ethnocentrism found out in the larger world.

Sometimes I wonder if I obsess about race too much. I buy her books that emphasise her Chinese heritage and, more importantly, have characters that look like her. When she began Early Head Start, I was secretly thrilled that there were no white children in her class. When she entered Head Start seven months later, I was delighted that ten of the fifteen kids running around were Chinese and that all spoke Cantonese. No one mispronounced Siu Loong's name, not even the non-Chinese teachers. However, the parents and caretakers of these children are not ones with whom I share anything except an ancestral homeland. For the most part, we do not share the same language and thus cannot talk with each other. Some of them do not return my tentative or "Jou sahn" when we pass each other in the hall or wait for the elevator together. I do not know their politics and opinions. After seeing my punk rock babysitter, they may have guessed mine, although this did not prevent them from electing me the chairperson of both the Class Committee and the Settlement House's Policy Committee. But because we have virtually nothing in common, we do not arrange for our children to see each other outside the classroom. Perhaps because their children are full-blooded Chinese, often raised in a community of other full-blooded Chinese, they do not see arranging play dates with the other Chinese children as a concern. Or perhaps they already do, but because my Cantonese is limited to ordering food and asking for prices, I am left out of the invitation loop.

In addition, despite my visible pleasure at Siu Loong being around children who share the more neglected half of her heritage, I feel as if I'm compromising some of my anti-authoritarian beliefs by placing her in a school-like atmosphere. She not only picks up the odd Cantonese phrase but also the seemingly senseless rules and regulations found in all classrooms. One evening, as I sat and talked with a friend, Siu Loong grabbed my legs. "Put your feet like this," she commanded, attempting to bend my legs into a cross-legged position. Then she grabbed my hands. "Put your hands like this," she demanded, intertwining my fingers and then folding my hands. This was not a comfortable position for a grown woman in a chair, so I promptly uncrossed my legs and unfolded my hands. Siu Loong tried to reposition me again. "This isn't comfortable," I protested. "It is comfortable," she insisted, trying to bend my fingers. "You need to sit like that so I can read you a story," she added.

That was when I realised that, for some unknown and probably nonsensical reason, Siu Loong's teachers were having their charges sit for story time with folded hands and crossed legs. The logic of this escapes me. Isn't it enough that the kids are seated and quiet? Why impose a needless rule? Especially one that she will parrot and annoy me with? Often, I feel as if my life is split. If I want to be around people who think as I do, who believe and are willing to fight for the same things, they will not look as I do. They will not share the same culture or upbringing. I will have to explain certain aspects of my life and sometimes have these aspects be misunderstood or distorted. If I choose to be with those who share my culture and collective history, I risk having my individuality misunderstood or ignored. During high school, I chose to be with other Chinese. We shared nothing except a common ancestry. In that circle of friends, my needs and wants as an individual and as an emerging anarchist were ignored. As an adult, I have been asked why I choose to be around so many white people, why I do not choose to be around "my own." In this circle, my needs and wants as a woman of color are ignored.

Sometimes I wonder if Siu Loong feels the split as acutely as I do. I wonder if she notices that, around white people, virtually anything is okay. She can run and climb and laugh and shout. She can even take all of her clothes off. No one will chastise her. The most that will happen is that the grown-ups will laugh. However, among those who look more like she does, whether they be schoolmates or relatives, such behavior is not only not laughed at, but actively discouraged and chastised.

When I try to talk with my anarchist friends about this split in my life and hers, they don't get it. Why is it important that I send Siu Loong to "school"? Why am I subjecting Siu Loong to regiment and restrictions at such an early age? Can't I find an alternative source of childcare for her – one that does not reinforce models of hierarchy and oppression? And why am I so hung up on race? One anarchist described my concerns about race and ethnicity as "nationalistic bullshit." How can I raise a baby anarchist of colour if my choices lay between a white, colour-blind movement or a gathering of those who can identify with her looks and heritage, but little else?

I'm still struggling to find some sort of balance between these two extremes. It's hard to think of solutions when those around me – both my peers and the parents of Siu Loong's peers – do not acknowledge that there is a problem. This reflects a larger issue-white anarchists' refusal to discuss race, racism and exclusivity in the movement. Knowing this doesn't make it any easier. I am still struggling alone with this concern.

End Youth Imprisonment

Ryan Calhoun

Last week president Obama put an end to the use of solitary confinement on youth locked up in the federal prison system. In an op-ed announcing a series of executive actions the president cited the particular psychological harms that young inmates face when being placed in solitary confinement. He rightly points out that a life in blossom under such conditions is robbed of its future potential. Obama's op-ed and his executive actions, which also put restrictions on adult solitary confinement, are no doubt laudable and a terrific step in the right direction.

However, his appeals to the severity of conditions for youth within solitary, at the federal level, apply also to juvenile detention generally. Right now there are well over 70,000 juveniles incarcerated in the United States. Fueled by an endless call for law-and-order and tough-on-crime policies, more children are being tried as adults and are being met with more severe sentences as a result. Juveniles are being arrested more and find themselves behind bars longer, and the consequences of their time spent in correctional facilities are disastrous.

First, children are not at all exempt from the sexual predation that pervades America's correctional facilities. The particularly disastrous effects of exposure to such predation at a young age is well documented and rightly universally condemned. However our cultural stereotype of pedophilic assault seems to never take place in incarceration, and the perpetrator is never cast as a detention centre employee. Yet that is who incarcerated youth are most likely to be sexually victimised by. Shockingly, children are even less safe in juvenile detention centers than in normal jails and prisons, where the rate of sexual assault is nearly twice what adult inmates face. 7.7 percent of inmates in juvenile facilities report sexual contact with staff members. With such uniquely horrendous conditions it is no wonder that 1/3rd of incarcerated youth diagnosed with depression track the onset of those conditions to when they were first incarcerated. The ordeal of being imprisoned does not teach youth to be peaceful, but fosters the mental characteristics of a lifelong offender.

Let us remember that juveniles are encumbered by criminal offences unique to them. Children can find themselves in the custody of the criminal justice system for consuming alcohol, purchasing cigarettes, consensual sexual interactions with fellow teenagers, refusing to go to school, and even persistent disobedience to their parents or legal guardians. When youths do show up to school they are often met with zero tolerance policies which start them on the path of the well-researched school-to-prison pipeline. Children are brought up in institutions often meant to mimic the atmosphere of prisons and jails, with the threat ever looming that misbehaviour may land them in the real deal.

Youth are stigmatised in our culture, with perceptions of criminality among minors increasing as rates of actual criminality decrease. We need to stop denying young people their agency while simultaneously exposing them to more severe treatment than many adults face. President Obama's policies do not go nearly far enough. Nothing less than a halt to the incarceration of children, the elimination of all laws that uniquely target and harm them, and the active opposition to a media and culture that criminalises them will suffice. If we wish to see a world which has done away with mass incarceration and focuses on peaceful alternatives we cannot afford to tolerate a system that makes so many people into convicts before they even possess the right to vote. End our prison-centric culture where it starts. Free all children now.

NO!

Issue 15

AGAINST
ADULT
SUPREMACY

FREE OF CHARGE OF COPYRIGHT

Mistrust and Things

Layla AbdelRahim

Since the 1950s of Soviet Russia, Lena Alexeevna Nikitina and Boris Pavlovich Nikitin, have been sounding the alarm that children's most vicious enemy is, in fact, adults' mistrust that begins with holding the child when she walks, helping her up when she falls, forbidding her to climb "dangerous" stairs even on the primitive children's playgrounds marked "for use between 0–3 years old", picking up the child and sticking her on the slide, constantly telling her what to do or not, what to wear, eat, feel, know, think, and so on, in other words, exercising total control. Mistrust is also manifested in speaking for the child, putting words in her mouth, branding, evaluating, "helping" and "teaching". Finally, it takes the form of siding with the institution in the adult endeavor to reconstruct the child from a curious individual to an obedient consumer of things and of instruction.

Protective behaviour on the part of adults may, at first glance, seem harmless, even benign. In the long run, it affects the physical, emotional, and mental development, where the child forfeits her right to learn to trust her own abilities and limitations. The absence of those inner mechanisms of self-regulation creates outright danger and is at the basis of much stress and "failure" of the future-adult. Moreover, mistrust sends children the following message: adults treat anyone smaller and weaker than themselves as frail, handicapped, even insipid (have you heard that baby-talk-intonation?). People call such behaviour "protective", "caring", "loving". Since this is love, many children learn to suppress their frustration and to accept others' control and their own failure. Later, they reproduce this love, care and protection with younger ones, but also with their own parents by then grown old, child-like and frail and thus continue the cycle.

The Nikitins call for trusting the child, providing her with an emotionally safe and enriching environment rather than limitations and control. Such an attitude would raise curiosity, creativity and confidence levels to the extent that parents would not need consumerism to replace family relations, because an independent child will know how to make toys, invent games or find answers to questions about the self and the world. There is an important distinction to make, though, between trust and neglect or between self-chosen independence or self-reliance and imposed neglect concealed by slaving parent substitutes, vocabulary, and things.

But how could the meaning of a child's freedom to investigate, experience and choose her own categories appear in a capitalist setting? For example, Francoise Dolto advises parents to pay children for household chores in order to help them become financially autonomous and concomitantly conscientious workers. Or, at the Childhoods 2005 conference in Oslo, numerous presentations focused on the "positive" aspects of consumerism and called for the participation of children in this sphere – they equated participation in consumerism with "empowerment" and "independence".

But the problem is that a child who receives a few dollars for washing dishes does not learn independence, rather the contrary: to succumb to the will of others, to do them services in return for a reward set by the more powerful. In this case, the child does not do the dishes because s/he uses them or to participate on an equal footing in family life. The child does them for a materialistic end in order to get something from materialistic parents. It goes without saying that having children do schoolwork for grades and for the promise of material bliss in the "future" is part of the same strategy that markets obedience, consumerism, misery and mistrust, a strategy that shuffles meanings, sells 500ml juice in 750ml bottles, substitutes bright packages of favourite monsters on TV with yoghurt derived from miserable cows and chemical laboratories, and so on, ad infinitum. In all of this, parents, instead of siding with their children and protecting them, end up being the prime vehicles of capitalist meaning.

Rays of Light

Bina Shah

In early March I had the privilege of meeting 90 young girls from the outskirts of Malir who had participated in the She Leads Campaign Against Child Marriage. They were trained by Rutgers-WPF, a Dutch NGO, to advocate against child marriage and for girls' education, amongst their friends and families in Jam Khanda, a rural part of Malir with dismal education rates, where many girls are married while still in their teens. Under the programme, 210 girls in Mohammed Bin Qasim town, Malir and Gadap, and another 250 had been trained in Sanghar; they, along with their teachers, had reached another 9,000 girls and their family members through the simple method of door-to-door visits and conversations.

The girls travelled to a five-star hotel in Karachi to participate in a workshop, receive tablet computers loaded with apps dealing with SRHR (sexual and reproductive health and rights), and to celebrate having completed the year-long programme. They had prepared short plays and speeches about the disapproval and difficulties they endured when trying to convince the elders of their communities that child marriage is a grave ill in Pakistani society that robs girls of both their health and their futures.

Dressed in school uniforms and bubbling with enthusiasm, these girls struck me by their willingness to put themselves forward as community leaders in order to help other girls in their neighbourhoods. Such is the power of grass-roots action, which is based entirely upon the power of the people. By standing up in this movement, these girls had actually taken the power into their own hands in a society which doesn't want to give power to young women like them. They were creating a revolution together, a grave threat to people who always wanted to keep young girls under their control by robbing them of the right to choose their own lives.

We heard from Sabr-un-Nissa, a 16-year-old student in Class 10, whose mother had died after giving birth to two stillborn children. Despite her personal pain, or perhaps channeling it in order to help others avoid her mother's fate, Sabr-un-Nissa joined the campaign and managed to convince her friend Sadia's family not to get her married off at the age of 15. In Pakistan today, 37% of its 90 million women are married before the age of 18. And one in 70 out of those young women and girls will die because of early pregnancy, not enough time between pregnancies, and other risks of teenage pregnancy. The risks are especially high for girls who get married and have children before their bodies are fully developed.

Traditionalists, socially conservative and deeply patriarchal, argue in favour of child marriage, asserting that when a girl reaches puberty, she is ready to be married. But her body is still growing, and her brain doesn't reach full development until she is 18. Pregnancy poses health risks for young girls because the foetus will leach off all the nutrients the girl still needs to achieve her full growth, which can ruin her health for life. Many families will press for a nikah while the girl is still in her mid-teens, promising that the rukhsati will not take place until much later so that she has time to finish her studies. Unfortunately, even if the girl's family agrees to this arrangement, the boy's family starts pressuring the girl's family to pull her out of school, claiming that she won't need an education once she's married to their son. The girl's family gives in to the pressure, fearing the consequences if they don't agree. In Pakistan, girls are still regarded as property, and once they are contracted in marriage to another family, that family hurries to seize that property and secure in its own possession.

By joining the She Leads campaign against child marriage, each girl declared she was not anyone's property, but a human being with hopes and dreams and ambitions: a person in her own right, with talents, abilities, and potential. They showed courage in the face of the personal risk they faced by espousing this cause, but they knew they were contributing to a major social change and taking responsibility for removing one of the greatest evils in our society. They were, in a word, unstoppable.

The campaign had given a special name to these girls: Kiran, or ray of light. And in that room in that five-star hotel, only a blind person could have remained unaffected by their radiance. Thrilled with the doors that were opening for them, they rushed around the hall afterwards, posing for photographs with their new tablets. Witnessing their new-found confidence, their sense of purpose, and their happiness, I too felt bright about the future of Pakistan.

Libertarian Child-Rearing (Excerpt)

Phil Dickens

Even within mainstream circles, the issue of educating children is a contentious one. Given "that it is through the channel of the child that the development of the mature man must go," in the words of Emma Goldman, this is understandable. The direction in which children develop affects the path they take as adults, and it is instinctive to want to ensure that our children "turn out right."

But what is "right?" Goldman argued that children should be raised to be "a well-rounded individuality," and not "a patient work slave, professional automaton, tax-paying citizen, or righteous moralist." Few anarchists would disagree. But how do we achieve such a thing?

The vital question in the raising of children, citing Goldman again, is whether "the child [is] to be considered as an individuality, or as an object to be moulded according to the whims and fancies of those about it?" The latter, it seems, fits with convention, whilst even basic and liberal attempts at educational reform are slammed as "trendy."

The TV show *Super Nanny* is a prime example of "traditional," authoritarian child rearing. On its website, it offers "why children need discipline." According to them, "many parents don't set rules for their kids because they don't want to be the villain but setting your child limits is vital for teaching him self-control."

Interestingly, the debate here becomes a microcosm of mainstream political debate on any issue. Many families are "failing to set rules because you don't want to be too tough on your kids," but in the process "they're too soft to enforce boundaries and follow up bad behaviour with consequences." The job of the parent, then, is to be to the child what the state is to the citizen. Just as with law enforcement for citizens, parental discipline "helps your child feel secure and determines what kind of person he'll grow up to be." Super Nanny advocates a liberal rather than conservative approach of "see[ing] discipline as a way of teaching your child self-control instead of a way of controlling your child." However the outcome, namely that the child is "moulded according to the whims and fancies of those about it," remains the same.

Just as statists are with the concept of anarchy, the *Super Nanny* team is aghast of childhood without rules. Rules, they argue, "impact on his academic success – think about how the discipline he learns from you is the basis for his behaviour at school – demonstrate that there are consequences to his actions and keep him safe." To the contrary, anarchists and libertarians would argue that "the free growth and development of the innate forces and tendencies of the child" is more vital. "In this way alone can we hope for the free individual and eventually also for a free community, which shall make interference and coercion of human growth impossible."

Wilhelm Reich, author of *Children of the Future*, argues that stifling the child's natural vocal expressions (shouting, screaming, bellowing, crying, etc.) not only affects the child's psychology but their physical motility:

> Small children go through a phase of development characterised by vigorous activity of the voice musculature. The joy the infant derives from loud noises (crying, shrieking, and forming a variety of sounds) is regarded by many parents as pathological aggressiveness. The children are accordingly admonished not to scream, to be 'still,' etc. The impulses of the voice apparatus are inhibited, its musculature becomes chronically contracted, and the child becomes quiet, 'well-brought-up,' and withdrawn. The effect of such mistreatment is soon manifested in eating disturbances, general apathy, pallor of the face, etc. Speech disturbances and retardation of speech development are presumably caused in this manner. In the adult we see the effects of such mistreatment in the form of spasms of the throat. The automatic constrictions of the glottis and the deep throat musculature, with subsequent inhibition of the aggressive impulses of the head and neck, seems to be particularly characteristic.

The effects of such stifling commands are most damaging on that minority of children who are "hyper active," and whose urge to move and shout is far harder to suppress. As such, Reich concludes "that small children must be allowed to 'shout themselves out' when the shouting is inspired by pleasure. This might be disagreeable to some parents, but questions of education must be decided exclusively in the interests of the child, not in those of the adults."

As anarchists argue with regards to society, self-regulation is much more effective than enforcement from without. Moreover, in children it is a natural part of their development. According to Reich, "psychoanalysts have failed to distinguish between primary natural and secondary perverse, cruel drives, and they are continuously killing nature in the new-born while they try to extinguish the 'brutish little animal.' They are completely ignorant of the fact that it is exactly this killing of the natural principle which creates the secondary perverse and cruel nature, human nature so called, and that these artificial cultural creations in turn make compulsive moralism and brutal laws necessary." Thus the use of punishment, coercion, threats, moralistic lectures and admonitions, withdrawal of love, etc. to inhibit "bad" behaviours overrides instincts towards self-regulation. Reich asserts that this trend has left virtually all adults in our society with some degree of psychological problem. Rather, without authoritarian measures, socialisation and the restriction of harmful activities occurs naturally:

> This close interrelation between biopathic behaviour and authoritarian countermeasures seems to be automatic. Self-regulation appears to have no place in and no influence upon emotions which do not come from the living core directly but only as if through a thick hard wall. Moreover, one has the impression that secondary drives cannot stand self-regulatory conditions of existence. They force sharp discipline on the part of the educator or parent. It is as if a child with an essentially secondary-drive structure feels that it cannot function or exist without disciplinary guidance. This is paralleled by the interlacing of self-regulation in the healthy child with self-regulation in the environment. Here the child cannot function unless it has freedom of decision and movement. It cannot tolerate discipline any more than the armoured child can tolerate freedom.

Further to which, "one cannot mix a bit of self-regulation with a bit of moral demand. Either we trust nature as basically decent and self-regulatory or we do not, and then there is only one way, that of training by compulsion. It is essential to grasp the fact that the two ways of upbringing do not go together."

A century before Reich, Mikhail Bakunin anticipated him when he argued that children "do not constitute anyone's property: they are neither the property of the parents nor even of society. They belong only to their own future freedom" and the "rights of the parents shall be confined to loving their children and exercising over them... authority [that] does not run counter to their morality, their mental development, or their future freedom." From this, "it follows that society, the whole future of which depends upon adequate education and upbringing of children... has not only the right but also the duty to watch over them." Thus, child rearing is not just a parental but a communal process, and "real freedom – that is, the full awareness and the realisation thereof in every individual, pre-eminently based upon a feeling of one's dignity and upon the genuine respect for someone else's freedom and dignity, i.e. upon justice – such freedom can develop in children only through the rational development of their minds, character and will."

Poverty and the Young Brain

Madeline Ostrander

The brain's foundation, frame, and walls are built in the womb. As an embryo grows into a foetus, some of its dividing cells turn into neurons, arranging themselves into layers and forming the first synapses, the organ's electrical wiring. Four or five months into gestation, the brain's outermost layer, the cerebral cortex, begins to develop its characteristic wrinkles, which deepen further after birth. It isn't until a child's infant and toddler years that the structures underlying higher-level cognition – will power, emotional self-control, decision-makin – begin to flourish; some of them continue to be fine-tuned throughout adolescence and into the first decade of adulthood.

Pat Levitt, a developmental neuroscientist at Children's Hospital Los Angeles, has spent much of his career studying the setbacks and accidents that can make this construction process go awry. In the nineteen-nineties, during the media panic over "crack babies," he was among a number of scientists who questioned whether the danger of cocaine exposure in utero was being overstated. (Levitt spent two decades examining the brains of rabbit mothers and their offspring that were dosed with the drug, and says that the alarm was "an exaggeration.") More recently, as the science director of the National Scientific Council on the Developing Child, he has become interested in another sort of neurotoxin: poverty.

As it turns out, the conditions that attend poverty – what a National Scientific Council report summarised as "overcrowding, noise, substandard housing, separation from parent(s), exposure to violence, family turmoil," and other forms of extreme stress – can be toxic to the developing brain, just like drug or alcohol abuse. These conditions provoke the body to release hormones such as cortisol, which is produced in the adrenal cortex. Brief bursts of cortisol can help a person manage difficult situations, but high stress over the long term can be disastrous. In a pregnant woman, the hormone can "get through the placenta into the foetus," Levitt told me, potentially influencing her baby's brain and tampering with its circuitry. Later, as the same child grows up, cortisol from his own body may continue to sabotage the development of his brain.

In March, in the journal Nature Neuroscience, a group of researchers from nine hospitals and universities published a major study of more than a thousand children. They took DNA samples, made MRI scans of the children's brains, collected data on their families' income level and educational background, and gave them a series of tests for skills like reading and memory. The DNA samples allowed the scientists to factor out the influence of genetic heritage and look more closely at how socioeconomic status affects a growing brain. The scans focussed on over-all brain surface area, determined partly from the depth of the folds on the cortex, and the size of the hippocampus, a lumpy, curled structure nestled in the middle of the brain that stores memories. As might be expected, more educated families produced children with greater brain surface area and a more voluminous hippocampus. But income had its own distinct effect: living in the lowest bracket left children with up to six per cent less brain surface area than children from high-income families. At the lowest end of the income spectrum, little increases in family earnings could mean larger differences in the brain. At the middle and upper income levels, though, the money-brain curve flattened. In other words, wealth can't necessarily buy a better brain, but deprivation can result in a weakened one.

A person whose brain has been undermined in this way can suffer long-term behavioural and cognitive difficulties. In March, a study appeared in the journal Acta Paediatrica showing eerie ultrasound images of foetuses that more frequently moved their mouths and touched their faces when their mothers were either stressed out or, even more so, when they smoked cigarettes – likely a sign of delayed nervous-system development. In a longer-term study published two years ago, neuroscientists at four universities scanned the brains of a group of twenty-four-year-olds and found that, in those who had lived in poverty at age nine, the brain's centres of negative emotion were more frequently buzzing with activity, whereas the areas that could rein in such emotions were quieter. Elsewhere, stress in childhood has been shown to make people prone to depression, heart disease, and addiction in adulthood.

Over the past decade, the scientific consensus has become clear: poverty perpetuates poverty, generation after generation, by acting on the brain. The National Scientific Council has been working directly with policymakers to support measures that break this cycle, including better prenatal and paediatric care and more accessible preschool education. Levitt and his colleagues have also been advocating for changing laws that criminalise drug abuse during pregnancy, since, as they pointed out in a review paper, arrest and incarceration can also trigger the "maternal stress response system." The story that science is now telling rearranges the morality of parenting and poverty, making it harder to blame problem children on problem parents. Building a healthy brain, it seems, is an act of barn raising.

NO!

ISSUE 16

AGAINST ADULT SUPREMACY

I Am

DAVID: A younger version of myself waits for the bus after school. My friend starts to tell me some of the jokes about "illegals" he knows. I look visibly uncomfortable and he acknowledges it: "You shouldn't take it personally" he says with a smirk, "I mean, unless you're 'illegal.'" I freeze and then fumble to change the subject. His reasoning is perfectly sound. Why would I be offended unless I was "illegal"? I take the bus home thinking what a close call that was, and I start to plan how I'll make it so that this never happens again. I become super-conscious of the potential trajectory of conversations. I try to avoid anything that can lead to someone asking me about my status, and in my mind everything leads there.

"Illegal is illegal" is straightforward logic to a kid, and at 12 it had paralysed me. It held me back and kept me isolated from others. Yes, I've done all the work and I want to go on our school trip, but "illegal is illegal." Yes, I'm a high achieving student and I want to go to a good school, but "illegal is illegal." My parents have sacrificed everything for me and I love them and I want to love them, but "illegal is illegal." That word was the afterthought of everything that I did, and it degraded anything positive in my life. The i-word created a wall between my human dignity and myself. The criminalising language didn't respect me and didn't allow me to respect myself.

Last year on March 10, those of us forced to sit in the shadow of that wall of disrespect stood up and confronted the slur. Along with immigrant youth across the nation, led by the Immigrant Youth Justice League, I declared that I am undocumented, and I am no longer afraid to defend my dignity. This year I continue to do so without apologies. By coming out, we're taking a hammer to the wall of ignorance that is confining us to the shadows. We're changing the popular narrative surrounding undocumented immigrants, and today as "illegal is illegal" fuels in more than a dozen states, it is more important for us to be out. You can help by making where you live a safer place for us to live with dignity. Help us make America a safer place for immigrant youth to share our stories. Help us drop the i-word.

TONY: I found out I was undocumented when I was about 13 years old. I used to play soccer and my coach at the time had informed me about these tryouts that were being held in Queens, to form a team that would go to Italy to compete. My coach insisted that I should go try out and I did. Tryouts were held for about two weeks and I made the final list. In my mind, I was going to Italy. I was so excited. All I could think of was to run home and tell my mother the great news. I got home and ran up the stairs calling out for mom. I told her the big news. She looked at me with this face that I will never forget.

Everything around me froze; time ceased to exist. It was just my mother and I in the living room staring at each other. She suddenly began to cry. She sat me down and explained that I was not going to be able to go because of my status in this country. I was confused. Status? She said we were not here legally in this country. I was more confused, "illegal"? She told me that life was not going to be easy for me. She told me that it was going to be hard to get into college, to find a job, to be able to get a driver's license, to travel. I always dreamed of getting into college, since no one in my family had ever graduated from high school let alone gone to college. I figured I would be the first, yet what she was telling me made my goal seem near impossible. My dream was to get into college and I sure wasn't going to let people tell me I couldn't get in. In high school I worked hard and got excellent grades. I was part of the soccer team and senior year I was offered four scholarships to universities based on my achievements in soccer and for my good grades. I had to decline because of my status did not allow me to get the funding.

Reality hit me in the face. I always reminded myself why my parents brought me here; all their hard work and sacrifice would not go in vain. I refused to give up and quit. I applied to colleges and finally I was accepted to John Jay College here in New York City, and was able to attend without a scholarship. But I still think of the words that blocked my scholarships: We don't give scholarships or monetary help to people who are "illegal." That word made me feel like dirt and made me feel worthless. I began to ask, how can humans be "illegal"? Why would media, society, and politicians use the i-word? They made it seem like we were a sickness that people should stay away from. The i-word is a terrible word that should not be used. It is a huge step back and we need to move forward. We are made to live in fear.

I no longer want to live in fear, no longer in the shadows. I exist. My dreams, my voice counts. We are no different from anyone else, we are not better than anyone, and no one is better than we are. Nine dumb numbers do not define us. We are people who have grown up here all our lives. This is our home. We can do something about creating a better future. It's time to make a change and to break all these racial barriers and learn to understand each other, learn to accept our differences and live free. Today, I come out publicly undocumented, unafraid, unapologetic and now I am FREE.

SONIA: Many times, when I am asked who I am, I respond with "I am undocumented." I haven't always identified as undocumented. When I was little my parents left me in the care of my grandparents, they migrated to the United States. I was too little to understand why my parents were not there to share birthdays with me, did not understand why they were not there walking me to school. I did not understand why phone calls were the vehicle in which my parents were able to express their love for me. Calling card after calling card, I asked them when will I be with them.

No one actually prefers to risk their life crossing the border, leaving behind memories and childhoods, leaving behind their mothers and fathers and leaving behind their children. No one comes to this country because they want to be exploited, and treated less than human. No one migrates to this country and wants to identify as "illegal". Their decision is not done out of thin air, there have been structures and policies that have pushed many to migrate (NAFTA, Bracero Program, Imperialism, privatisation). My parents migrated to the United States because they wanted a better life for their children. My mom worked in factories, and my dad worked as a cook. They paid taxes (still do), hired lawyers, paid fines, got robbed by lawyers. But most of all, they lost many nights of tucking me to bed, many nights of reading me books, and combing my hair and seeing me walk for the first time. They sacrificed those nights for a better future for me. They are not illegals, they are my parents. They are strong courageous and admirable.

I remember the time I was reunited with my parents; I was about 5 years old. I arrived in Harlem. They pushed me to be the best I can be, making sure education was a priority, motivating me to always be honour roll. And that is what I did, I excelled in school. I hoped time would soften the difference between others and me. I always knew that I was undocumented, but I trusted there was a fair system that would fix that up. My dad promised me my status would soon change, lawyers promised him that too. But no results. I knew my undocumented status put me on a different path than those friends I hung out with. There would be no Cornell University, no going away, no trips abroad, no teaching, no career, no fraternities, and no peaceful nights that did not consist of thinking of "deportation" or "illegal". I am undocumented. I do not speak on behalf of undocumented youth across the country. I speak of my experience, a similar experience shared across states.

When I say I am undocumented, I own my liberation, I own my humanity and the power I have. I stand with the undocumented youth across the states because we are beautiful amazing leaders. I am not the "model dreamer." I am undocumented. I stand with youth that are not high honour roll in Harvard. I stand with youth who are marginalised out as not fitting what the "American Dream" looks like. I stand with my brothers and sisters who organize 24/7 with no pay, who are about community and not politicians. I stand with my mother and father because they are not the reason that I am undocumented. They and I are not "illegals". I am undocumented, unafraid and unapologetic.

Meeting Parents

Lily Schapira

Eight days after my daughter was born, I sent this message to the organising committee members of the Seattle Solidarity Network:

"I wanted to let you all know that I need to take a few weeks hiatus from coming to SeaSol meetings... Baby is doing well, we just need to clear the decks while I recover and while we figure out this whole nursing thing. Thanks for understanding, and we'll see you in a few weeks! (I'd estimate three.)"

Four months later, I had still not returned to SeaSol meetings more than a handful of times. I was an I.W.W. member and had been organising with SeaSol since our first fight in 2008. I was the only female-identified person to consistently attend SeaSol meetings for our entire first year and for several more years for the IWW branch in Seattle. Both groups planned to pay for childcare, and I was committed to continuing my activism after giving birth, but somehow I was not managing to make it happen. What was the problem?

What follows are some reflections on becoming a mom while trying to continue work as a class warrior. Because my daughter is only six months old now, I can only base my reflections on these first months of parenthood. While I will mostly present ideas about how to make our organising "baby friendly," I'm sure there are many more topics to come about becoming "kid friendly". The following suggestions are also influenced by the fact that while my partner is on baby duty from 10am to 4pm, I am on duty from 4pm to 10pm every day. This system of "watches" is how we both manage to keep our sanity and our part-time jobs, but it also means that I am responsible for the bulk of childcare during prime meeting times. This advice is for other individuals who would like to help support new parents in organisations such as SeaSol and the IWW, as well as newly expecting parents who might appreciate some suggestions to help smooth the transition from activist to parent + activist.

Step One Childcare in meetings. Childcare is obviously an important part of helping any organisation become parent- and baby-friendly. However, I'm not a believer in the "build it and they will come" style of organisation building. If you start offering childcare in meetings, I wouldn't expect moms, dads, babies and kids to just appear out of the woodwork. In SeaSol and the Seattle IWW branch we started providing childcare after four very active members of both organisations became parents within weeks of each other. That is, we based our actions on a current, felt need in the organisations rather than a hypothetical future need. (If anyone does the opposite and finds out that parent activists do come out of the woodwork, please let me know. That would be great!)

We also decided to do advance fundraising in order to pay for childcare. While several members (often women) volunteered to do the childcare for free, we didn't want to lose out on the possibility of having those people participate in the meetings. We need everyone we can to do the organising work of SeaSol and the IWW, so we decided it would be better to have the childcare done by someone who would not otherwise be involved with our organisations.

This is all well and good, but unfortunately, childcare isn't really what I needed to come back to organising. I've come to believe there's a difference between being truly baby-friendly in meetings and simply providing childcare (however important that is). What I needed as a new mom was not just someone to hand the baby off to so that I could participate in meetings in a "normal" way. What I needed and still need is support for my new normal, which involves being in an extremely dependent and time-consuming nutritional and emotional relationship with a tiny human. Steps Two through Six are about supporting this new normal.

Step Two Help with meals. It's really hard finding time to cook any kind of meal, let alone a healthy one, while taking care of an infant. I mean, impossibly hard. Add to that the fact that our meetings are right at dinner time and you have me between a rock (hungry baby) and a hard place (hungry mama).

One of the best things helpers can do for new parents is to have food waiting for them at meetings. This would probably work best as a shift system where interested individuals could sign up to bring a dinner for one or two hungry mamas or papas per meeting. Shifts would not be as logistically challenging as providing food for everyone at the meeting, but I guarantee it would make it far more likely that your new mamas could attend meetings. (The breastfeeding ones are extra hungry, too!) We have not tried this in SeaSol, but we do have a monthly potluck meeting with food provided, and I am much more likely to attend those meetings.

Step Three Help with rides or packing. I have a car but am still daunted by all the logistical challenges of getting out of the house with a baby. This includes everything from making sure she is fed and changed to visiting with her in the car seat so she doesn't scream her head off on the way to the meeting. I also sometimes bring a giant exercise ball to meetings for bouncing her to sleep, a baby carrier, and so much other stuff that I feel like a pack mule trying to make my way into meetings. Helpers can offer rides and/or offer to show up early to help the parents gather things together. I've been lucky enough to have a fabulous SeaSol organiser helping me out with these sorts of pre-meeting preparations.

Step Four Have supplies on hand at meetings. Parents and helpers can keep supplies on hand to help reduce the burden of packing before meetings. These care packages should contain extra diapers in several sizes, wipes, a couple of toys, and a few changes of clothing. There should also be snacks for emergency parent feeding as well. A very motivated helper could even show up at the parents' house to help them pack such a bag.

Step Five Volunteer to do childcare for events other than meetings. Meetings aren't the only events that new parents want to attend. Often the help I most need is just an extra pair of hands, or someone to sit beside me and entertain the baby during an event. My baby never wants to be banished off to some "kid room" with just herself and a non-parental adult – she wants to be where the action is! A helper can simply offer to sit by a parent and entertain their kid for a little while, if needed.

Step Six Don't push it. It's an understatement to say that new parents are "adjusting" to their new role. For me, especially for the first several months, it felt like my new life was a Picasso painting of my old life – there were many recognisable elements, but they were all mashed up and weird looking. I'm now figuring out how to weave activities I value back into my life, but there's no going "back to normal." I'm not going to be able to participate in exactly the same way I did before I became a mom. For example, I used to facilitate meetings regularly. Now, I will absolutely abandon that duty for a crying baby with no qualms whatsoever. But I can contribute in other ways that are meaningful and useful for the organisation, such as writing, graphic design, and other activities that I can do during nap times or off duty. This is all to say: don't feel too disappointed if your new parents can't contribute to your organising in their old way; hopefully they can find new ways that suit their new schedules and responsibilities.

In the first months of motherhood, I was too discombobulated to think of any of these suggestions. As a potential helper, you may find that new parents are too overwhelmed to think of these things or ask you for them. But if you offer, they will sometimes take you up on it. I can guarantee you it's worth the effort. I might be biased, but I think during a tense moment in a meeting, there's hardly anything better than having a baby go, "Fffpppptt!"

Neurodivergence and Kindergarten

Nick Walker

In August 2012, as many families prepared for the start of a new school year, the editorial team of the Thinking Person's Guide to Autism blog contacted a few autistic people who'd survived the public school system, and a few non-autistic parents who'd worked hard to help their autistic children survive the public school system. What, they asked us, did we wish that we had known, back when we (or our kids) were first starting school?

There's a lot that I learned later on, in adolescence and adulthood, that I wish I'd known in kindergarten and elementary school. I wish I'd known the things that I later learned through aikido training: the self-regulation and self-defence skills; the ability to both inwardly access and outwardly convey calm centeredness and physical confidence.

And I wish I'd known that I wasn't alone, that I would eventually find more and more people like me. By this I mean not only the autistic community, and the friends I made as a teenager and adult who weren't autistic but to whom I could relate in other ways. I also mean that I wish I'd known there were others out there who'd seen what I was seeing and experiencing: the dynamics of institutionalised oppression, privilege, marginalisation, injustice, and abuse; the fact that school was clearly constructed to brutalise children into soulless conformity and unquestioning compliance, and to crush, rather than cultivate, genuine creativity and curiosity.

I could see all of this clearly, but I had no words for it, and the fact that I didn't have the words for it and that no one else seemed to be seeing it left me feeling alienated and furious; the frustration ate at me every day, throughout my elementary school years.

I wish someone had said to me, back then, "Yes, what you're witnessing and experiencing is institutionalised social injustice; it's everywhere in the world and it follows the same basic patterns that it has followed throughout history. There are other people who've seen it for what it is, who've come up with words for it and written about it. These systems of injustice dominate human society, and yes, most people are largely oblivious and complicit. But some people have woken up, and more people will; you're not alone." I wish someone had said all of that to me on my first day of kindergarten.

Never assume that a child isn't ready to understand such things. Especially not an autistic or otherwise neurodivergent child (not because we're necessarily any smarter than neurotypical children, but because there are more likely to be unpredictable discrepancies between what we know and what we're capable of communicating that we know). To quote one of the common maxims of the Neurodiversity Movement: presume competence. Sometimes what's causing meltdowns and rages and "behaviour issues" is that a child really does understand.

The Boy Who Is Free

Laura Gottesdiener

Fifteen years after the uprising, a child named Diego was born in Zapatista territory. He was the youngest member of the household where I was staying, and during my week with the family, he was always up to something. He agitated the chickens, peeked his head through the window to surprise his father at the breakfast table, and amused the family by telling me long stories in Ch'ol that I couldn't possibly understand. He also, unknowingly, defied the government's claim that he does not exist.

Diego is part of the first generation of Zapatista children whose births are registered by one of the organisation's own civil judges. In the eyes of his father, he is one of the first fully independent human beings. He was born in Zapatista territory, attends a Zapatista school, lives on unregistered land, and his body is free of pesticides and genetically modified organisms. Adding to his autonomy is the fact that nothing about him – not his name, weight, eye colour, or birth date – is officially registered with the Mexican government. His family does not receive a peso of government aid, nor does it pay a peso worth of taxes. Not even the name of Diego's town appears on any official map. By first-world standards, this autonomy comes at a steep price: some serious poverty. Diego's home has electricity but no running water or indoor plumbing. The outhouse is a hole in the ground concealed by waist-high tarp walls. The bathtub is the small stream in the backyard. Their chickens often free-range it right through their one-room, dirt-floor house. Eating them is considered a luxury.

The population of the town is split between Apostatises and government loyalists, whom the Apostatises call "priipriistas" in reference to Mexico's ruling political party, the PRI. To discern who is who, all you have to do is check whether or not a family's roof sports a satellite dish. Then again, the Apostatises aren't focused on accumulating wealth, but on living with dignity. Most of the movement's work over the last two decades has involved patiently building autonomous structures for Diego and his generation. Today, children like him grow up in a community with its own Zapatista schools; communal businesses; banks; hospitals; clinics; judicial processes; birth, death, and marriage certificates; annual censuses; transportation systems; sports teams; musical bands; art collectives; and a three-tiered system of government. There are no prisons. Students learn both Spanish and their own indigenous language in school. An operation in the autonomous hospital can cost one-tenth that in an official hospital. Members of the Zapatista government, elected through town assemblies, serve without receiving any monetary compensation.

Economic independence is considered the cornerstone of autonomy – especially for a movement that opposes the dominant global model of neoliberal capitalism. In

Diego's town, the Zapatista families have organised a handful of small collectives: a pig-raising operation, a bakery, a shared field for farming, and a chicken coop. The twenty-odd chickens had all been sold just before Christmas, so the coop was empty when we visited. The three women who ran the collective explained, somewhat bashfully, that they would soon purchase more chicks to raise. As they spoke in the outdoor chicken coop, there were squealing noises beneath a nearby table. A tangled cluster of four newly born puppies, eyes still crusted shut against the light, were squirming to stay warm. Their mother was nowhere in sight, and the whole world was new and cold, and everything was unknown. I watched them for a moment and thought about how, although it seemed impossible, they would undoubtedly survive and grow.

Unlike Diego, the majority of young children on the planet today are born into densely packed cities without access to land, animals, crops, or almost any of the natural resources that are required to sustain human life. Instead, we city dwellers often need a ridiculous amount of money simply to meet our basic needs. My first apartment in New York City, a studio smaller than my host family's thatched-roof house, cost more per month than the family has likely spent in Diego's entire lifetime. As a result, many wonder if the example of the Apostatises has anything to offer an urbanised planet in search of change. Then again, this movement resisted defeat by the military of a modern state and built its own school, medical, and governmental systems for the next generation without even having the convenience of running water. So perhaps a more appropriate question is: What's the rest of the world waiting for?

Around six o'clock, when night falls in Oventic, the music for the celebration begins. On stage, a band of guitar-strumming men wear hats that look like lampshades with brightly colored tassels. Younger boys perform Spanish rap. Women, probably from the nearby state of Veracruz, play son jarocho, a type of folk music featuring miniature guitar-like instruments. It's raining gently in the open field. The mist clings to shawls and skirts and pasamontañas, the face-covering ski masks that have become iconic imagery for the Apostatises. "We cover our faces so that you can see us" is a famous Zapatista saying. And it's true: for a group of people often erased by politicians and exploited by global economies, the ski-masks have the curious effect of making previously invisible faces visible. Still, there are many strategies to make dissent disappear, of which the least effective may be violence. The most ingenious is undoubtedly to make the rest of the world – and even the dissenter herself – dismissive of what's being accomplished. Since curtailing its military offensive, the government has waged a propaganda war focused on convincing the rest of Mexico, the world, and even Zapatista communities themselves that the movement and its vision no longer exists.

But there are just as many strategies for keeping dissent and dissenters going. One way is certainly to invite thousands of outsiders to visit your communities and see firsthand that they are real, that in every way that matters they are thriving, and that they have something to teach the rest of us. As Diego's father said in an uncharacteristic moment of boastfulness, "I think by now that the whole world has heard of our organisation."

NO!

Issue 17

AGAINST
ADULT
SUPREMACY

There is a Better Way

Vicki Larson

The pressures and pace of modern life has made parents and children stressed and miserable. With the rise of dual-earning families, mothers, and increasingly, fathers are struggling with work-life issues, forcing many to lean in or opt out. But is it truly modern life that's at fault or is it our expectation that two people – whether hetero or same-sex – can do it alone and do it well? Is the nuclear family all it's cracked up to be?

Despite the belief that monogamous male-female bonding is how mothers and children were supported and thrived, the anthropologist Sarah Blaffer Hrdy and others believe it was actually female cooperative breeding, or alloparenting – 'sharing and caring derived from the pooled energy' of a network of 'grandparents, aunts, uncles, siblings, distantly related kin, and non-kin' – that shaped our evolution. Shared parenting is likely in our genes. It works. So why do we cling to the idea that the nuclear family is the best way to raise children?

The nuclear family can be extraordinarily dangerous for children. Some – often children of educated and privileged families – are buckling under pressure to succeed and are committing suicide at alarming rates. Those in the United States who experience parental divorce are overwhelmingly being raised in poverty, which has lifelong ramifications on their health, wealth and education. At the extreme, some 500 children a year are murdered by their parents in the US, and millions more are abused and neglected, with inadequate systems to help them until damage is done. But even in so-called 'normal' families, children can't escape some sort of dysfunction, whether they're being raised by a parent who is depressed, adulterous, emotionally cold, smothering, absent, angry, passive-aggressive, narcissistic or addicted. The moral philosophers Samantha Brennan and Bill Cameron suggest that love-based marriage, with the 'instability, tension, and even violence that too often forms a central part of romantic conflict,' doesn't always offer children the stability and security they need.

Parents, too, struggle. It is a lonely, isolating and exhausting business, especially for mothers, who still typically do the bulk of childcare. They pay a huge price for it. Not only do many forsake career opportunities and income, but they also are subject to societal idealisation of motherhood and then shamed and blamed for any perceived failings, most often by their own children.

With all that, can we raise children better? Yes. Rather than leave childrearing solely in the hands of one or two people, it would help everyone if we approached it more along the lines of the old African proverb: 'It takes a village to raise a child.' We should take alloparenting to the next level: quality and trained caregiving that is shared, continuous and, most important, mandatory. For the philosopher Anca Gheaus, communal childrearing makes a lot of sense. In a series of papers, Gheaus explores what childrearing ideally would look like based on children's rights and emotional needs. While acknowledging that some parental power and decision-making is essential until children can care for themselves, parents often use their power arbitrarily and in their own best interest – not necessarily their child's. Being a parent shouldn't automatically give someone a 'monopoly of care' over a child, she says, especially since anyone can become a parent without having any training or undergoing any testing to see if he or she's up for the job. Which is why Gheaus suggests that some non-parental care should be mandatory. If childrearing became more of a communal obligation, all children, whether subject to disadvantaged socio-economic backgrounds or just bad parenting, would benefit. More people would be invested in their lives, and the children would be exposed to a variety of opinions and lifestyles that would enhance their budding autonomy. Having numerous caregivers would expose bad parenting earlier, too, and help to mitigate it. And as they grew into adulthood, children would be more likely to be compassionate – or at least open-minded – toward people whose beliefs and values differed from their parents'. But how to make that happen?

The collective childrearing on Israel's kibbutzim has been lauded for giving children high-quality care in a supportive environment, despite problems with its approach to communal sleeping in its early years. While many parents might not opt to live in a communal setting, there are other ways to provide children with a network of people, ideally not related, who care for them. It could take the form of formalised, but non-religious god-parenting, in which children are assigned caregivers who live outside the family home and are willing and able to help care for them several hours a week while they are young, and then become trusted confidantes as they age. There are many men and women who either don't have children or whose children are grown – or perhaps disenfranchised – but still want to make a difference in a child's life. Allowing more people to be involved with the lives of children would create a real, communal investment in the future.

It's easy to see how parents would benefit. Having a trusted, loving network of caregivers would give moms and dads a much-needed break to spend time with each other or alone. They would feel less overwhelmed, especially if they have children with learning challenges or physical disabilities, or have erratic work schedules. It would also help them better manage the ambivalent feelings that parenting elicits, which is 'inevitably accompanied by anger, frustration, and occasionally even hatred,' Gheaus writes.

In some ways, we are already doing a form of alloparenting. Many children are raised with multiple parents, whether through same-sex coupling, divorce, open adoption, polyamory or reproductive technology. The sociologist Karen Hansen notes that dual-employed parents rely on friends, paid caregivers and relatives to help. Teachers, coaches, tutors and mentors often fill in the gaps. But many come and go. And that's the problem. Children can be cut off from loving caregivers, often because of parental needs or whims. Sometimes they lose access to relatives after a divorce, or to beloved neighbours because of moves or rifts; long-term nannies or babysitters are fired with no regard to a child's desire to continue the relationship. Parents have no moral right to do that.

Besides helping children and parents, allotments would benefit, too; they'd have richer, deeper relationships with more younger people who just might be more inclined to care for their caregivers as they age. It would, of course, require a revolution in childrearing, Gheaus admits. And parents would have to get over the jealousy they often feel when their child loves someone else. But as parents struggle with work-life issues and the divide between the haves and have-nots grows, who is truly keeping our children's best interests in mind? Alloparenting is the best way for both children and parents to flourish.

oling as Genocide

In the late summer, as villages began the preparation for winter, the trucks would tour the villages. They knew where to go and what to say. The man from the government would explain the children were being removed, taken away from their homes and their families and given a place at a residential school. If anyone complained or protested, they were told they were blocking what was best for the child. If that didn't stop the words of dissent, they were warned they'd be arrested and they could spend the year in jail. So the children left, with tears in their eyes and confusion at what they had done and where they were going.

Across Canada, for more than 100 years, children of the indigenous population, or First Nation as they are known here, were taken away as part of the policy of "aggressive assimilation", or as one survivor put it, "They tried to beat the Indian out of us." The idea was simple. The government would provide the money and the church would provide the education. Children were easier to mould, and the education they received would prepare them for life in Canadian society. Their traditions, their language and the heritage would be ignored. "I said hi in my local language to a priest as I walked into the school on my first day. He lifted me by the ears and beat me unconscious. I was six," said one survivor. Canada's first prime minister, Sir John Macdonald, believed the system was the future: "When the school is on the reserve, the child lives with his parents who are savages; he is surrounded by savages."

The abuse was rampant. Children were raped. Children were abused physically and emotionally. Children were tortured. And children were unloved. In one school, there was even a crudely put together electric chair where "unruly" boys were made to sit and a current was sent shocking through their body. One man choking back the tears said: "I used to look at the sky and know my parents were looking at the same stars. But I felt alone in the world." Another said "the priest told us we were uncivilised. Then he would take us into a back room and rape us".

The final school closed in 1996. More than 150,000 children had been forced to attend. It's thought up to 6,000 children died during that time. It may be more. Record-keeping was poor and the guilty could hide their secrets. Finally, the survivors as they called themselves realised they had been the victims of abuse. They banded together and took the government to court and won. They received a settlement, the largest of its kind in the world. But they also won the right to a Truth and Reconciliation Commission where they could tell their stories.

For more than five years, the Commission travelled all over the country, gathering evidence and hearing testimony. In a packed function room in a hotel in the Canadian capital, Ottawa, many of those who'd been abused gathered to hear the report. Among them was Annie Johnston. She was sent to a school near her home in British Columbia at the age of five "but it could have been on the moon, I was so removed from my family". The abuse was constant, the humiliation unforgiving. "My brother was at the same school on the boys side. We were forbidden to talk to one another," she told me, her eyes welling with tears. "The messages that they gave, that we were heathens, we were pagans, my way of life was no good. At five years old you believe everything." It's 50 years since Annie left the school but every day she remembers something; a moment, a smell or a sound and she returns. She said she fed her experiences to her children. "I didn't know how to be a mother, how could I?" And so another generation felt the pain and the anger.

Justice Murray Sinclair – himself from the First Nations – chaired the commission. As he stood and acknowledged Canada was guilty of cultural genocide, those in the room rose with a roar. Their hurt, their anger, their pain had finally been acknowledged. The standing ovation lasted for minutes. People cried, perhaps unable to absorb the history of the moment. "It was nothing less than the systematic and concerted attempt to extinguish the spirit of the aboriginal peoples," Sinclair continued. "But as the survivors have shown us, they have survived."

Beside me a woman rocked back and forth. "Thank you, thank you," she said almost silently. "Too long, too long." The commission has made 94 recommendations. This, it believes, will help redress the problems the residential schools have caused, will begin to make amends for past evils, and aid the reconciliation so desperately needed. "It's time to start a new chapter in Canada where everyone is treated equally," said Justice Sinclair. "This is not an aboriginal issue, it's a Canadian issue." The government has said it will look at the findings of the commission, which is short of accepting what needs to be changed.

But for many who made the journey to Ottawa, the report is not the end of the process. It is merely a beginning. For them, for their people and for the country which has always been their home.

Little Suns

Asadah Kirkland

The power of a parent does not come from telling a child what to do, or from having "possession" of a child. And it surely does not manifest itself in the form of hitting a child in order to "discipline" him by instilling fear. It is not having "control" over children, but rather, knowing what characteristics and actions will, when combined, be the perfect recipe for helping a child grow into a good, contributing citizen.

All too often, parents desire to have "power over" young people. Have you even been in a job situation in which a person misused his power and always nagged you, made you do things you didn't want to do, or constantly looked over your shoulder? Annoying, right? What was your feeling? What did you really want to say to him? What did you want to do to him? The behaviour he displayed did not make you more powerful. His behavior was disempowering, because it showed lack of confidence in your abilities. It demonstrated a lack of trust. Overall, it made you resent him. Hmmm, does that boss' behavior sound similar to anything a child might experience?

At the top of my concern list is the route parents take when they say they're "pushed to the limit." I have heard it referred to as "the last resort," when a parent feels she has to show her power by yelling at or hitting her child to discipline him. Parents say things like, "I have to talk to them five and six times!" or "He thinks just because he's getting older, he can talk to me any old kind of way?" Yes, parents, I hear you. But there's a reason behind a child blocking out your communication, and there's a way to make sure he doesn't block you out – and it doesn't involve hitting.

Think of it like this: there are people you genuinely like speaking to, because they have things to say that you like to hear, while there are others who may be less appealing to speak to, because they either can't relate to you, or they're saying things that are adverse to your beliefs. Nonetheless, as an adult, you have the power to tune a person out, or cut communication all together. Unfortunately, children can seldom do that with their parents. Just imagine always being questioned by someone, always having someone tell you what to do, always having someone suggesting her way is the best way, and invalidating your point of view. That's a demonstration of being spoken TO or AT. Being spoken WITH feels much different. There's an actual exchange of communication in the latter. If more adults had conversations WITH children, both parties would benefit from the understanding that would result.

The communication we have with children does not always have to be about jurisdiction, giving orders, implications, inspection, and other "adult interest" topics. Children don't always have the same concerns adults have. Cleaning up the house and finishing homework may be really important topics for adults to address, but it's not about addressing them. It's about being wise enough to cater to a child's interest by finding out what is important to him, and talking about that for a change. The busy schedule and life challenges of a parent cannot supersede the importance of her children's interests. If adults don't lend importance to what children say and think, children will quickly lose interest in what adults say and think. Getting the respect and trust of children cannot be forced. Those values develop out of their experiences with and observations of adults. Children's ideas count, and their viewpoints are valid. Adults only have to listen, watch, and use their wisdom to direct the paths of children.

During a recent book discussion, a wise gentleman likened babies to little suns. He said that when children are born, they shine brightly, and life experiences tend to dim those lights over time. "That's it!" I thought. Can we, as parents and educators, motivate and cultivate children so that those rays KEEP shining brightly, well into their teen years? Can we give them enough tools and happiness to shine brightly as adults? During that discussion, I think everyone involved realised that we could be doing more to foster more growth in these little lights. Hitting a child to discipline him dims the lights. Yelling at a child dims the lights. Invalidating the efforts of a child dims the lights. We only have to think of the things in our lives that make us feel bright. Once we do that, then we can look at whether or not we give out the behavior we'd like to take in.

Many adults rationalise the spankings they got as children and say, "Well, those spankings did OK by me – I turned out to be a better person because of them." The idea here is that being hit by their parents kept them from doing harmful things. But, people, was the decision to not repeat the harmful acts done out of fear, or out of reason? Children will only make good decisions if they have the ability to REASON – to think or argue logically. A parent who does not take the time to give a child thinking and negotiating skills will raise a child who will become a less powerful adult. Think about it: not being able to reason and negotiate as an adult will cost the adult a job and a good relationship – all because the parent took more time to discipline the child and make him STOP things, rather than taking the time to allow the child to experience and explore things. Granting a child freedom has nothing to do with letting him run all over the place, it means helping the child feel liberated with the ability to eliminate life's barriers – with the skills you give him.

Those in power lead easier lives. There is nothing wrong with granting children easier lives. Whether you envision others having all the power, or whether you equip your child with the ability to harness his power, and use it, is only a decision. Power, when displayed, shapes and moulds the way one thinks, sees or acts. Power inspires. It lends vision and fortifies faith. Dig deep and find your power. It's that stuff that makes you creative, confident, able, and loved by others. Then, look at your child, and REALLY observe the power he was born with, and find ways to strengthen what you discover. Put a new twist on the power exerted in your home. Don't let it be about your control over anyone. Let it be about how much light all of you can muster up and give out to the rest of the world.

Psychiatry and Resistance

Bruce Levine

The mass media equates anarchism with chaos and violence. However, the social philosophy of anarchism rejects authoritarian government, opposes coercion, strives for greatest freedom, works toward "mutual aid" and voluntary cooperation, and maintains that people organising themselves without hierarchies creates the most satisfying social arrangement. Many anarchists adhere to the principle of nonviolence (though the question of violence has historically divided anarchists in their battle to eliminate authoritarianism). Nonviolent anarchists have energised the Occupy Movement and other struggles for economic justice and freedom.

In practice, anarchism is not a dogmatic system. So for example, "practical anarchist" parents will use their authority to grab their child who has begun to run out into traffic. However, practical anarchists strongly believe that all authorities have the burden of proof to justify control, and that most authorities in modern society cannot bear that burden and are thus illegitimate – and should be eliminated and replaced by non-coercive, freely participating relationships.

My experience as a clinical psychologist for almost three decades is that many young people labeled with psychiatric diagnoses are essentially anarchists in spirit who are pained, anxious, depressed, and angered by coercion, unnecessary rules, and illegitimate authority. An often used psychiatric diagnosis for children and adolescents is oppositional defiant disorder (ODD); its symptoms include "often actively defies or refuses to comply with adult requests or rules" and "often argues with adults."

Among young people diagnosed with attention deficit hyperactivity disorder (ADHD), psychologist Russell Barkley, one of mainstream mental health's leading ADHD authorities, says that they have deficits in "rule-governed behaviour," as they are less responsive to rules of authorities and less sensitive to positive or negative consequences. A frequently used research tool that distinguishes alcohol/drug abuser personalities was developed by Craig MacAndrew (commonly called the MAC scale), and it reveals that the most significant "addictive personality type" have discipline problems at school, are less tolerant of boredom, are less compliant with authorities and some laws, and engage in more disapproved sexual practices.

I have encountered many people who had been diagnosed with bipolar disorder, schizophrenia, and other psychoses, and who are now politically conscious anarchists, including Sascha Altman DuBrul, author of *Maps to the Other Side: The Adventures of a Bipolar Cartographer*. DuBrul, several times diagnosed with bipolar disorder, has lived in rebel communities in Mexico, Central America, and Manhattan's Lower

East Side, worked on community farms, participated in Earth First! road blockades, demonstrated on the streets in the Battle for Seattle, and he reports that many of his anti-authoritarian friends also have been diagnosed with mental illness. Teenagers, as evidenced by their musical tastes, often have an affinity for anti-authoritarianism, but most do not act on their beliefs in a manner that would make them vulnerable to violent reprisals by authorities. However, I have found that many young people diagnosed with mental disorders – perhaps owing to some combination of integrity, fearlessness, and naïvety – have acted on their beliefs in ways that threaten authorities. Historically in American society, there is often a steep price paid by those who have this combination of integrity, fearlessness, and naïvety.

While DuBrul and his friends have political consciousness, my experience is that most rebellious young people diagnosed with mental disorders do not, and so they become excited to hear that there is actual political ideology that encompasses their point of view. They immediately become more whole after they discover that answering "yes" to the following questions does not mean that they suffer from a mental disorder but instead have a certain social philosophy:

Do you hate coercion and domination?

Do you love freedom?

Are you willing to risk punishments to gain freedom?

Do you instinctively distrust large, impersonal, and distant authorities?

Do you think people should organise themselves rather than submit to authorities?

Do you dislike being either an employer or an employee?

Do you smile after reading the Walt Whitman quote "Obey little, resist much"?

Young people who oppose inequality and exploitation, reject a capitalist economy, and aim for a society based on cooperative, mutually-owned enterprise are essentially left-anarchists – perhaps calling themselves "anarcho-syndicalists" or "anarcho-communitarians." When they discover what Noam Chomsky, Peter Kropotkin, Kirkpatrick Sale, or Emma Goldman have to say, they may identify with them. These young people have a strong moral streak of egalitarianism and a desire for social and economic justice. Not only are they not mentally ill but, from my perspective, they are the hope of society.

There is another group of freedom-loving young people who hate the coercion of parents, schools, and the state but lack an egalitarian moral streak, and are very much into money and capitalism. Some of them may have been dragged into the mental health system after having been caught drug dealing, and are labeled with conduct disorder and/or a personality disorder. While these young people rebel against they themselves being controlled and exploited, many of them are not averse to controlling and exploiting others, and so are not anarchists, but some have spiritual transformations and become so.

There are at least two ways that mental health professionals can join the resistance: (1) speak out about the political role of mental health institutions in maintaining the status quo in society, (2) depathologise and repoliticise rebellion in one's clinical practice, which includes helping young anarchists navigate an authoritarian society without becoming self-destructive or destructive to others, and helping families build respectful, non-coercive relationships. If a nonviolent anarcho-communitarian (politically conscious or otherwise) is dragged by parents into my office for failing to take school seriously but is otherwise pleasant and excited by learning, I tell parents that I do not believe that there is anything essentially "disordered" with their child. This sometimes gets me fired, but not all that often. It is my experience that most parents may think that believing a society can function without coercion is naive but they agree that it's not a mental illness, and they're open to suggestions that will create greater harmony and joy within their family.

I work hard with parents to have them understand that their attempt to coerce their child to take school seriously not only has failed – that's why they're in my office – but will likely continue to fail. And increasingly, the pain of their failed coercion will be compounded by the pain of their child's resentment, which will destroy their relationship with their child and create even more family pain. Many parents acknowledge that this resentment already exists. I ask liberal parents, for example, if they would try to coerce a homosexual child into being heterosexual or vice versa, and most say, "Of course not!" And so they begin to see that temperamentally anarchist children cannot be similarly coerced without great resentment.

It has been my experience that many rebellious young people labeled with psychiatric disorders and substance abuse don't reject all authorities, simply those they've assessed to be illegitimate ones, which just happens to be a great deal of society's authorities. Often, these young people are craving a relationship with mutual respect in which they can receive help navigating the authoritarian society around them.

NO!

ISSUE 18

AGAINST
ADULT
SUPREMACY

Adult Education

Adora Svitak

TED Transcript

Now, I want to start with a question: When was the last time you were called "childish"? For kids like me, being called childish can be a frequent occurrence. Every time we make irrational demands, exhibit irresponsible behavior, or display any other signs of being normal American citizens, we are called childish. Which really bothers me. After all, take a look at these events: Imperialism and colonisation, world wars, George W. Bush. Ask yourself, who's responsible? Adults.

Now, what have kids done? Well, Anne Frank touched millions with her powerful account of the Holocaust. Ruby Bridges helped to end segregation in the United States. And, most recently, Charlie Simpson helped to raise 120,000 pounds for Haiti, on his little bike. So as you can see evidenced by such examples, age has absolutely nothing to do with it. The traits the word "childish" addresses are seen so often in adults, that we should abolish this age-discriminatory word, when it comes to criticising behavior associated with irresponsibility and irrational thinking.

Then again, who's to say that certain types of irrational thinking aren't exactly what the world needs? Maybe you've had grand plans before, but stopped yourself, thinking, "That's impossible," or "That costs too much," or "That won't benefit me." For better or worse, we kids aren't hampered as much when it comes to thinking about reasons why not to do things. Kids can be full of inspiring aspirations and hopeful thinking, like my wish that no one went hungry, or that everything were free, a kind of utopia. How many of you still dream like that, and believe in the possibilities? Sometimes a knowledge of history and the past failures of Utopian ideals can be a burden, because you know that if everything were free, then the food stocks would become depleted and scarce and lead to chaos. On the other hand, we kids still dream about perfection. And that's a good thing, because in order to make anything a reality, you have to dream about it first.

In many ways, our audacity to imagine helps push the boundaries of possibility. For instance, the Museum of Glass in Tacoma, Washington, my home state, has a program called Kids Design Glass, and kids draw their own ideas for glass art. The resident artist said they got some of their best ideas from the program, because kids don't think about the limitations of how hard it can be to blow glass into certain shapes, they just think of good ideas. Now, when you think of glass, you might think of colourful Chihuly designs, or maybe Italian vases, but kids challenge glass artists to go beyond that, into the realm of brokenhearted snakes and bacon boys, who you can see has meat vision.

Now, our inherent wisdom doesn't have to be insider's knowledge. Kids already do a lot of learning from adults, and we have a lot to share. I think that adults should start learning from kids. Now, I do most of my speaking in front of an education crowd - teachers and students, and I like this analogy: It shouldn't be a teacher at the head of the class, telling students, "Do this, do that." The students should teach their teachers. Learning between grown-ups and kids should be reciprocal. The reality, unfortunately, is a little different, and it has a lot to do with trust, or a lack of it. Now, if you don't trust someone, you place restrictions on them, right? If I doubt my older sister's ability to pay back the 10 percent interest I established on her last loan, I'm going to withhold her ability to get more money from me, until she pays it back. True story, by the way.

Now, adults seem to have a prevalently restrictive attitude towards kids, from every "Don't do that, don't do this" in the school handbook, to restrictions on school Internet use. As history points out, regimes become oppressive when they're fearful about keeping control. And although adults may not be quite at the level of totalitarian regimes, kids have no or very little say in making the rules, when really, the attitude should be reciprocal, meaning that the adult population should learn and take into account the wishes of the younger population. Now, what's even worse than restriction, is that adults often underestimate kids' abilities. We love challenges, but when expectations are low, trust me, we will sink to them. My own parents had anything but low expectations for me and my sister. Okay, so they didn't tell us to become doctors or lawyers or anything like that, but my dad did read to us about Aristotle and pioneer germ-fighters, when lots of other kids were hearing "The Wheels on the Bus Go Round and Round." Well, we heard that one too, but "Pioneer Germ Fighters" totally rules.

I loved to write from the age of four, and when I was six, my mom bought me my own laptop equipped with Microsoft Word. Thank you, Bill Gates, and thank you, Ma. I wrote over 300 short stories on that little laptop, and I wanted to get published. Instead of just scoffing at this heresy that a kid wanted to get published, or saying wait until you're older, my parents were really supportive. Many publishers were not quite so encouraging. One large children's publisher ironically said that they didn't work with children. Children's publisher not working with children? I don't know, you're kind of alienating a large client there. One publisher, Action Publishing, was willing to take that leap and trust me, and to listen to what I had to say. They published my first book, "Flying Fingers," you see it here. And from there on, it's gone to speaking at hundreds of schools, keynoting to thousands of educators, and finally, today, speaking to you.

I appreciate your attention today, because to show that you truly care, you listen. But there's a problem with this rosy picture of kids being so much better than adults. Kids grow up and become adults just like you. Or just like you? Really? The goal is not to turn kids into your kind of adult, but rather, better adults than you have been, which may be a little challenging, considering your guys' credentials. But the way progress happens, is because new generations and new eras grow and develop and become better than the previous ones. It's the reason we're not in the Dark Ages anymore. No matter your position or place in life, it is imperative to create opportunities for children, so that we can grow up to blow you away.

Adults and fellow TEDsters, you need to listen and learn from kids, and trust us and expect more from us. You must lend an ear today, because we are the leaders of tomorrow, which means we're going to take care of you when you're old and senile. No, just kidding. No, really, we are going to be the next generation, the ones who will bring this world forward. And in case you don't think that this really has meaning for you, remember that cloning is possible, and that involves going through childhood again, in which case you'll want to be heard, just like my generation. Now, the world needs opportunities for new leaders and new ideas. Kids need opportunities to lead and succeed. Are you ready to make the match? Because the world's problems shouldn't be the human family's heirloom.

Thank you.

Class Dismissed (Excerpt: Sex, Race and Class)

Selma James

If the relation of caste to class where women are concerned presents itself in a hidden, mystified form, this mystification is not unique to women. The least powerful in the society are our children, also unwaged in a wage labour society. They were once accepted as an integral part of the productive activity of the community. The work they did was part of the total social labour and was acknowledged as such. Where capital is extending or has extended its rule, children are taken away from others in the community and forced to go to schools, against which the number of rebels is growing daily. Is their powerlessness a class question? Is their struggle against school the class struggle? We believe it is. Schools are institutions organised by capital to achieve its purpose through and against the child.

Capital sent them to school not only because they are in the way of others' more "productive" labour or only to indoctrinate them. The rule of capital through the wage compels every able-bodied person to function, under the law of division of labour, and to function in ways that are if not immediately, then ultimately profitable to the expansion and extension of the rule of capital. That, fundamentally, is the meaning of school. Where children are concerned, their labour appears to be learning for their own benefit.

So here are two sections of the working class whose activities, one in the home, the other in the school, appear to be outside of the capitalist wage labour relation because the workers themselves are wageless. In reality, their activities are facets of capitalist production and its division of labour. One, housewives, are involved in the production and reproduction of workers, what Marx calls labour power. They service those who are daily destroyed by working for wages and who need to be daily renewed; and they care for and discipline those who are being prepared to work when they grow up. The other, children, are those who from birth are the objects of this care and discipline, who are trained in homes, in schools and in front of the telly to be future workers.

But this has two aspects. In the first place, for labour power to be reproduced in the form of children, these children must be coerced into accepting discipline and especially the discipline of working, of being exploited in order to be able to eat. In addition, however, they must be disciplined and trained to perform a certain kind of work. The labour that capital wants done is divided and each category parcelled out internationally as the life work, the destiny, the identity of specific sets of workers.

Power, Patriarchy and Parenting

bell hooks

Feminist focus on children was a central component of contemporary radical feminist movement. By raising children without sexism women hoped to create a future world where there would be no need for an anti-sexist movement. Initially the focus on children primarily highlighted sexist sex roles and the way in which they were imposed on children from birth on. Feminist attention to children almost always focused on girl children, on attacking sexist biases and promoting alternative images. Now and then feminists would call attention to the need to raise boys in an anti-sexist manner but for the most part the critique of male patriarchy, the insistence that all men had it better than all women, trickled down. The assumption that boys always had more privilege and power than girls furled feminists prioritising a focus on girls.

One of the primary difficulties feminist thinkers faced when confronting sexism within families was that more often than not female parents were the transmitters of sexist thinking. Even in households where no adult male parental caregiver was present, women taught and teach children sexist thinking. Ironically, many people assume that any female-headed household is automatically matriarchal. In actuality women who head households in patriarchal society often feel guilty about the absence of a male figure and are hyper-vigilant about imparting sexist values to children, especially males. In recent times mainstream conservative pundits have responded to a wellspring of violent acts by young males of all classes and races by suggesting that single women cannot possible raise a healthy male child. This is just simply not true. The facts show that some of the most loving and powerful men in our society were raised by single mothers. Again it must be reiterated that most people assume that a woman raising children alone, especially sons, will fail to teach a male child how to become a patriarchal male. This is simply not the case.

Within white supremacist capitalist patriarchal cultures of domination, children do not have rights. The feminist movement was the first movement for social justice in this society to call attention to the fact that ours is a culture that does not love children, that continues to see children as the property of parents to do with as they will. Adult violence against children is a norm in our society. Problematically, for the most part feminist thinkers have never wanted to call attention to the reality that women are often the primary culprits in everyday violence against children simply because they are the primary parental caregivers. While it was crucial and revolutionary that feminist movement called attention to the fact that male domination in the home often creates an autocracy where men sexually abuse children, the fact is that masses of children are daily abused verbally and physically by women and men. Maternal sadism often leads women to emotionally abuse children, and feminist theory has not yet offered both feminist critique and feminist intervention when the issue is adult female violence against children.

In a culture of domination where children have no civil rights, those who are powerful, adult males and females, can exert autocratic rule of children. All the medical facts show that children are violently abused daily in this society. Much of that abuse is life threatening. Many children die. Women perpetuate this violence as much as men if not more. A serious gap in feminist thinking and practice has been the refusal of the movement to confront head-on adult female violence against children. Emphasising male domination makes it easy for women, including feminist thinkers, to ignore the ways women abuse children because we have all been socialised to embrace patriarchal thinking, to embrace an ethics of domination which says the powerful have the right to rule over the powerless and can use any means to subordinate them. In the hierarchies of white supremacist capitalist patriarchy, male domination of females is condoned, but so is adult domination of children. And no one really wants to call attention to mothers who abuse.

Often I tell the story of being at a fancy dinner party where a woman is describing the way she disciplines her young son by pinching him hard, clamping down on his little flesh for as long as it takes to control him. And how everyone applauded her willingness to be a disciplinarian. I shared the awareness that her behavior was abusive, that she was potentially planting the seeds for this male child to grow up and be abusive to women. Significantly, I told the audience of listeners that if we had heard a man telling us how he just clamps down on a woman's flesh, pinching her hard to control her behaviour it would have been immediately acknowledged as abusive. Yet when a child is being hurt this form of negative domination is condoned. This is not an isolated incident – much more severe violence against children is enacted daily by mothers and fathers.

Indeed the crisis the children of this nation face is that patriarchal thinking clashing with feminist changes is making the family even more of a war zone than it was when male domination was the norm in every household. The feminist movement served as the catalyst, uncovering and revealing the grave extent to which male sexual abuse of children has been and is taking place in the patriarchal family. It started with grown women in feminist movement receiving therapeutic care acknowledging that they were abuse survivors and bringing this acknowledgment out of the private realm of therapy into public discourse. These revelations created the positive ethical and moral context for children to confront abuse taking place in the present. However, simply calling attention to male sexual abuse of children has not created the climate where masses of people understand that this abuse is linked to male domination, that it will end only when patriarchy is eliminated. Male sexual abuse of children happens more often and is reported more often than female abuse, but female sexual coercion of children must be seen as just as horrendous as male abuse. And feminist movement must critique women who abuse as harshly as we critique male abuse. Beyond the realm of sexual abuse, violence against children takes many forms; the most commonplace forms are acts of verbal and psychological abuse.

Abusive shaming lays the foundation for other forms of abuse. Male children are often subjected to abuse when their behavior does not conform to sexist notions of masculinity. They are often shamed by sexist adults (particularly mothers) and other children. When male parental caregivers embody anti-sexist thought and behaviour boys and girls have the opportunity to see feminism in action. When feminist thinkers and activists provide children with educational arenas where anti-sexist biases are not the standards used to judge behaviour, boys and girls are able to develop healthy self-esteem. One of the most positive interventions the feminist movement made on behalf of children was to create greater cultural awareness of the need for men to participate equally in parenting not just to create gender equity but to build better relationships with children. Future feminist studies will document all the ways anti-sexist male parenting enhances the lives of children. Concurrently, we need to know more about feminist parenting in general, about the practical ways one can raise a child in an anti-sexist environment, and most importantly we need to know more about what type of people the children who are raised in these homes become.

Visionary feminist activists have never denied the importance and value of male parental caregivers even as we continually work to create greater cultural appreciation of motherhood and the work done by women who mother. A disservice is done to all females when praise for male participation in parenting leads to disparagement and devaluation of the positive job of mothering women do. At the beginning of the feminist movement feminists were harsh critics of mothering, pitting that task against careers which were deemed more liberating, more self-affirming. However, as early as the mid-'80s some feminist thinkers were challenging feminist devaluation of motherhood and the overvaluation of work outside the home. Writing on this subject in Feminist Theory: From Margin to Centre I made the point that:

> Working within a social context where sexism is still the norm, where there is unnecessary competition promoting envy, distrust, antagonism, and malice between individuals, makes work stressful, frustrating, and often totally unsatisfying… any women who like and enjoy the wage work they do feel that it takes too much of their time, leaving little space for other satisfying pursuits. While work may help women gain a degree of financial

independence or even financial self-sufficiency, for most women it has not adequately fulfilled human needs. As a consequence women's search for fulfilling labour done in an environment of care has led to re-emphasising the importance of family and the positive aspects of motherhood.

Ironically just when feminist thinkers had worked to create a more balanced portrait of mothering patriarchal mainstream culture launched a vicious critique of single-parent, female-headed households. That critique was most harsh when it came to the question of welfare. Ignoring all the data which shows how skilfully loving single mothers parent with very little income whether they receive state assistance or work for a wage, patriarchal critiques call attention to dysfunctional female-headed households, act as though these are the norm, then suggest the problem can be solved if men were in the picture as patriarchal providers and heads of households.

No anti-feminist backlash has been as detrimental to the well-being of children as societal disparagement of single mothers. In a culture which holds the two-parent patriarchal family in higher esteem than any other arrangement, all children feel emotionally insecure when their family does not measure up to the standard. A utopian vision of the patriarchal family remains intact despite all the evidence which proves that the well-being of children is no more secure in the dysfunctional male-headed household than in the dysfunctional female-headed household. Children need to be raised in loving environments. Whenever domination is present love is lacking. Loving parents, be they single or coupled, gay or straight, headed by females or males, are more likely to raise healthy, happy children with sound self-esteem. In future feminist movement we need to work harder to show parents the ways ending sexism positively changes family life. The feminist movement is pro-family. Ending patriarchal domination of children, by men or women, is the only way to make the family a place where children can be safe, where they can be free, where they can know love.

"Child Privilege"

Joy

Note: This is very US-centric. So to be clear, I know that what I write is not universal.

This is a fucked up notion for many reasons. First. Privilege is not about whose life is better. Privilege is SYSTEMIC POWER, which adults DO possess. Parents exercise control over every aspect of their children's lives. Think about it: the entire premise of a punishments/rewards relationship, of a "stern love," of "parenting" in general, is CONTROL. Young people are regularly stripped of our autonomy – to move, communicate, and interact on our own terms – by adults (not just parents, but also the state, private institutions, and adult society at large). Adult privilege IS the power to violate our autonomy, which every adult posses. Adult privilege is NOT having an easier life.

Second. "Having everything provided for" is NOT a justification for control. It's benevolent abuse. Which is, you know, not actually benevolent. Adult abusers regularly use the economic dependence of their children as justification for controlling them. I've also heard this gem: "Children are a protected class." Protected from what, exactly? From abuse? By giving adults absolute and exclusive control over kids' lives, you are enabling abuse. End of discussion.

Third. All of these so-called "adult responsibilities" stem from capitalism. If you actually have a problem with the stress and uncertainty that come with trying to survive in a capitalist society, you should turn your attention toward capitalism. Do NOT weaponise your situation against youth. Being oppressed (or just affected) on the axis of capitalism does NOT negate your social power as an adult. And it's not like capitalism doesn't affect youth. Being born into a poor family? Affects one's quality of life. Significantly. Even without "adult responsibilities." (I am middle-class myself and not speaking from lived experience… but this seems like common sense. Correct me if I'm wrong.) And then schools are becoming increasingly neoliberal… you see third grade test scores being used by private contractors to predict the number of prisons they need to build. (To be clear, I know this doesn't affect me as a white person. The prison industrial complex is anti-Black at its core.)

To summarise. "Adult responsibilities" are real. They do not entitle you to violate our autonomy. Fuck you. IMPORTANT P.S. (cw: paedophilia) I haven't seen this on tumblr (yet) but inevitably some dickwads will find this post and latch onto the idea of "full personhood" / "full autonomy" as an excuse for their paedophilia. FUCK THOSE PEOPLE.

Adulthood as Oppressor Identity

Adultism could not exist without the social classes of "child" and "adult." John Holt suggests that to end the dehumanisation of children, we abolish "the institution of childhood" i.e. we focus on ending the situation of children. But this ignores the people who actually put children in that situation. I suggest that we instead abolish adulthood.

Adulthood is a mindset. It is constructed at the individual level. While there are institutional factors that encourage its construction, it is ultimately not an institution in and of itself. Children are stereotyped as self-centred, irrational, unreasonable, entitled, manipulative, untrustworthy; while adults are thought to be empathetic, rational, reasonable, honest, trustworthy. The qualities ascribed to children suggest that they need to be controlled, while those ascribed to adults suggest their ability to control children. Adulthood is thus constructed in opposition to childhood.

These stereotypes are perpetuated by mass media as much as – perhaps even more than – by individuals. But this cannot obscure the fact that the internalisation of these stereotypes is individual. The individual grows up surrounded by the message "adults good, children bad." Unable to claim adulthood, they construct a specific notion of childhood that excludes themselves. "I'm not an adult… but at least I'm not a child!"

> The toddler insists "I'm not a baby, I'm a big boy!"; the 11th grade student avoids the stigma of hanging out with a 10th-grader. (S Bonnischen)

The individual enters adulthood having constantly constructed and re-constructed childhood in this way. Their entry into adulthood completes the oppositional child/adult construction because they (the individual) no longer occupy an ambiguous middle ground. "Not child", always synonymous with "me", is now also synonymous with "adult". There is another more potent construction of adulthood, which also happens at the individual level.

> Stepping into [the role of "the adult"] grants privilege and prestige – but it's dependent on wielding power over one or more actual young people. […] Interacting [with their children on an] equal basis is a threat to parents' sense of their own adulthood. Many parents are deeply invested in being a "good mother" or "good father" – putting that identity in jeopardy strikes at the very heart of who they see themselves as. To be a good parent, to be "the adult" at all, requires that they feel they are actively supervising / guiding / controlling their children's lives. (S Bonnischen)

Thus adulthood is constructed both as the opposite of childhood (being "an adult"), and as the power-wielder in an unequal relationship with a young person (being "the adult"). Both constructions of adulthood feed into a mentality of superiority and control which only harms young people. Therefore, they need abolishing. I emphasise the individual nature of adulthood because I believe its abolition begins when young people recognise its construction within themselves.

NO!

ISSUE 19

**AGAINST
ADULT
SUPREMACY**

Bullying Health

Elena Hagopyan

As soon as you got any "bigger" health problem, you're basically in trouble, not only by the things you're facing by your condition, but actually the opinion is far harder. Today it is better to be some picture perfect child, young person or adult, as otherwise, you will be looked down upon by others. The silly of it is the fact no one is picture perfect, everyone who seems this way, it is just an act.

Myself, I have epilepsy, it always has been a problem, basically because I have to hide it every single day. If you have epilepsy, you better have the version of seizures most know, tonic-clonic seizures, even while it probably is horrible to have them, people at least understand it. I don't, I have 2 types of seizures, ones most ever will rarely notice, atypical absence seizures, and much more obvious ones, atonic seizures. Most around me will know, friends and family, and yet, I am in actual fact not open about it at all. Yes, very often it is better to not tell people than to actually tell people there is something "wrong" with you, as while it is not really wrong, people will see you as actually wrong.

And in too many ways that is stupid, fact is that I should be open about it, as otherwise bad things could in fact happen, and yet by the stigma people create, I wouldn't even want to do so. Yet, that is not even all, as I have to take medication because of my condition, and the only thing you will think of when doing so, is how people will react, as too often it is not nice. Still, it actually gets worse by the fact adults should protect children and youth who are in these situations, yet most often they will just join in the bullying that happens if you have any health problem.

It is an obvious problem, adults bullying children and youth over health problems, and it happens very often. The silly fact is that it happens even at schools, teachers who will bully or just treat children and youth differently because they aren't the same according to the teacher's eyes. Ending up in many children and youth getting into depression and even committing suicide, with the actual cause being teachers. As if the life isn't hard enough if you have any health problem, if you are a child or youth, you will get the added horror called school. While school should be the place of education, and getting to a bright and happy future, it is in many ways a hell on earth, and to a huge amount of children and youth, the most dreaded thing of the day.

It is actually also one of the biggest reasons of children and youth dropping out of schools, being bullied at school. While most parents try to look at the reasons and quite often get blamed when a child drops out of school, it is almost always the school that is the actual problem. And that is problematic, yet, far too often still ignored, and you can get this happening even without any health condition. The crazy thing is that children and youth are far too often already in very troubled situations, we get thrown the troubles of school on top of it, and if you got a health problem, it only gets unbearable. And eventually, it never actually stops, instead of searching for solutions, it all gets stigma dropped upon it, it is a disgrace to ever openly talk about these problems. No, instead the problems continue and continue, and as noted for far too long now, suicide ratings of children and youth are only increasing and increasing, and adults basically keep searching for the problem, while it always has been right in front of them.

All children and youth are stigmatised in ways, we are all a disgrace to a part of the adult society, and as the years go on, it seems to only get worse and worse. Instead of us being seen for who we are, which always is different, we are rather seen as ways of campaigns to help adults, while all this time, our problems, the things we really would like to be solved, they are overlooked, not important enough, as basically, we are not important enough to adults, even while they think they are showing this by certain statements.

Independence or Respect for Elders

One of the reasons that Donald Trump has flummoxed pollsters and political analysts is that his supporters seem to have nothing in common. He appeals to evangelical and secular voters, conservative and moderate Republicans, independents and even some Democrats. Many of his supporters are white and don't have a college degree, but he also does well with some highly educated voters, too.

What's bringing all these different people together, new research shows, is a shared type of personality – a personality that in many ways has nothing to do with politics. Indeed, it turns out that your views on raising children better predict whether you support Trump than just about anything else about you.

Matthew MacWilliams, a doctoral candidate at the University of Massachusetts, Amherst, conducted a poll in which Republicans were asked four questions about child-rearing. With each question, respondents were asked which of two traits were more important in children:

– independence or respect for their elders
– curiosity or good manners
– self-reliance or obedience
– being considerate or being well-behaved

Psychologists use these questions to identify people who are disposed to favour hierarchy, loyalty and strong leadership – those who picked the second trait in each set – what experts call "authoritarianism." That many of Trump's supporters share this trait helps explain the success of his unconventional candidacy and suggests that his rivals will have a hard time winning over his adherents. When it comes to politics, authoritarians tend to prefer clarity and unity to ambiguity and difference. They're amenable to restricting the rights of foreigners, members of a political party in the minority and anyone whose culture or lifestyle deviates from their own community's.

"For authoritarians, things are black and white," MacWilliams said. "Authoritarians obey." While some scholars have argued that authoritarianism is associated with conservatism, there are certainly authoritarians in both parties. And MacWilliams found that the likelihood that participants in his poll supported Trump had little to do with how conservative they were – no surprise, as Trump's positions on many issues are relatively moderate. Trump also appealed more or less equally to the likely Republican primary voters in MacWilliams's sample regardless of their age or sex, income and level of education. Regular churchgoers and evangelicals were no more or less likely to support Trump, either.

Those with authoritarian views on raising children were, however. Among Republicans who are otherwise similar, authoritarians – those who chose the second option in each of the four questions above – have nearly 50-50 odds of supporting Trump. The odds are much lower for those who chose the first option on all four questions: Assuming they were similar in other respects to the authoritarians, the chance that Republicans in this group supported Trump were just 1 in 6. By contrast, how respondents answered the questions about child-rearing had little or nothing to do with their likelihood of supporting one of Trump's rivals. The authoritarians were somewhat more likely to support Sen. Ted Cruz (R-Tex.) but not by much.

Now, you might think that how a parent raises a child has little to do with how they vote. After all, roughly half of the people with authoritarian views on all four questions did not support Trump. So MacWilliams checked to make sure that his questions about child-rearing were in fact predictive of authoritarian political attitudes. In the poll, respondents were also asked whether they thought that it is sometimes necessary to keep other groups in their place, whether opposition from the political minority sometimes needs to be circumscribed, and whether they think the minority's rights must be protected from the majority's power. Trump's supporters were much more likely to oppose protections for the minority, while the other candidates' supporters didn't have strong opinions one way or another. For example, the chance that a Republican who agreed that other groups sometimes need to be put in place also supported Trump was about 3 in 5.

MacWilliams also found that respondents who said they felt threatened by terrorism were also significantly more likely to support Trump, and polling by The Washington Post has found that opposition to immigration is something else that unites many of his supporters. Authoritarians, given their aversion to outsiders, are more likely both to perceive threats from terrorism and to oppose immigration. That Trump's support is based partly on personality rather than policy helps explain why his supporters are so enthusiastic about some of his most widely mocked ideas – such as banning all Muslims from entering the country, a proposal that his opponent Jeb Bush called "unhinged." "This is in people's guts, not their brains," said Marc Hetherington, a political scientist and an expert on authoritarianism at Vanderbilt University. "This is much more primal."

And the findings are bad news for the other contenders in the GOP primary, since authoritarians tend to be set in their ways. What they have in common is an aversion to new kinds of experiences. "Some people eat at Thai and Indian restaurants, and some people eat at steak houses," Hetherington said. That aversion could also extend to politicians they don't know as well as Trump. "It's not worth it to attack him," said MacWilliams, who spent many years as a progressive political consultant before going to graduate school. "A large segment of his base is like 'granite,'" MacWilliams added, quoting an anonymous adviser to Sen. Marco Rubio (R-Fla.) who was interviewed by Jeremy W. Peters of the New York Times. Analysts have conventionally divided the Republican primary race into "lanes" – candidates who appeal to evangelicals run in the "evangelical lane," for example. There might also be an "establishment lane" and a "libertarian lane." Some have argued that Trump is taking up all of the lanes at once.

"Maybe the future of the GOP is this one wide, luxurious lane, allowing the Trump steamroller easy passage," wrote The Washington Post's Philip Bump. Another interpretation is just that Trump has discovered a new lane – the authoritarian lane – that other candidates might seek to exploit in the future. "Does that become an activated part of the party moving forward or not?" MacWilliams asked. "I think that is a key question. Is it specific to his ability to speak to them and activate them, or not?" Authoritarianism isn't always a negative trait, noted Vanderbilt's Hetherington. Authoritarians can be more direct and decisive when the situation calls for it. "There's this notion that all the nuanced navel gazing that liberals do is superior," he said. "Not always." Nonetheless, research on authoritarianism is extremely sensitive, since it began after World War II, when psychologists and social scientists wanted to understand how so many people could support repressive, homicidal dictatorships in Europe and elsewhere. "I'm not saying they're fascists," MacWilliams said of Trump's supporters, "but authoritarians obey."

One of the greatest breakthroughs in anarchist theory and practice first appeared six years ago, and hardly any anarchists even know of its existence. Not only that, but most of the anarchists who do know of its existence either disregard it or dismiss it with comments containing hierarchical and authoritarian language. I am referring to the philosophy and practice known as Taking Children Seriously or TCS.

Taking Children Seriously is an educational and parenting philosophy which uses Karl Popper's views on epistemology, critical rationalism and a belief in fallibilism to reach a conclusion that coercion of any form is bad for the growth of knowledge and psychologically damaging to people, especially children. From this conclusion, Taking Children Seriously creates the framework for a methodology through which parents can cooperate with their children to find mutually preferable solutions to problems and disagreements that arise between them. The TCS movement has over a thousand participants all over the world, has produced two books and maintains a journal and a number of active e-mail discussion lists.

TCS takes parenting, a subject which is hardly ever discussed or thought about in anarchist circles, and provides an approach to it which is consistent with anarchist principles that oppose hierarchy and domination. TCS also lends a sharply critical eye towards contemporary authoritarian parenting philosophies and practices. The lack of such a critical approach to parenting, as well as the lack of an alternative parenting methodology consistent with anarchist principles, creates one of the most discouraging situations within the anarchist movement. Namely, anarchists end up inexplicably conveying messages to their children of acceptance of the "necessity" of relationships of domination.

TCS combines educational philosophy, epistemology and parenting and transforms them into a unified and inter-dependent system. This is of great value to anarchists, since most anarchists strive for a holistic outlook and approach towards people and society, and tend to shun laundry lists of forms of oppression and anarchist principles. Along with providing a holistic approach to child-raising, TCS provides a rational approach, as well as an emphasis on peoples innate fallibility. Given the fact that many defenders of authority often use the inequality of knowledge as a justification for those with the greater knowledge to assume positions of authority, TCS sees the explicit recognition of ones own fallibility as being essential for preventing one from becoming an authority over children. TCS also sees this as vital for the growth of knowledge, since if one realises that one may be making a mistake, one is left more open to new and better ideas which can be of more use for both parent and child alike.

Most people, anarchists included, unconsciously view children as being products in the process of being assembled. Schooling, parental advice, life experience and sometimes religious indoctrination are supposed to supply the product with the appropriate software necessary for functioning, while parental control and "discipline" are supposed to ensure that the product does not damage itself or leave the factory during the assembly process. This view of children comes about from a lack of faith in the abilities of children to use reason or make their own decisions. Instead of this, the TCS approach contends that every action that one does comes from an individual choice, either explicitly or implicitly. The choice one chooses may or may not be the right one, but it is through the use of one's abilities to reason that one is able to eventually find the choice that works best for them at the moment, and as a result create or grow their own knowledge.

TCS says that children can and should live outside the factory/product paradigm of childhood. TCS sees authority of any kind as being detrimental to the growth of knowledge by discouraging one to think for themselves, since such activity is futile under authority. With no certain or secure environment through which one could put ones thoughts into practice and test out the validity of one's ideas, one has no safe grounds on which to grow one's knowledge. Furthermore, any "education" or "advice" given by an authority figure to a child has no deep value for the child, other than that of being a tool through which the child can appease the authority or use to score points to gain some reward (psychological or tangible) which is offered as an "incentive" by the authority. Outside of the social construct of the parent/child or school relationships, the "knowledge" or behaviours one is supposed to carry out no longer has any apparent use-value to the child, and therefore can be forgotten without any negative consequences. These behaviours or "knowledge" were never something which the child used to satisfy their own curiosities or interests, and therefore have no personal significance to them.

TCS' conception of the ideal role that a parent should play is in many ways similar to that of many anarchists conceptions of the role that anarchists should play in society. TCS believes that parental advice can still be very useful to children and that parents should offer their advice and useful information to the child whenever the child is willing to receive it. TCS sees the role of parents as being that of a "helper" for the child. The parent is not supposed to be a "guide" or set an example, but instead should be a supplier of good ideas, useful information, resources, and materials. Parents should also actively work to make sure that their child does not become trapped in a coercive situation that they do not want to be in and to make sure that their children are well-informed of any potentially coercive situation that they could become involved with, so that the child does not stumble onto a coercive situation without warning. Parents are not necessarily "protectors" of their children, but rather people who use their special advantages of being a parent to help their children live in as open and free an environment as possible. This will probably mean that the parent may end up playing the role of the "protector", but it would only be done so at the expressed (verbally or otherwise) desire of the child for protection.

Now, some people may look at this and think that TCS asks for the parent to be an amazing, always-working, self-sacrificing saint. TCS is actually very much against that idea. TCS is opposed to parents sacrificing themselves for their children, and sees the desires and preferences of both the parent and the child as being of equal importance. TCS instead posits that great effort should be made to find mutually preferred solutions to problems and disagreements. With authority damaging a lot of our current abilities for independent and creative thought, the potential for common preference finding may seem small to none. However TCS contends that with lots of practice and discovering what practical and self-imposed barriers exist within ourselves, we can eventually discover how to be creative and be more effective at finding common preferences. The trick is to always honestly strive to find common preferences between parents and children, and not give into the authority-based myths that it is "impossible".

One of the major failings of anarchism is that it has so far overwhelmingly examined and analysed big picture things like institutions, class, civilisation, and society, and has paid next to no attention to smaller scale things, like psychology, epistemology, interpersonal relations and face-to-face interactions. One of the major failings of TCS is that it has had the exact opposite problem. An example of this problem is the fact that TCS considers parental authority to be something which could be eliminated by the parent simply thinking and behaving differently. This outlook pays no attention to the fact that parental authority is also an institutional creation. With the State using laws that force every child to live under the dictates of a legal guardian, a police force that will find and bring back every "runaway" child, and an economic system that forces every child to be materially dependent upon a parent, a parent will have authority over their child regardless of what parenting style they practice. With this being the case, a child can not genuinely trust a parent to be non-authoritarian with them, for at any time and for any reason the parent could impose rules upon them and have the full force of the State to back them up. To truly abolish authority, it needs to be simultaneously eliminated at an institutional and social level as well as at an interpersonal and psychological level.

Another example of TCS' lack of social consciousness, is that it pays no attention to how race, class, patriarchy and other forms of social oppression coerce and dominate children. If one truly wants to eliminate coercion from children's lives, and from the practice of parenting, one needs to have a clear analysis of how all the various spheres of life effect and relate to the lives of children and parents. Taking this into account, it could be said that race, class and patriarchy coerce children just as much as the State and schools do, and that parents actions are just as guided by considerations of race, class and patriarchy as they are by the dictates of the State.

arn. Resist. Escape. Imagine.

School teaches us a lot of crap. Not just in boring textbook lessons, but in its day to day activities. It teaches obedience and submission to authority. It teaches that academic intelligence is more important than our passion in life, that getting a job and having an income is more important than building and nurturing a healthy community. Difference in economic class is also a large factor in the quality of a learning environment. But regardless of wealth or poverty, mass education based on compulsion and competition will never result in self-empowered, and cooperative people. We need to get the schoolin' mentality outta our heads!

Challenging authority can be very empowering. In a society where alienation and frustration often lead people to find release in drug abuse or misdirected aggression, we need to seek ways to channel our rage and attack the root causes of our problems. Rebellion is healthy, now let's make it strategic, too. Get with a group of trusted friends or work alone. Make an underground newsletter. Write inspiring graffiti. Play pranks. Hand out flyers. Make posters. Plan walkouts or skip days. Do phone/fax jams to the administration office. Just be aware of who you are affecting and play safe!

What are our options? What would we do without schools?! Look around, kids everywhere are leaving the school institution and taking education back into their own hands. There are tons of home school groups around. Many are conservative, but often they have tools and resources that may help you start a more radical unschooling support group. If it is the question of pleasing the parents, check out the GED option, or a structured mail-in homeschool course. If they won't be satisfied with your decision then maybe you should look into legal emancipation. Parents abuse their authority, it is what they've learned to do all their lives. They need some unlearning of their own, but in the meantime don't endure any sort of abuse. We have to find ways out of these self-perpetuating cycles.

Imagine what the world would be like if kids were free to pursue their own interests, instead of being locked up in a school all day, for 12 years, and force fed 'knowledge.' School doesn't only affect youth, it affects anyone who has hope for the future. School is the breeding ground for the domination, competition, and violence in society. Getting out of school and fighting it is a big step in the direction of freedom and equality. We need to challenge authority and social privilege wherever it is found. Youth have a strong tradition of igniting movements. The potential for a new world lives inside you…

NO!

ISSUE 20

AGAINST
ADULT
SUPREMACY

Condemned and Hated

Isis Nelson

Adults have consistently ignored young opinions and voices forever. It's taught to us that we should respect our elders, because they're old, and not speak unless spoken to by an adult. They constantly fail to protect and help us. The history of our world is filled with young people and children being failed by adults and losing their rights. From birth, we're told that we are inherently inferior. Year after year, young people's ideas are shot down by older relatives, older siblings, teachers, professors, leaders, bosses, etc. Our ambitious, often progressive, ideals and values are instantly invalid because we're "young and inexperienced", full of "idealism", or told older people "know better". Love, compassion, inclusivity, and ideas of acceptance are laughed off by adults.

We're compared to communists, socialists, "feminists" (with very negative denotations), "hippies", "SJWs" (whatever that means to them), and oppressed by systematic, visible, active values older people have against the young. We're constantly told that change has to be incremental and slow; almost-like how the U.S. government allowed states to adjust, meaning it took years for schools, mostly in the South, to desegregate. Incremental change is inefficient and never-enough for the most ignored people in this world. I am absolutely tired of waiting for older people to catch up with our always changing, diverse planet and inhabitants. We cannot allow older, ignorant actions and opinions to blind us from the humanity of others. I don't have any patience for adults' failings, stale, failures to acknowledge oppression, and absolutist ways. I am tired of having to respect people older than me without ever knowing their actions or inactions. Too many adults in my life have failed me to let me allow this to continue. I, for one, refuse to give in the oppressive, stagnant actions and views elders and adults have against us. As if we're not educated, socially aware, smart, and worthy of respect. I'm tired of being yelled at because "not everything is about race", or how "unrealistic" my ideas are.

Children and teenagers have rights, just as every human does. We cannot be made silenced or ignored due to older peoples' unchanging values. Just because they lived in the 60s or 70s and are alive doesn't make me respect, and/or like them. I do not care for people that think I should like them because they're older than me. I judge others by their character, actions, and views, not age. I like and respect people for their actions, inactions, attitudes, ethics, and ways of thinking. I don't like or respect others when they oppress/harm children, and then actively allow for their generation to destroy that which is around us, promote hawkish ideals and inhumane actions. My snarl will be vicious and my voice louder when I'm discounted just because of my age. As if my years and experiences on Earth confirm my ideas and views.

Age discrimination against young individuals is called "adultism" and is currently defined as "positive bias toward adults, addictions to adults, and discrimination toward the young". At the heart of most conversations and actions between adults and youth have positive adult bias. Education, youth work, business, schools, government organisations, or elsewhere, adultism is motivation behind behavior. It is present in attitudes, cultures, systems, physical places, and much more. Adultism also goes hand-in-hand with ephebiphobia, the fear of youth. This phobia is full-blown in modern media. Academics, government agencies, educators, and youth advocacy organisations describe ephbiphobia as "any loathing, paranoia, or fear of young people, or the time of life called 'youth'". This widespread feeling among adults affects everything, and it's a legitimate issue. Don't let anyone tell you otherwise. Denying young people their right to vote and representation, creating policies, laws, and structures excluding youth voices very well might be ephebiphobia. Along with legislation, agencies and libraries that exclude or deny youth participation as an outreach method is an act of discrimination. This applies to police, government personnel and administrators that act in overbearing or misguided ways.

Ephebiphobia, unfortunately, has a large affect on politics. Once young individuals connect with their community through forms of civic engagement like volunteering and activism, they're far more likely to be become and remain active voters for the rest of their lives. Fear of youth has led legislators and voting organisations to ignore young peoples' concerns and enthusiasm to influence the world around them. In culture, media networks and publishers often demonise young people's interests, activities, and ideas. Through this, we feel ashamed to be involved with our own peers and communities. To add onto that, young PoC are neglected by youth leadership programs, and are then locked up in juvenile detention centres, making their experiences of racism and sexism much worse. This reinforces stereotypes of minorities, meanwhile forcing young PoC to silence themselves and their cultures in fear of being persecuted.

June Jordan, a Caribbean-American feminist poet and activist, in her book Passion, a set of poems from 1977 – 1980, said this about hippies in the 1970s: "When we heard about the hippies, the barely more than boys and girls who decided to try something different... we laughed at them. We condemned them, our children, for seeking a different future. We hated them for their flowers, for their love, and for their unmistakable rejection of every hideous, mistaken compromise that we had made throughout our hollow, money-bitten, frightened, adult lives..." Does this not ring true about current socially and politically aware teenagers and young adults? We're condemned for dreaming about better and different futures filled with acceptance, love, and new values, free of any discrimination. Why is that a bad thing? Why must we be so hated for thinking forward about our own future and the children that will inhabit it? Why is positive progress suddenly so appalling that we're shamed for even thinking about it? Does democracy not apply to us too?

Ephebiphobia and adultism have existed for thousands of years. Plato once remarked, "What is happening to our young people? They disrespect their elders, they disobey their parents. They ignore the law. They riot in the streets, inflamed with wild notions. Their morals are decaying. What is to become of them?" Versions of this are continually echoed throughout time. Hatred of young people is very real and very damaging. Because of our continually risk-adverse culture, most children's behaviours are constrained and restricted by their parents. We're raised and educated, then kept "safe" due to our parents' own anxieties, which are fuelled by stories and images of violent, aggressive crimes. Young people are labeled as "troublemakers" and "failures" because societies fail to even notice our bright, and sometimes hidden, potentials.

These fears of youth culture and prejudices against us lessen the chances of the youngest generations to succeed in the future. I despair for my fellow minors every day. A violent, aggressive, anti-social minority, one that's always existed, causes us to be viewed through slanted lenses. This view is so distorted, young people face a self-fulfilling prophecy: why even bother to try when you're told that you're a failure? Why try to strive when your very existence is seen as an annoying nuisance? Adult paternalism wants to protect young people, and if this process curtails freedoms, damages potential, and destroys civil liberties, it's viewed as merely incidental. Most of the old do not care about us, or our experiences. We're barely human at all to them, just naive children who don't learn or think.

My message to other young people: rebel, liberate yourselves and peers. Do not allow adults or elders to treat you as sub-human. You are your own being, with your own thoughts, feelings, values, and ideas. Do your best and fight against a society that was not made for you. Be fair, kind, compassionate, and accepting of those different than you. Please don't be ashamed to be who you are. You are valuable and just as human as your parents, teachers, or anyone else. We, like every other person, deserve to be respected and only judged by our character, not by our age, race, religion, nationality, etc. Being a "special snowflake" isn't a bad thing. Shed the ugly labels those who're older than you embedded in your skin. Aspire to be better than the generations before us. Don't let oppression remain in your homes. We have the potential to make the world a better place, so we will. We are the future, after all, and we know the world is better when we work together. Show hateful adults what the future looks like.

Akilah S. Richards

I often hear people talk about pregnancy from a space of gratitude – and sometimes excitement. Though I agree that the journey is incredible and enriching, there is another, perhaps less embraced aspect: For me, pregnancy was also full of moments of intense vulnerability, fear, and at times, anger. I felt fearful about my own safety, it being so inextricably linked with the safety of the person growing in my belly.

Inadvertent pushes from someone who stood in a line behind me, an overly-ambitious driver who darted across me at an intersection, a woman who threatened me because she (wrongly) assumed I stole her parking spot – all those instances of intense vulnerability and primal fear, stemming from my need to protect my future child. Even more unnerving were the instances where physical contact with my belly wasn't just implied, it was accomplished. This is where my anger would rise to the surface – I'd get angry at the people who felt completely within their rights to touch my belly, to touch my baby. Whether from an elderly man or a woman who was also a mother, I resented them for feeling okay with touching my child without permission, even when she was in utero. For sure, I felt uncomfortable with them trying to touch my body – and all that that says about being a woman in public space. But more than that, it clued me in to many adults' idea that they don't need children's permission to touch them – or to require that they touch someone else.

Today, my daughters are twelve and ten, and I still feel the need to protect them physically – and to advocate for their right to govern their own bodies. But I have to do more than advocate for them. In a world that constantly sends messages to women about connecting their value with their physicality and desirability, I need to help them operate with an awareness of their right to reject or accept physical touch, or any act that affects their personal space or feeling of safety, from any adult or child. And that means I have to be honest about the ways that I, myself, might infringe on their personal boundaries, and I have to facilitate these conversations with the adults around me. And I don't just mean conversations about what we can do to protect children, but what we must do to help children understand their options for protecting their physical and emotional selves.

One way we can approach this goal is to explore some of the common mistakes we adults make when it comes to helping children practice bodily autonomy, which is at the root of consent culture for children. Otherwise, we will continue to do the things that compromise the self-confidence, the sense of safety/bodily autonomy, and the mental wellness of the children we love. Because the reality is that children are coerced into situations where their bodies are treated as the property of their parents. The instances vary from making them hug a family member to trading their body for sex, drugs, or even food. All of these instances can send a message to children that their bodies are not their own. They also blur the lines between safe and unsafe touch, or consent versus coercion, and make it difficult for many children to identify when they're being inappropriately or uncomfortably touched by an adult or another child. Many of us send messages that lessen their ability to recognise and trust what feels safe and uncomfortable for them, as well as how to confidently communicate with an adult that they trust when their personal boundaries are violated by anyone, including an adult or child they know and trust.

Statistically, the percentages are wildly unnerving: 90% of child sexual abuse victims know the perpetrator in some way, and 68% are abused by family members. What's more staggering is that 90% are abused by someone they know, love, or trust, and that 20% of child sexual abuse victims are under the age of eight. Most of them don't tell until they become adults. One of the reasons for this is that as children, they didn't have language around those feelings. No one was talking to them about their right to feel safe in their own bodies – to have and assert personal boundaries as a way of protecting themselves.

Consent culture is often confined to the topic of consensual sex or intimacy among adults, but it should extend toward all behaviours and to children. Similarly, the term bodily autonomy tends to be more widely recognised under a specific topic: reproductive justice advocacy – and more specifically, the pro-choice movement among abortion rights. So as to extend these important concepts beyond the scope of sex and reproduction, let's look how parents' mistakes around bodily autonomy can contradict the practice of consent culture among children. Because when children don't feel sure about inappropriate touch, we must look at the narratives around body ownership and consent. For this reason, we must look at confident body autonomy for all people, even before they become adults, and outside of the context of sex.

Teaching Children to Ignore Personal Boundaries

In the US, we have a subtle history of showing children that their bodies are owned by their parents. Forced physical contact with relatives reinforce the dangerously wrong message that relatives can't be abusers. "Grandpa just wants to hug you – don't back away," or other similar verbal prompts, tell children to ignore their feelings about a person (whether based on intuition or past experience) and listen to what an adult says instead. As well-meaning observers, we adults often infringe on personal boundaries within children's interactions. Coercing a reserved child to hold hands and dance around with an outgoing child may feel like we're helping that child develop good social skills. But what we may actually do is teach them that it's okay for other people to force them to do what makes them (or other people) comfortable.

In later years, that can cause some children to feel that they need to be forced to do things, or that their natural tendency is somehow not okay. This can also have long-term negative effects on their social skills because self-esteem and authentic friendships are difficult to form and maintain when a person isn't okay with who and how they innately are. Also, many children who endure sexual abuse in particular don't tell because they're afraid of being blamed for being complicit in the abuse. This tells us that children don't understand abuse. That's in part because we, the adults, don't give them the language to name these experiences, and to feel safe coming to us about them.

Difficult aspects of personal boundary violation, particularly peer-to-peer abuse, make it extra complicated for adults to feel clear on how to broach the topic with children. But children need to know that other children can be abusers and that they can abuse another child by touching them without permission, even if that child told them yes in the past. Whether subtle or overt, the effects of childhood body violations are that we don't feel that we own ourselves. I know this from personal experience. We feel uncomfortable, unsure, or even afraid about asserting dominion over our own bodies. And again, it's important to realise that our bodies and our boundaries exist outside of sex, and consent is required for anything having to do with our bodies.

A solution to the blurred lines of personal boundaries is to practice parenting without coercion. Consent culture should start with children – and when children grow up believing that all people have the right to control and protect their own bodies, then they're likely to respect other people's boundaries, and to speak up when boundaries – whether their own or those of others – are being violated.

Reinforcing Shame or Silence Around Body-Related Feelings

Instead of starting positive, developmentally appropriate conversation about bodies, sex, and intimacy in general, many parents tend to omit those terms when conversing with their children. But getting comfortable with saying penis, vagina, anus, or even the more popular (and maybe less easy to hear from a child) slang terms like butthole, for example, can lessen the feeling of shame around talking about private body parts or body-related feelings.

These same types of conversations can also help children feel equipped to communicate with someone they trust if they are being sexually violated, for example. This way, we're not just giving them language about what's happening with them, we're also helping them express what's happening to them. If they're comfortable naming them, then they have language to utilise when those body parts are affected by anyone in any way.

Another word that often goes unspoken among parents to children in healthy ways is masturbation. It's normal for children's curiosity to include their own bodies, sometimes showing up as self-pleasuring. Labelling that form of self-exploration as bad, or avoiding the topic with your child altogether, can make it difficult for a child to feel comfortable with their own bodies and physical feelings. As caring adults, one way we can nurture safe space for children is to educate ourselves on taboo topics like masturbation and children, particularly prepubescent children. Some of us may have incorrect ideas about masturbation based on our parents' perspectives or other aspects of our own introduction to sexuality. But our children are not us, and though they are our responsibility, their bodies and experiences are their own. In support of that, we can read, discuss, and watch our way towards a sex-positive approach to parenting so that our children feel safe asking questions, and knowing (from experience) that they can discuss any aspect of their bodies with us, including sensations and thoughts that they may find pleasurable.

Personally, I address masturbation with my daughters in part because I don't ever want to set the precedent that anyone (not even their mother) needs to validate how to explore aspects of their sexuality. My intention is to avoid making masturbation an issue of morality or appropriateness, and instead focus on what is socially safe and personally hygienic. In other words, as Lea Grover so perfectly stated, "We don't play with our vulvas at the table."

Neglecting to Teach Your Child the Importance of Their Intuition

Intuition is not exclusive to adulthood, and it can play a very helpful role in helping a child develop a healthy sense of bodily autonomy. At any age, we have feelings in our bellies or chests, for example, that are directly triggered by feelings of safety or lack thereof. Help children to name and acknowledge those feelings – and to trust them.

One way I practice nurturing intuition is to help children understand what intuition does. For my girls, I like the simple definition of intuition as a kind of internal safety alarm. I give them specific examples of times that I listened to my intuition and kept myself safe, and times that I ignored my intuition, and wasn't sure how to protect myself when I faced danger. I'm not always sure if this is effective, but it helps me be sure that I'm practicing what I believe will work, and what has worked with them in prior instances. Asking them how intuition feels for them is good, too. That way, they've verbalised the feelings and can more easily recognise and even share them when they show up.

Some parents tend to direct their child on how they should interact with a new adult, instead of watching and seeing how their child responds to them and going from there. That's an example of intuitive interference. In order for a child to develop a sense of trust in their own intuition, we as parents have to respect their choices, and decide on a safe place and time to discuss the interaction and see if our child has questions. This is where we parents can be advocates and allies for our children.

For example, if I meet up with a friend who has an outgoing child and I have my bona fide introvert in tow, I let that parent know that my daughter may or may not play with their child. Or that she may not hug them, nor participate in any well-meaning small talk. I often bring books, games, and even art supplies along so that my daughter can feel comfortable in that setting (where she's accompanying me somewhere) without feeling pushed to engage with anyone, child or adult, unless she chooses to do so. We can also tell them about your own experiences with intuition and encourage them to talk, write about, or act out moments when they recognised intuitive feelings. When we parent without addressing intuitive feelings and how to express them, we can miss opportunities to convey the importance of words like "no" and "stop," or phrases like "I don't want to" or "I don't like that."

If a child is playing with someone whose body language or verbal cues lead a child to start feeling uncomfortable, we can tell them that an uneasy feeling in their belly or chest is enough to warrant them saying "no," "stop," or "I don't like that," because their bodies are their own, and they get to choose what is done to it. And more than that, they get to express their choice through consent or refusal. Also tell them that it's important they stop whatever they're doing to someone else's body when that person uses those key terms. This way, we help children to start exploring the reality that they may not agree with or understand why someone is saying "no" to them, and that the person does not need to explain whatever they're declining. Saying "no" is enough.

There are examples among children in all parts of the world that stem from lack of consent where children are concerned. Certainly, this includes sexual abuse, as is the normal conversation around consent culture, but it includes more. It also includes non-sexual activities and daily occurrences that offer opportunity to practice consent culture in all aspects of living. The point here is to become much more proactive about preventing sexual and other forms of physical abuse by adults to children, and among children as well.

We may not be able to prevent all instances, but if we raise young people who are clear about personal boundaries and armed with the language and clarity about their feelings and bodily rights, then we can minimise these instances, as well as the harm done by them. And we can stop the cycle of children who become adults wrestling with unresolved pain and trauma from their bodies not being treated as their own property.

As a Trans Boy

Sometimes when I read crappy articles, I like to go through them and make sure I understand why they're so crappy.

Daycare Workers Fired for Not Acknowledging 6-Year-Old as Transgender Boy:
At what age should a child be allowed to express themselves as transgendered?

This phrasing implies that children should be punished until a certain age for behaviours that are manifestations of transgenderism. That's worked out really well for gayness, has it not? Maybe the way parents respond to manifestations of transgenderism might differ based on the child's age, but you can't get away from the fact that "disallowing" transgender expression is oppression.

> That is the question surrounding a wrongful termination lawsuit in Katy, TX over a six-year-old girl whose parents now wants to be recognised as a transgendered boy.

Their six-year-old trans boy who wants to be recognised as a boy. It's cis-sexism privilege that lets the writer think he knows better than the boy (and his parents) and state that this story is about a girl.

> The privately-owned learning centre that the child attended for over four months as a girl disagrees. Until recently, all interaction with her was as a young girl.

It's a common misconception, I think, that trans people are one sex until we one day decide to be another. Just like cis people, trans people are one sex their entire lives. What changes is the ability to recognise and manifest this. The point is that even if he attended the daycare presenting as a girl, his experience there was still different than that of cis girls. It's inaccurate to say that he attended "as a girl". He attended as a trans boy presenting as a girl.

> In recent weeks, the child's appearance changed, including a short boyish haircut, and the parents told the daycare staff to now treat her as a boy because she was transgendered.

The order of this sentence is telling. The writer seems to think the change in appearance is more important than the declaration of identity. Of course this serves to trivialise transgenderism and frame it as something artificial. While the external changes that come with a transition are important for many reasons, they're also technically irrelevant. The kid would be a boy whether or not his hair was short.

This included a name masculine change.

I can see how someone might see this as trivial as well. It's like when you take a foreign language class in elementary school and everyone picks a "Spanish" name. It's gender class and everyone gets to choose a boy name. In reality, choosing a name is about acknowledging that the medical industrial complex coercively assigns sex at birth, and one of the clearest and most symbolic ways it does this is by demanding that infants be given gendered names before their genders can even be determined. Working through this and choosing a new name, it seems to me, is an important part of understanding cis-sexism and coming to terms with transgender identity.

> Two members of the Children's Lighthouse Learning Centre's staff disagreed with this.

They've been taught simplistic messages about what sex and gender are and what purposes they serve, and they've been told that transgenderism is an unnecessary and possibly harmful denial of those messages. Their privilege protects them from the need to examine those messages. And privilege always makes the beholder think they have an objective view on the marginalised position. It's some impressive cis-sexist ignorance and arrogance to think that it's any of their business or in any way their place to even have an opinion about this boy's identity.

> The manager of the daycare, Madeline Kirkse, and worker Akesha Wyatt refused the parent's request.

It's also some impressive arrogance that they think they know better than the parents how to take care of the child. Of course, we're not exactly getting the whole story here, but one would think there would have been a discussion wherein the parents request that the caretakers respect the boy's identity. And when the parents are informed that the caretakers refuse to do this, it seems very logical that the parents should withdraw him from their care. You have to be pretty full of yourself to think that you know so much better than the parents (and your employer) that you bring a suit.

> Both women voiced concerns about possible bullying from other children and parents towards the child because of the sudden turn of events.

Bullying that it would have been their responsibility to call out. It's some backwards bullshit to put the onus on the kid for being oppressed rather than on the oppressors for oppressing.

> Additionally, Kirske opposed the request due to religious beliefs.

I know the Pope hates trans people, but I still call bullshit. If your religion requires you to oppress people, then your religion is bullshit. Oops my atheism.

> Both were terminated and are now suing the daycare for wrongful termination, represented by noted attorney Houston attorney Andy Taylor.

It occurs to me that the cause and effect alluded to in the title of this piece isn't really accurate. They were fired for being privileged bigots and they're suing their employers because their privilege tells them they have the right to be privileged bigots. The boy is almost beside the point. Whether or not the suit is successful, those two women aren't going to be looking after this child. Trying to blame this kid's parents (or his transgenderism at large) for these women being fired is a gross oversimplification of the situation.

> According to Taylor, "This case involves a little 6-year-old girl who has been attending a private school in Katy, Texas for the last four months as a little girl. She has parents who are a same-sex couple, two men, who decided that she was transgender. On Friday, that little girl left school. I'm not going to use names, but (she was) known to everybody as 'Sally,' and on Monday, this little girl returns to school calling herself 'Johnny.'" But according to Dr. Johanna Olson, Adolescent Medicine, Assistant Professor, Children's Hospital Los Angeles, just because a child exhibits behaviours of the opposite sex does not necessarily mean a child is transgendered.

But? This statement is in line with everything else written so far. Where do you get off saying but?

> In an article for Human Rights Campaign, Dr. Olson states "I think you have to follow the affirmative approach to care – so what does that child need to feel safest and to feel the most whole in that moment in time? And, the biggest question is do you support a child going through a social transition in early childhood? The reality about these kids who are asking to live as gender different than their assigned sex at birth is that they usually have immense amounts of gender dysphoria. We do know that kids who are more gender dysphonic in childhood are more likely to have trans-identities as adolescents and adults."

I suppose it's good that the writer felt the need to include some sort of counterpoint, but some vague quote from a cis person parading around as an expert on trans people's needs is the opposite of useful. It's more of privileged cis people acting as if they have the objective view on our experience. Fuck off.

Here's the thing, if the world weren't so fucking cis-sexist, it wouldn't matter. Especially for such young children who aren't doing hormone therapy or surgical intervention. Children should be able to experiment with their hair and their clothes and their names and their pronouns. They should be safe to figure out how gender works and how they fit within that structure without having to worry about bullying and bigots and lawsuits. Because seriously, who cares whether this kid is a boy or not. It has no impact on anyone except him. It's no one else's business.

No Homes on Our Horizon

Laboria Cuboniks

Excerpt: XenoFeminism

From the street to the home, domestic space too must not escape our tentacles. So profoundly ingrained, domestic space has been deemed impossible to dis-embed, where the home as norm has been conflated with home as fact, as an unremarkable given. Stultifying 'domestic realism' has no home on our horizon. Let us set sights on augmented homes of shared laboratories, of communal media and technical facilities. The home is ripe for spatial transformation as an integral component in any process of feminist futurity. But this cannot stop at the garden gates. We see too well that reinventions of family structure and domestic life are currently only possible at the cost of either withdrawing from the economic sphere – the way of the commune – or bearing its burdens manyfold – the way of the single parent. If we want to break the inertia that has kept the moribund figure of the nuclear family unit in place, which has stubbornly worked to isolate women from the public sphere, and men from the lives of their children, while penalising those who stray from it, we must overhaul the material infrastructure and break the economic cycles that lock it in place.

DOG SECTION PRESS